PRACTICAL WAX MODELING

Advanced Techniques For Wax Modelers

By Hiroshi Tsuyuki and Yoko Ohba

ARTISAN IDEAS

Published by Artisan Ideas, 2019.
By Hiroshi Tsuyuki and Yoko Ohba
ISBN 978-0-9979798-8-6
Library of Congress Control Number: 2019947449
Printed in China.
Artisan Ideas is an imprint of **Artisan North America, Inc**
Tel: 800-843-9567
Info@ArtisanIdeas.com

For a selection of reference books for jewelers visit our website: www.ArtisanIdeas.com.

Artisan North America
753 Valley Road
Watchung, NJ 07069-6120

Ordering information:
Quantity sales. Special discounts are available on quantity purchases by corporations, associations, and others. For details, contact the publisher at the address above.
For single copies, please try your bookstore or jewelry supply store first. If unavailable this book can be ordered through: www.ArtisanIdeas.com.
To see our complete selection of books and DVDs on this and other subjects visit our website listed above.

Authors!

If you have an idea for a book please contact us at: Info@ArtisanIdeas.com.
We'll be glad to hear from you.

www.ArtisanIdeas.com

CONTENTS

Samples of Wax Modeling Techniques.

Samples of Finished Products.

Samples of Finished Products.

Samples of Finished Products.

WAX FOR PROFESSIONALS

Scope of the Utilization of Wax Modeling

It is given that technicians of jewelry manufacturers are taught wax modeling, but it is less evident that designers and small business persons have become more involved with wax. The use of wax modeling has spread greatly, not only at the manufacturing level, but also as an aid to designers and in sales promotion. Ordinarily this type of publication attracts only readers who are specialists, but the art of wax modeling seems to attract a variety of people who have an interest in jewelry.

Wax Modeling Meeting the Needs of the Times

Touched on in the book ***Basic Wax Modeling***, the properties found in wax are many, including rapid production without waste, softness, ease of shaping, and flexibility. These properties meet the user's needs and today's requirements at the manufacturing level.

Moreover, one reason wax has become so popular is that anyone is capable of working wax. For this reason, amateurs with little experience are captivated by wax when producing jewelry.

How To Keep Wax Alive in the Workplace

The popularity of wax is now widespread within the jewelry industry. Because little time is required for learning the skill, most people will thoroughly digest wax technology within a few years. There may come a time when most wax techniques and designs are of the same quality. But to prepare for this time, professional craftspersons should consider incorporating other skills. For example, devising methods of assembling metal parts and wax parts, or learning engraving skills. Small business owners who use wax obviously cannot compete with large manufacturing technologists or design professionals, but one method to consider is incorporating your customers' ideas into customized products.

SPECIAL FEATURES AND SUGGESTIONS FOR USING THIS BOOK

In this book, new wax modeling techniques are introduced for the first time. Developed in our classroom, these techniques are explained in detail and illustrated with step-by-step photographs.

The purpose of introducing these techniques is threefold:

1. To assist product designers,
2. To offer readily usable ideas for those already involved in the production of jewelry,
3. To offer progressive techniques that may be useful well into the future.

The special features of this book include: practical applications when using a combination of waxes, *mitsuro* and its uses, demonstrations of a variety of textures, and methodology of finishing castings. We recommend beginners to follow this step-by-step from the beginning. Although each heading is arranged separately, the text is structured so that it is permissible for one familiar with hard wax modeling to go directly to soft wax modeling.

A WORD FROM THE TRANSLATOR:

The words *mitsuro* and *hikime* have been adequately explained in the text. However, I have carried through with the words *takegushi* and *kisage* as well because they are unique to American wax modelers. Furthermore, these tools offer certain advantages (I feel) as explained in the following.

Takegushi are pointed bamboo dowels. They may be altered to ball points or even small flat chisels. *Takehera* are bamboo spatulas. They may be altered over and over again with the use of files and abrasive papers to fit your particular needs, thereby eliminating the cost of more expensive steel tools.

Kisage is a steel tool shaped much like a barrette file. The base is polished smoothly and the edges provide the cutting action. Cutting is done in a lateral motion, resulting in a wake that is as smooth as the polished base of the tool. Because there is so little base, it is prone to digging when used improperly. For that reason, its use was discouraged for beginners in the book ***"Basic Wax Modeling"***.

I

HARD WAX MODELING TECHNIQUES

TEXTURED RING

WORK DESCRIPTION:

To this gently curved ring of flat construction, with a wave-like engraving inserted in the center, an "ostrich-like-skin" texture is applied to both sides of the ring. Using the techniques introduced in the book ***Basic Wax Modeling***, we learn how to apply texture and produce the open portion of this ring. Pay careful attention to the esthetics of the texture and exert every effort to carefully complete, to the smallest detail.

WORK HINTS:

1. Establish a work routine.
2. Grasp the sense of texturing
3. Master the method of creating openings.

MATERIALS AND TOOLS:

Off-centered hole wax ring tube	Abrasive paper	Needle
Dividers	Spatula	Spring gauge
Jeweler's saw	Graver	Ring mandrel
File	Bur	Nylon (burnisher)

Use a piece of off-centered wax ring tube slightly wider than the piece shown. True up the surfaces smoothly with a wax file. Scribe all pertinent lines on the surfaces, top, front, and rear.

The design layout will commence from the top. First, draw the outline with a fine-point marking pen and lightly trace over with a scribe. This procedure is more accurate than point marking.

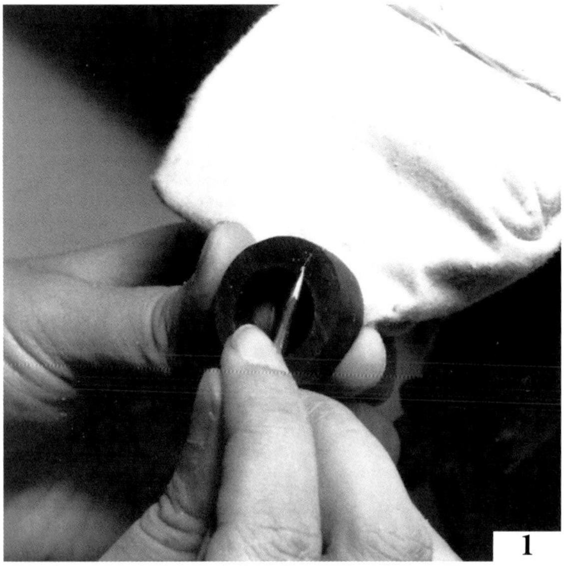
1

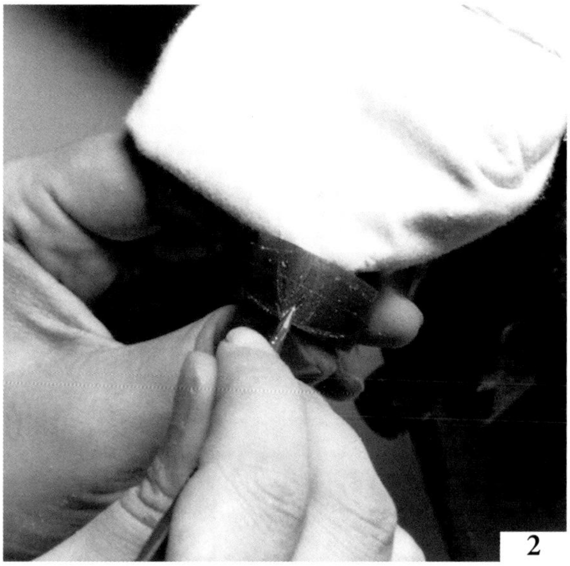
2

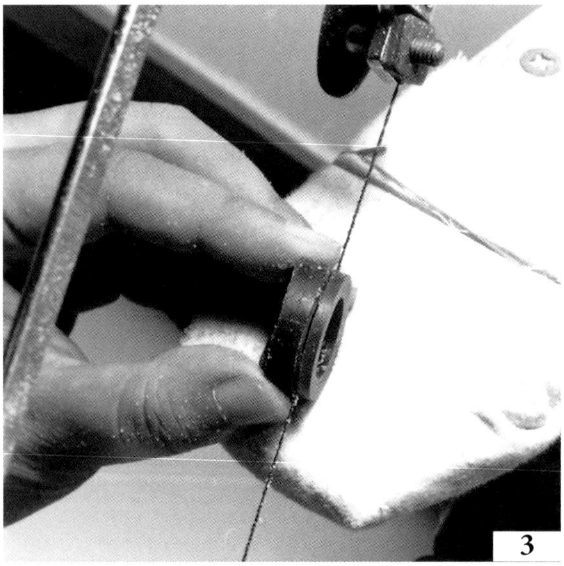
3

4

Extend the scribed lines all the way around the shank. As the saw will be canted in the cutting process, be careful not to over cut. Always cut outside the scribed lines.

Smoothen the cuts to the edge of the scribed lines with a coarse wax file. Always replace scribed lines eradicated due to material removal.

As the design is slightly domed, use a coarse file to trim the sharp corners, then, gradually move to a finer file to form a gently curved surface.

To size the ring, begin by filing just short of the desired size. Finish by rotating the ring around a dowel, wrapped in abrasive paper (400 - 1000 grit) inserted in the hole.

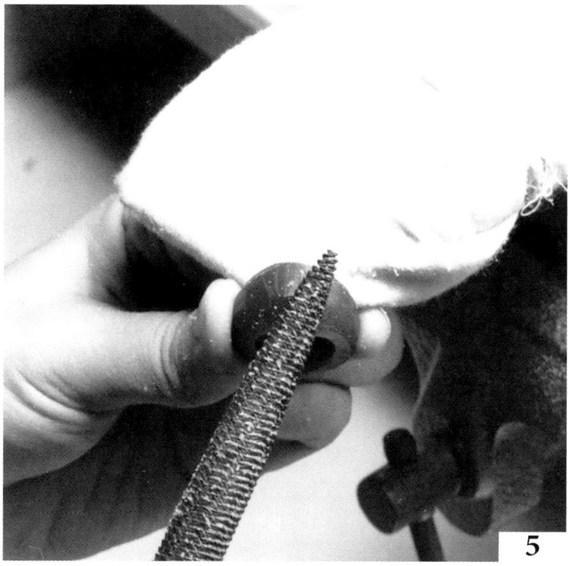

5

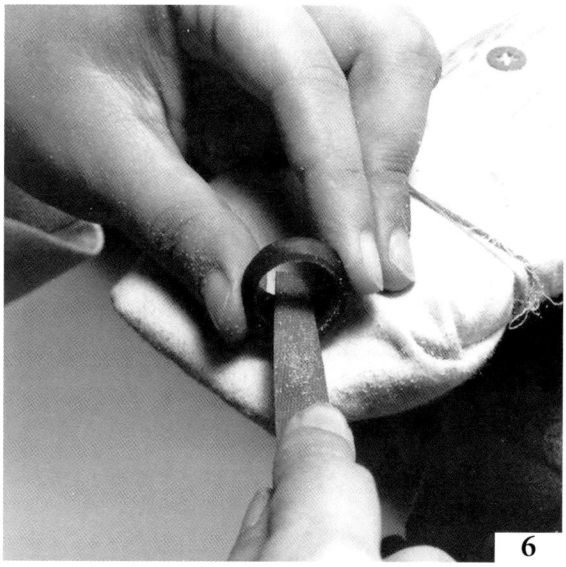

6

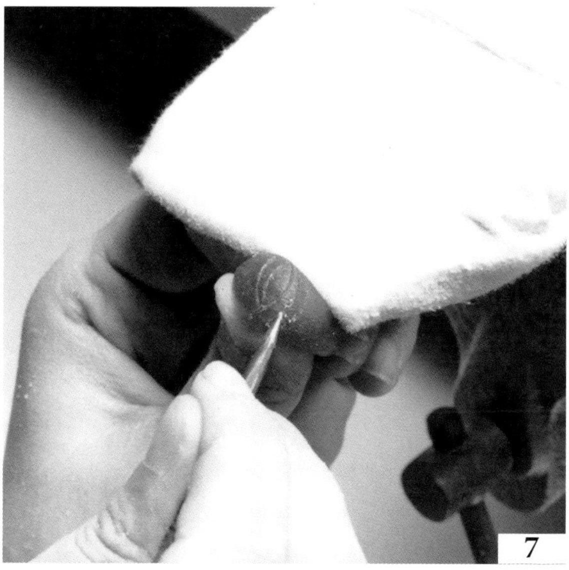

7

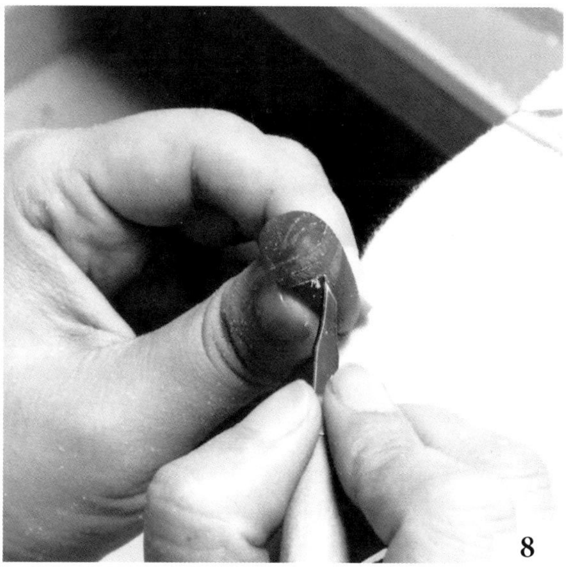

8

Scribe in the small details on the top portion of the ring again. Giving thought to the curvature of the surface, scribe a "natural flow" to the wave. To prevent errors, use a fine point marking pen before scribing.

To give a 3-dimensional appearance to the waves, shave away the lower portions to make them stand out. Be careful not to cut too deeply. Use caution as you cut.

After the waves (heart of the design) are well defined, smoothen the knife cut portions with a file. Use a fine cut file to finish the upper parts of the waves. Since this is fine work, a shortened grip on the file is preferred.

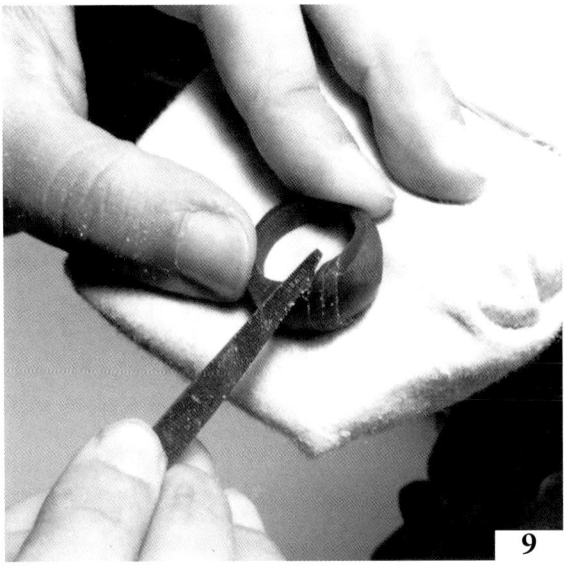

9

Next, create raised borders along the shoulders of the ring. First, scribe lines along both sides with a divider. At this time, pay attention to the uniformity of the widths. The border will extend to the mid-point of the ring. Texture will be applied to the area within the border.

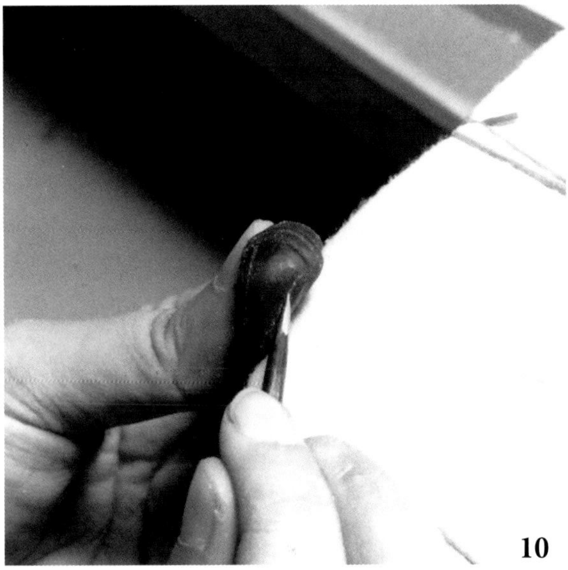

10

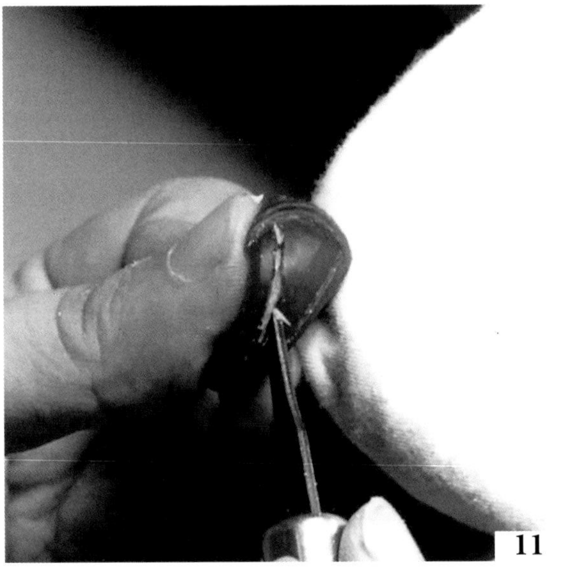

11

Lower the area inside the borders by taking thin cuts. Proceed carefully and neatly. A flat carver may help here.

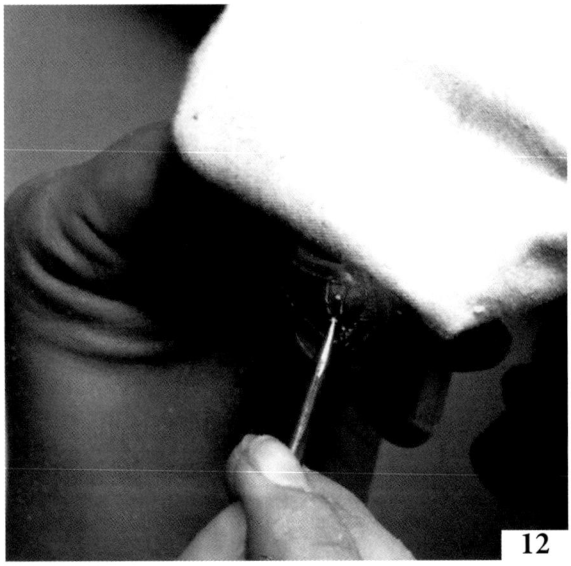

12

On the opposite side of the main waves, create the wave extension which will appear about halfway down from the top. Check for "balance" as the design is scribed. The flow of the lines should form pleasing curves.

Proceed by cutting the lower portion of the wave a step lower. It is better to use the tip portion of the blade. **Recommendation**: Exacto #16 or wax/rubber mold blade.

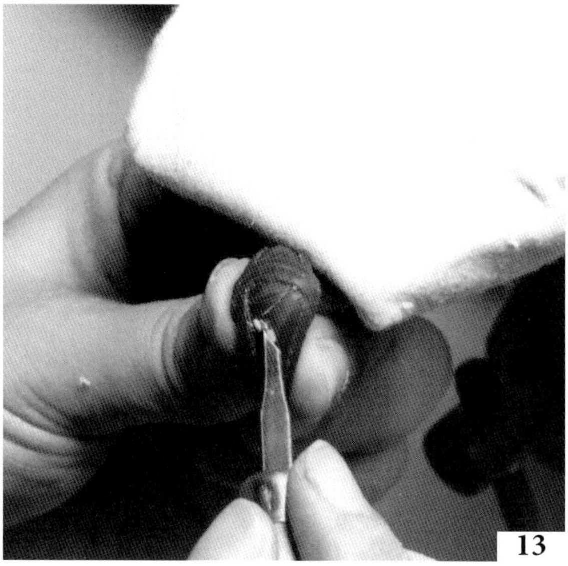

13

The space in the center will be used for an opening; for now bur the opening part down about 2 - 3 mm deep.

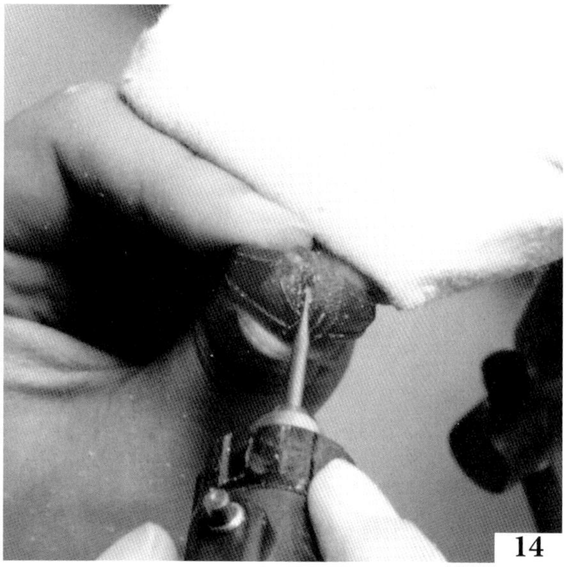

14

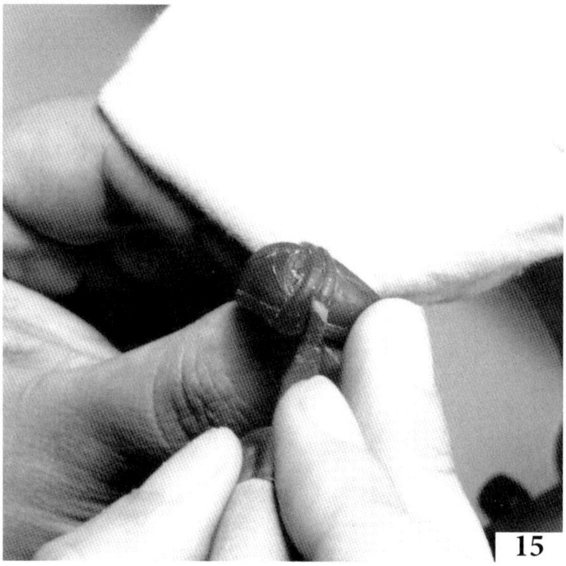

15

The rough shaping is now finished. Complete the profile of the wave. Incise a V groove, rounding as you proceed.

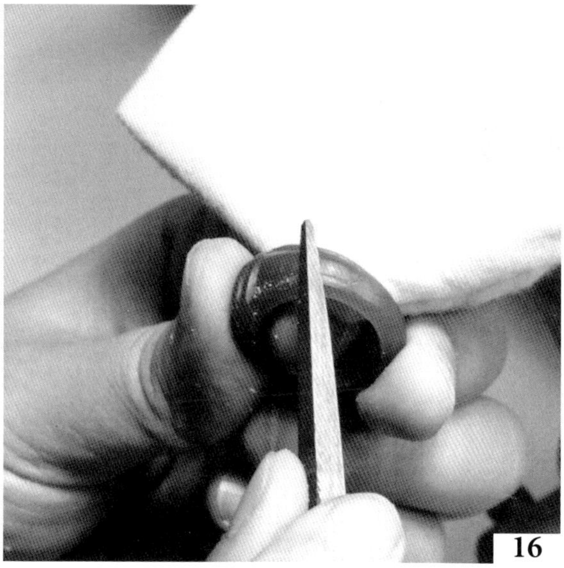

16

Using a fine cut file, round the outer edges as neatly as possible.

Smoothen the inner surface of the borders accurately with a fine file, right down to the corners. Use a *takegushi* (pointed bamboo dowel) or the like and finish neatly.

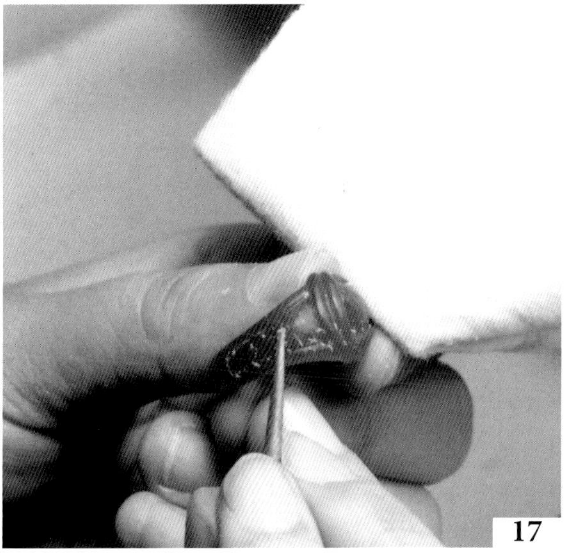

17

In an orderly fashion sand the surfaces with 400 grit paper progressing to 1000 grit paper. Cut small pieces of abrasive paper, fit into and sand parallel with the grooves.

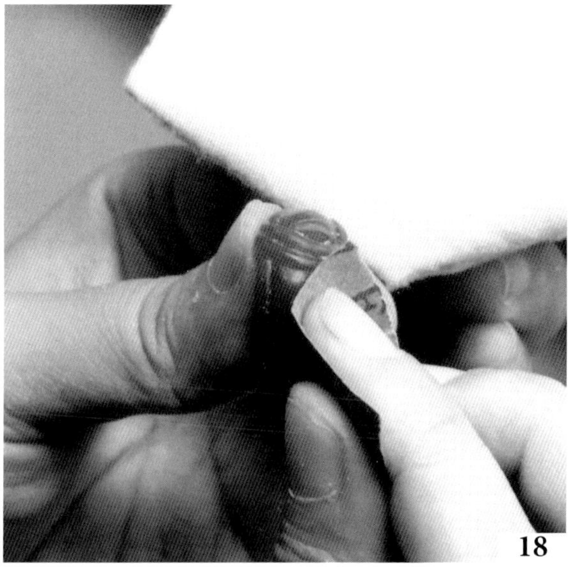

18

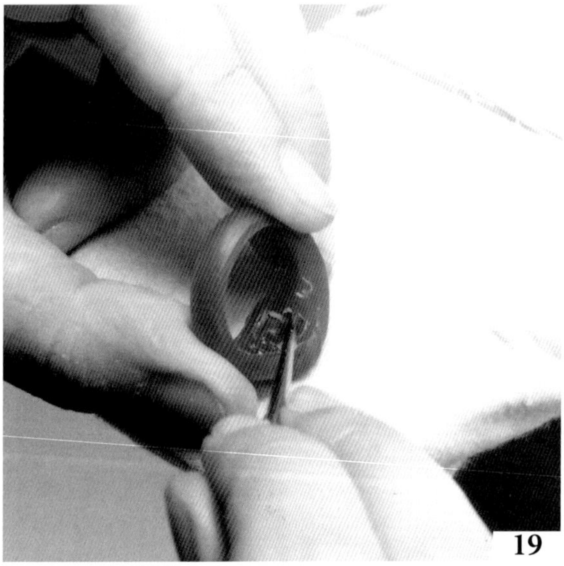

19

The previously created opening may now be completed by cutting through from the underside. Gouge out about two thirds of the material to reduce the thickness. This way the opening will be easier to finish.

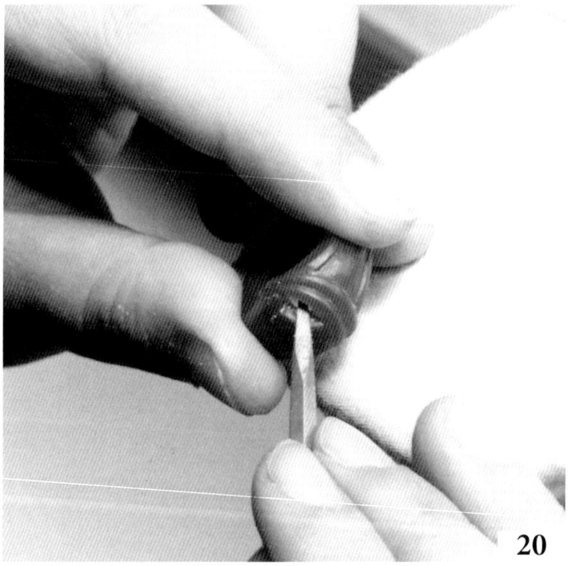

20

Next begin the work on the top. Using files and a *kisage* (pointed specialty tool for cutting), cut in carefully, especially along the edges.

Apply texture to the area within the borders. At this point we shall look into the "ostrich skin" texture. The graining can be created with a *takegushi* by line carving not unlike the uneveness of waves. Brushing away wax dust, carve these lines one at a time.

To create the little "bumps", pick up small quantities of wax on a hot needle; apply to the surface in a balanced manner. Watch the temperature of the needle; if it is too hot, the wax will run.

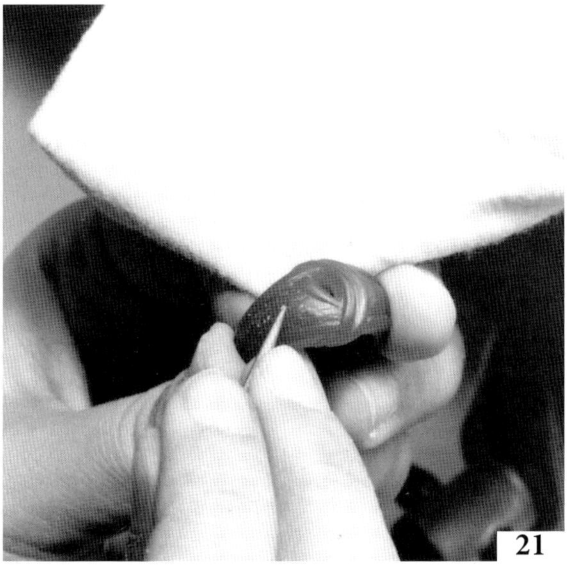
21

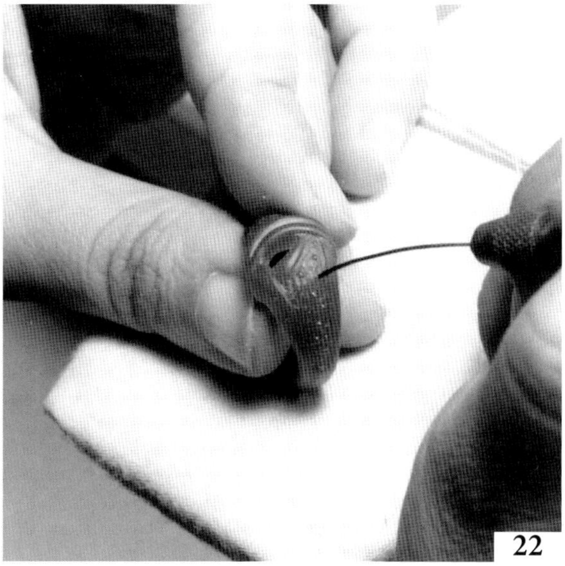
22

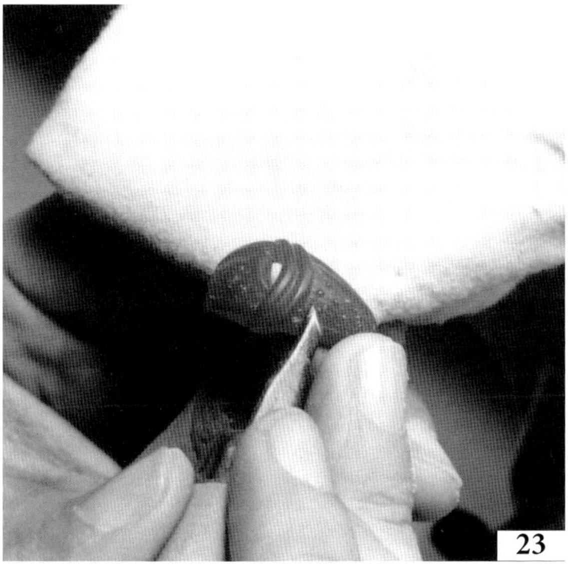
23

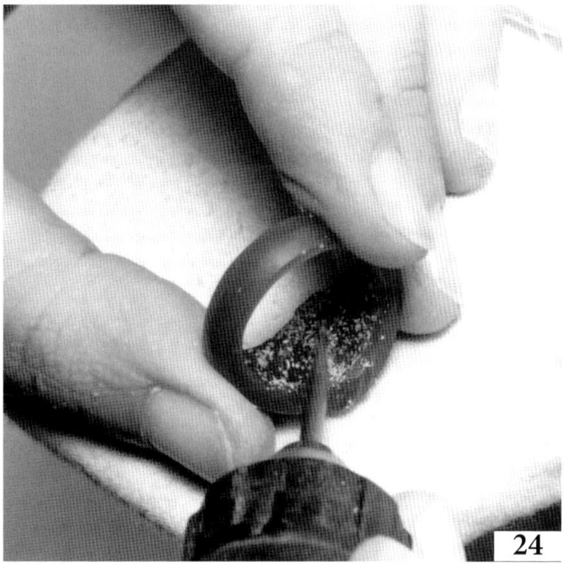
24

To make the "bumps" uniform, trim them with a knife. Repair the base, graining where required.

Remove the balance of excess material from the underside. Place a 1.0 - 1.2 mm width marker along the outer edges with a scriber (see Proj. 1, Fig. 1 of ***Basic Wax Modeling***). Remove the material to the mark with a bur. Finish up neatly with a small round gouge to the thickness of 0.8 - 1.0 mm.

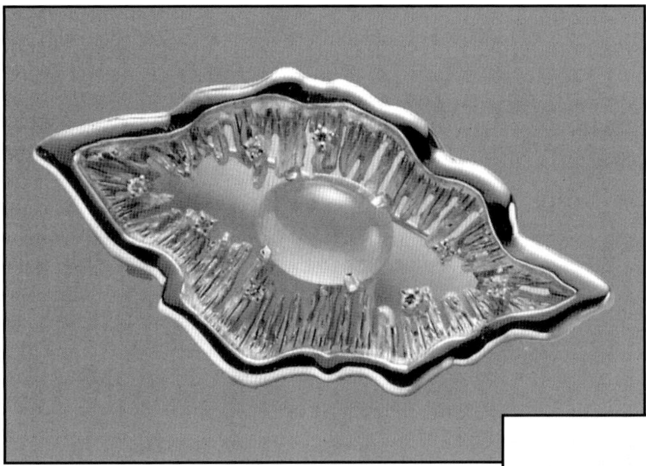

Creased and Carved Texture.

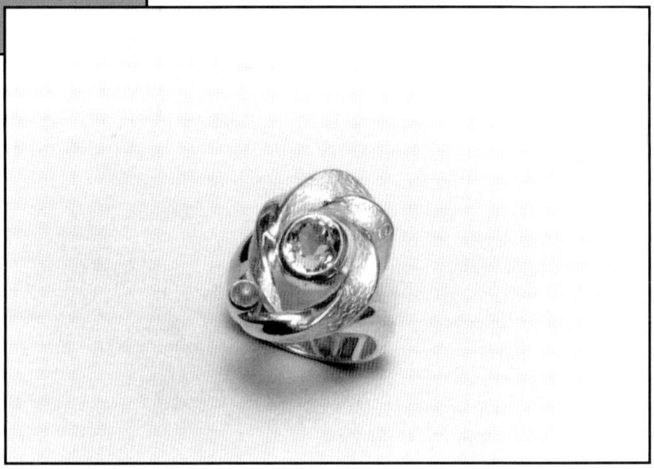

Ostrich Skin Texture.

Cloth Texture.

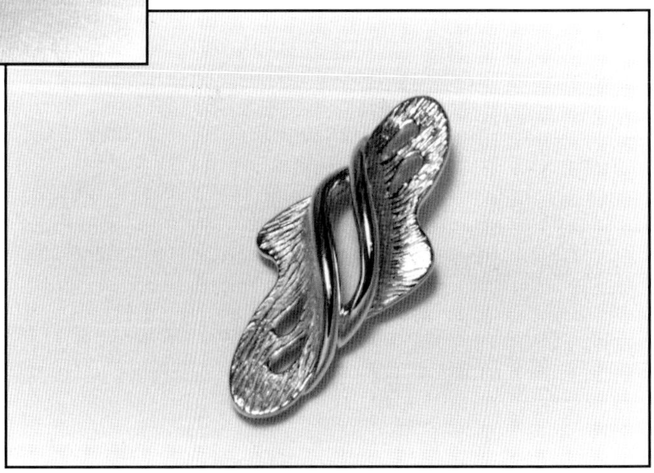

Creased Texture.

TWO PART RING

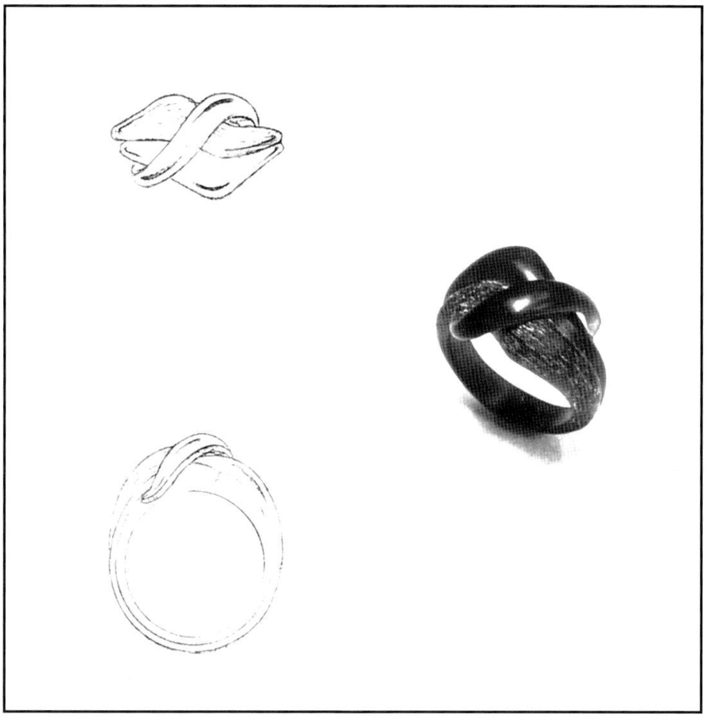

WORK DESCRIPTION:

Some designs with open spaces or solid bodied designs are more conveniently constructed in parts and assembled afterward. For this project learn the method of attaching a portion of the top to the balance of the model. This method is well suited for platinum/gold combinations, intricate complex designs, and designs with difficult underside removal of wax. This method of assembling parts greatly widens the scope of design capabilities.

WORK HINTS:

1. Master the application of texture.
2. Study ways of dividing a project into parts.
3. Devise methods to make and assemble parts.

MATERIALS AND TOOLS:

Centered hole wax ring tube	Block of wax
Dividers	Jeweler's saw
Files	Abrasive paper
Knife	Bur
Kisage spring gauge	Ring mandrel

Construct the ring to which the part will be attached. After taking height/ width measurements from the plan, cut a slightly oversize piece of centered hole ring tube. Scribe reference center line and the design about these line.

Cut the shank portion. As the saw will be in the canted position take care not to over cut. As you become experienced, you will be able to remove other excess material at one time with the saw.

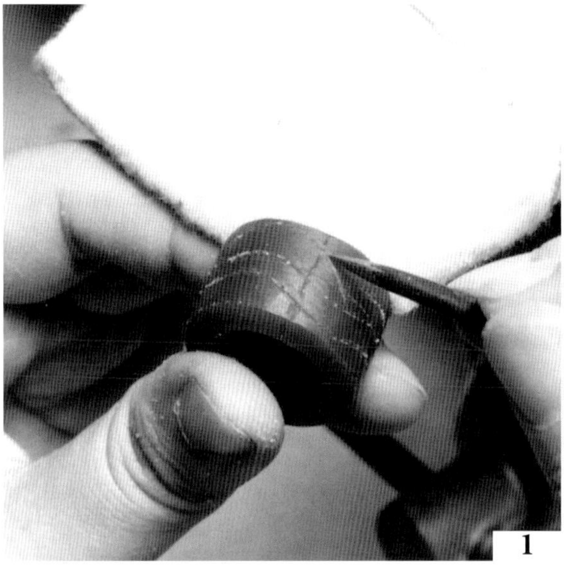

1

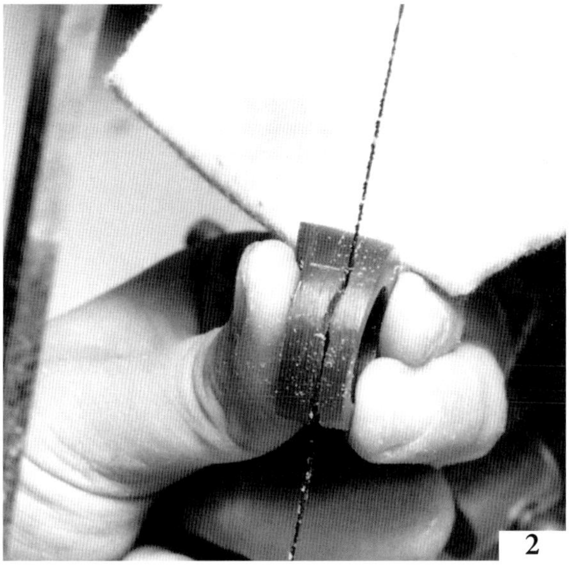

2

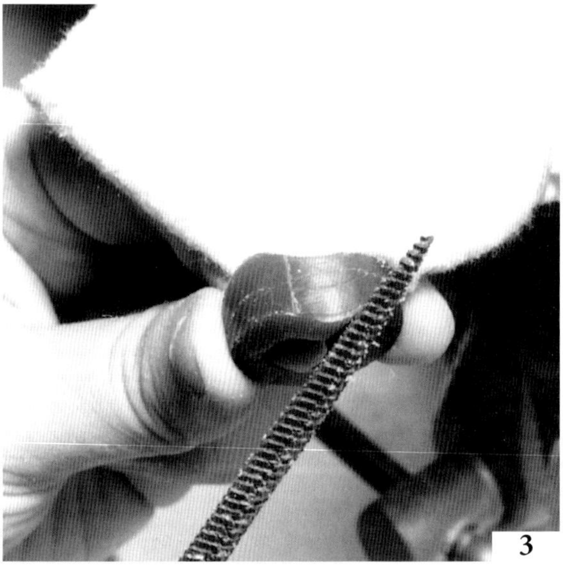

3

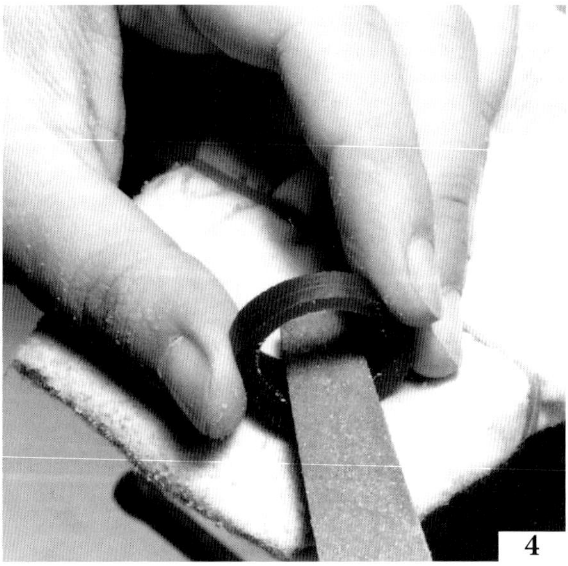

4

Coarse file to the scribed line, taking care not to go beyond. As the shank can be easily distorted at this time, mount the ring on a sizing stick, checking (design) as you proceed.

Next, size the ring. Use a half round file to just short of the desired size. Finish with dowel wrapped with 400 grit abrasive paper using progressively finer paper to 1000 grit until the desired size is reached.

Deepen the scribed lines. Cutting little-by-little, establish the contours. Give careful attention to the uniformity of the "flow". Height difference in the contours of 2 mm at the deepest part is okay.

Run a fairly deep V groove along the center contour line. As the inner surfaces will become a part of the wave structure, work a knife and *kisage* along the surfaces neatly.

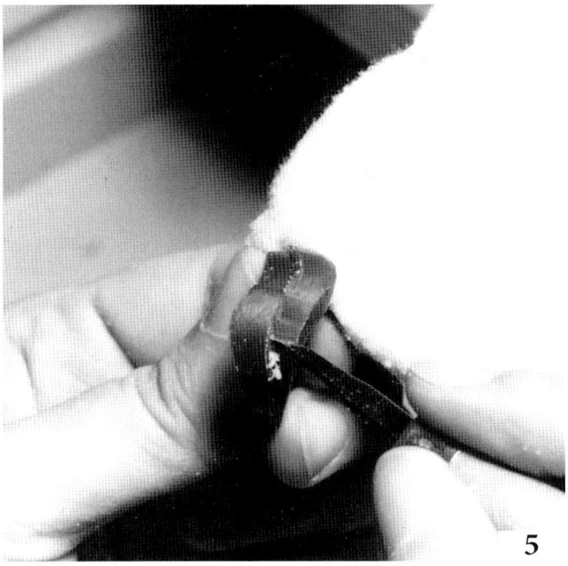

5

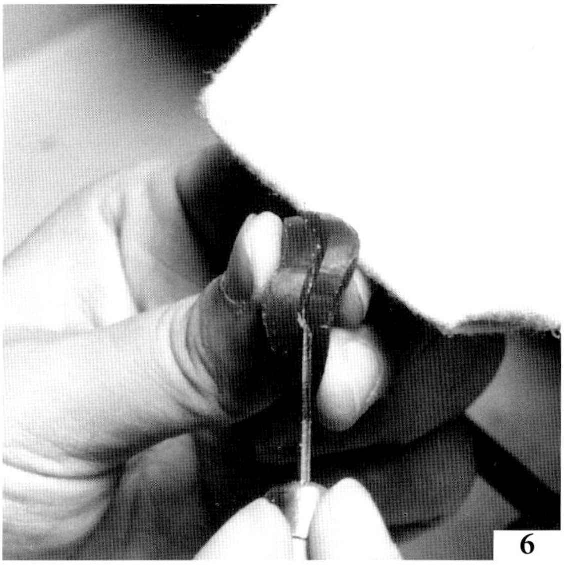

6

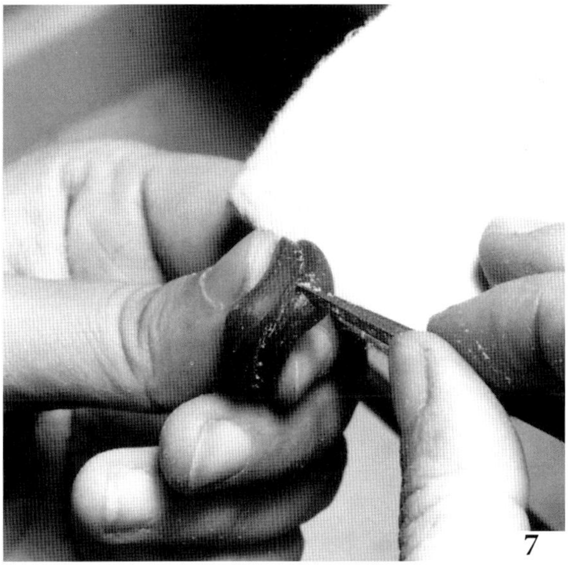

7

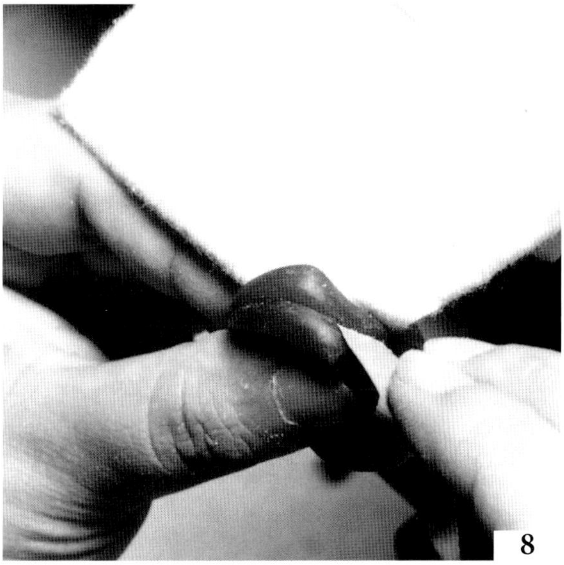

8

Use a needle file, progressing from coarse to fine, round out the divided parts. Utilize the pointed portion of the file to finish the groove.

Next, finish with abrasive paper, progressing from coarse to fine. Cut small strips of abrasive paper beforehand. Finish neatly into the groove using the corners of abrasive papers.

Sujime (crease) type texture is applied to one of the curved parts. Use the knife edge of a warm (not hot) carver in a pull stroke; the deeper and closer the creases, the more attractive the appearance.

Next, to remove the excess material from the underside, mark the area to be removed with a scriber and bur out the material. Follow up with a carver, smoothing the area to a uniform thickness of 0.8 - 1.0 mm.

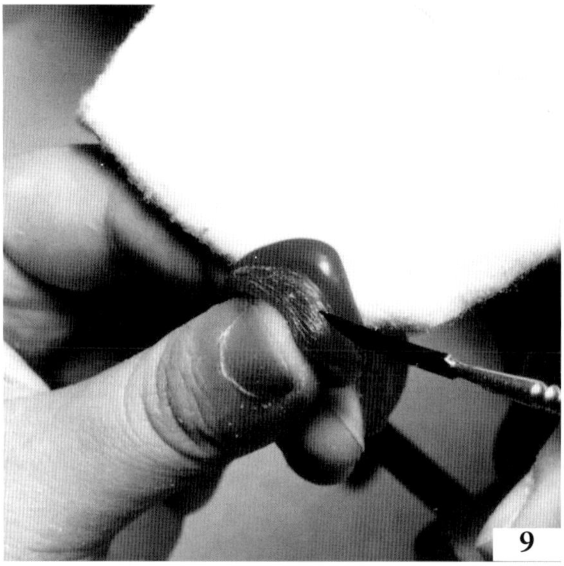
9

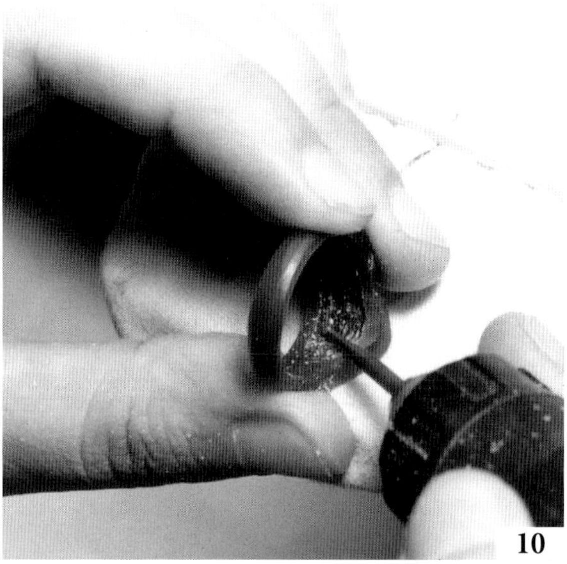
10

11

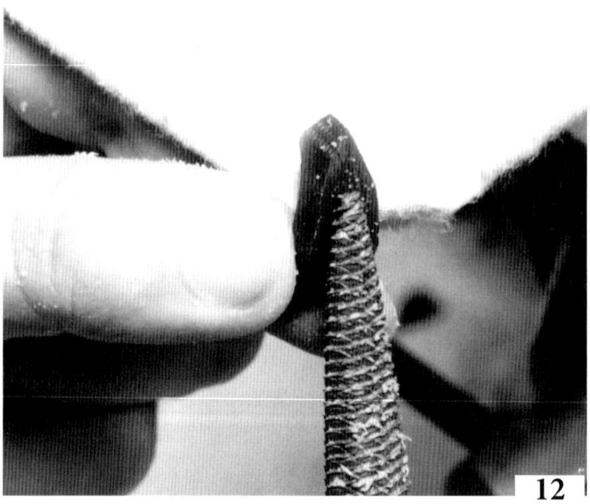
12

After the ring, which will serve as the base is finished, start on the upper part. From the design determine the size of the piece necessary; scribe the shape slightly larger on the wax. Cut out carefully.

Shape the part with a coarse file. The shape of the lower curve will be determined by its contact to the curved surface of the ring. The upper curve will then be parallel to bottom.

Place the part on top of the ring; mark the shape with a scriber again. Check for excessive gap between the two pieces. If necessary use the half round file and reshape to fit perfectly.

After the shape is fairly well set remove material to the scribed lines with a small file. Round the upper portion. Finish with the *kisage* and abrasive paper, checking the fit to the ring from time to time.

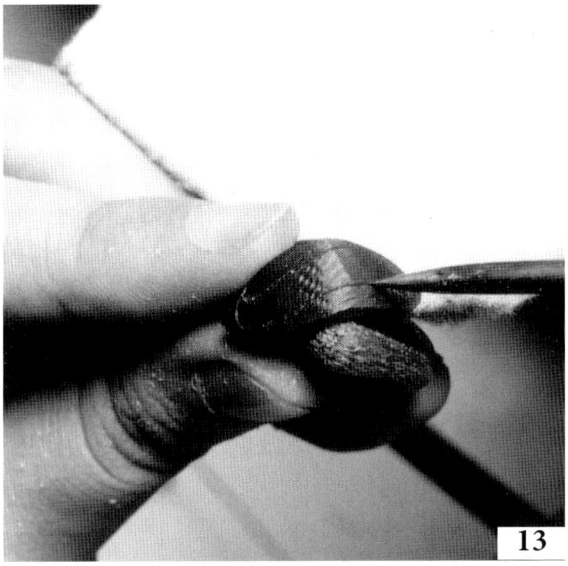

13

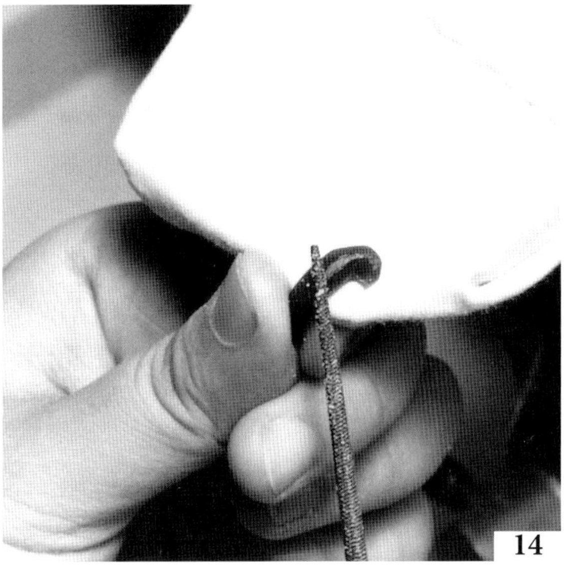

14

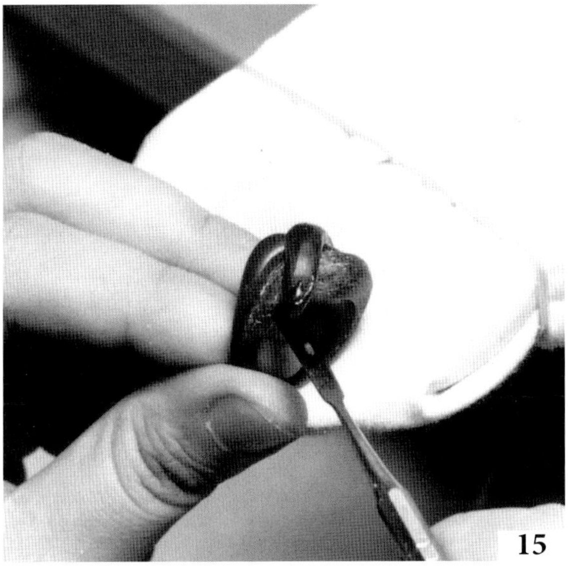

15

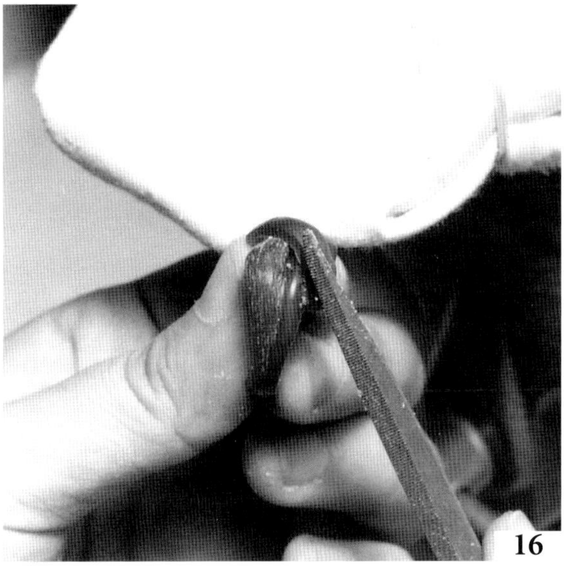

16

With the part in near finish condition mount it temporarily onto the ring. Use a heated spatula, a small amount of wax: lightly tack (ends) into place. Note carefully the position of the piece, apply additional wax if required.

Examine the assembly for appearance. If the part is too high or distorted, use a file to conform. When satisfied with overall balance, finish up with a *kisage* and abrasive papers.

Remove the part carefully with a knife. Using force may damage the part; draw the cutting edge lightly along the seam as many times as required to separate the piece.

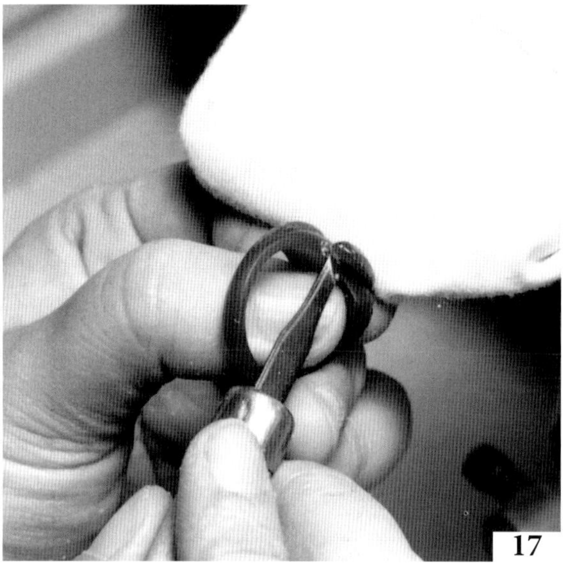

17

Put the finishing touches on the piece and remove (gouge) the material from the underside. As this portion is difficult to polish after casting, take the time to achieve a good finish in the wax stage. Strive to finish the part with a thickness of 0.8 mm.

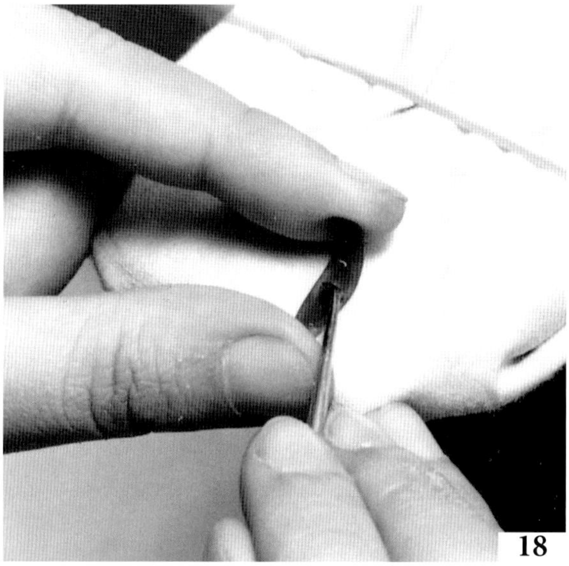

18

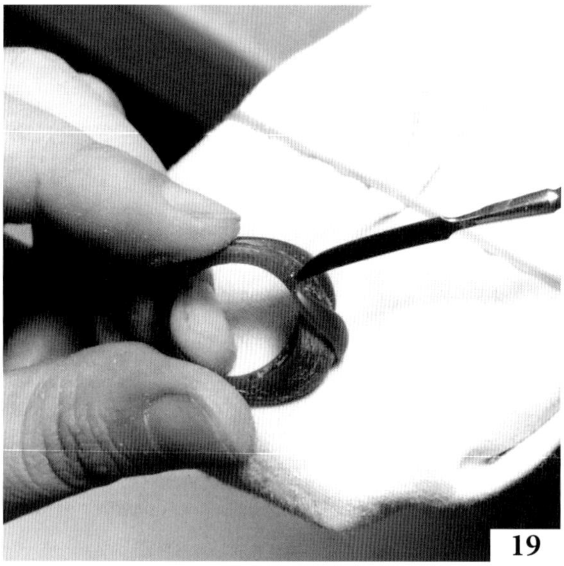

19

After the part is completely finished, affix the part to the ring permanently. Use the tip end of a spatula or a welding needle. Apply wax as smoothly as possible where the pieces contact.

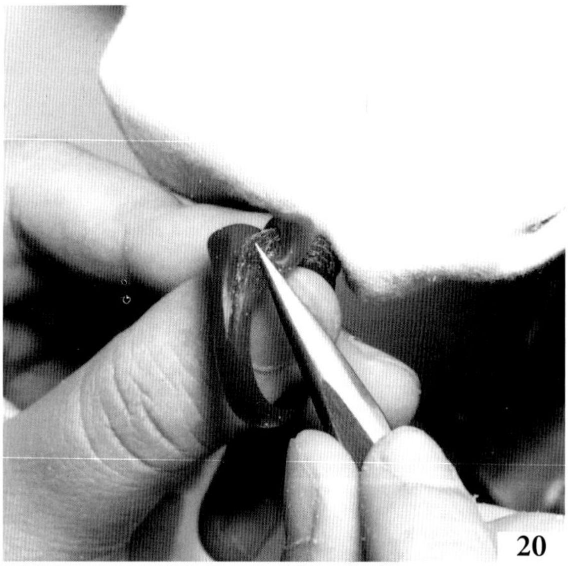

20

The last step. Clean up the contact joints. Repair scratches and other mars. Repair the texture at the welded areas.

RING WITH A FLOATING TWIST

GENERAL DESCRIPTION:

Similar to the High Domed ring with a wave pattern introduced in "***Basic Wax Modeling***", this is a large sized ring with an added twist.
Representing smooth flowing waves, the carved-out portion also images a natural flow into the open space. Here, as the domed waves form the base, much attention is devoted to create this natural flow. Also, be aware that this design is an expression with movement and substance without losing the sensation of "volume". An acute, deep cut will be placed at the edge of the opening.

WORK HINTS:

1. Examine the method of creating flow to the waves.
2. How to manage the deep cut.
3. Reduce the waves to a uniform thickness by gouging out the underside.

MATERIALS AND TOOLS:

Wax ring tube with flat side	Scriber
Jeweler's saw	Files
Abrasive paper	Spatulas
Carvers	Knife
Spring gauge	Ring sizer

From the design drawing determine the width of flat side ring tube required. Cut out the piece. While looking at the plan, rough in the outline with a needle file, over which draw the center lines with a scriber and copy the design. Copy slightly oversize.

Saw out the shank portion; trim the shank close to the scribed lines with a coarse file. In this step size the ring also, using files, abrasive papers.

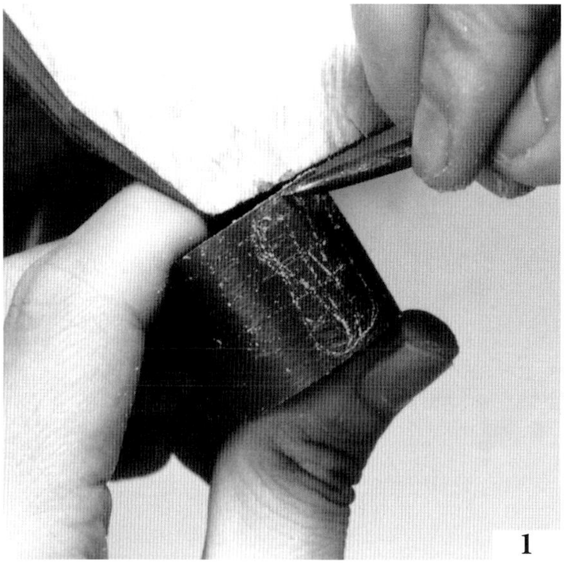

1

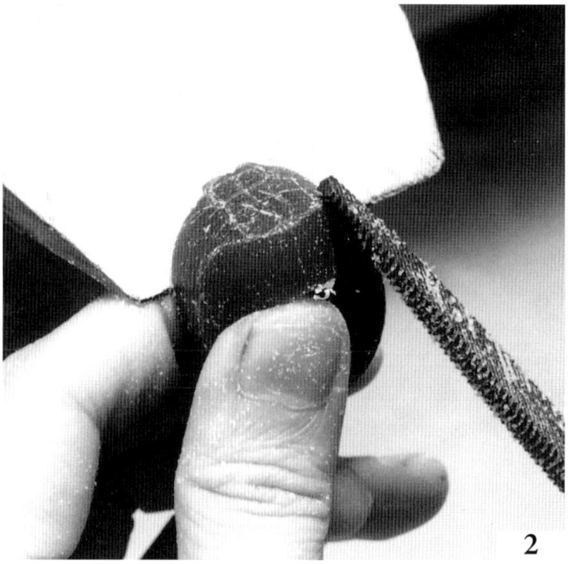

2

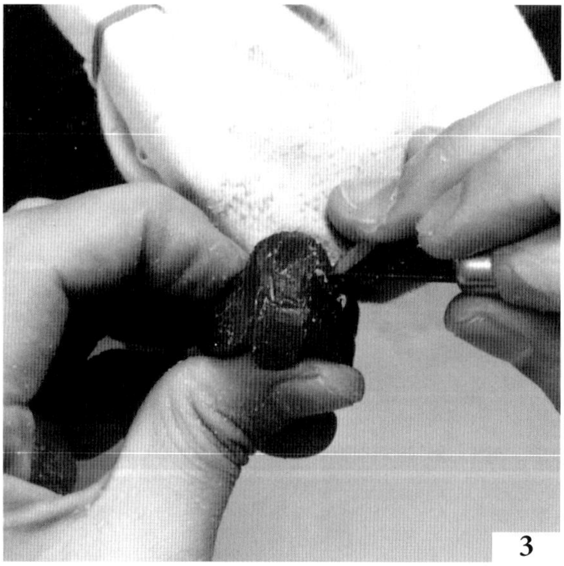

3

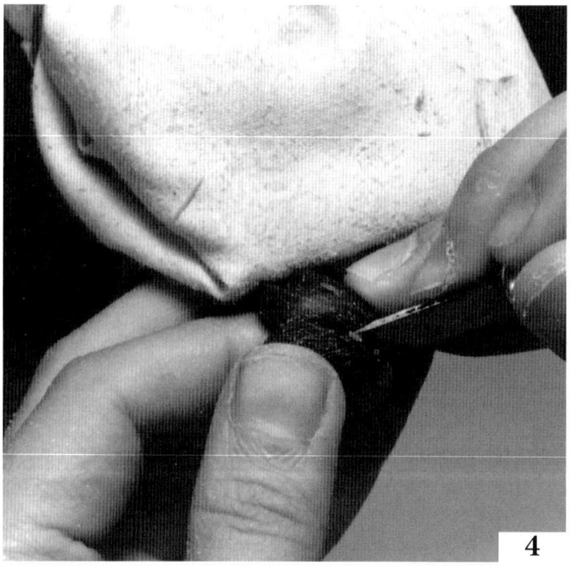

4

Study the design; determine the high/low differences. Begin cutting down from the highest point with a knife carver. Use a file to surface the shank area.

Run V grooves to define the central wave. Cut the grooves slightly deeper as you proceed rounding the wave. Giving flow to the wave using spatulas and wax carvers is a demanding technique.

After the central wave is roughed-in start the work on the 4 domed rows on both sides of the shank. Delineate them with a scriber: follow up with a V groover. Use the tip of a needle file to create a rounded cross section.

Use the end of a spatula to finish perfectly the portion where the large wave rides over the smaller ones. A *takegushi* sharpened to a point will yield good results as well. After the abutting edges have been cleaned up, sand the entire area with abrasive papers and an abrasive containing eraser, removing small scratches as you proceed.

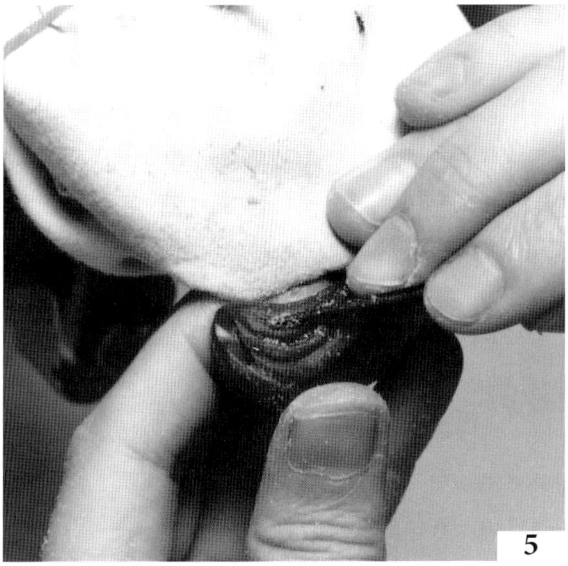

5

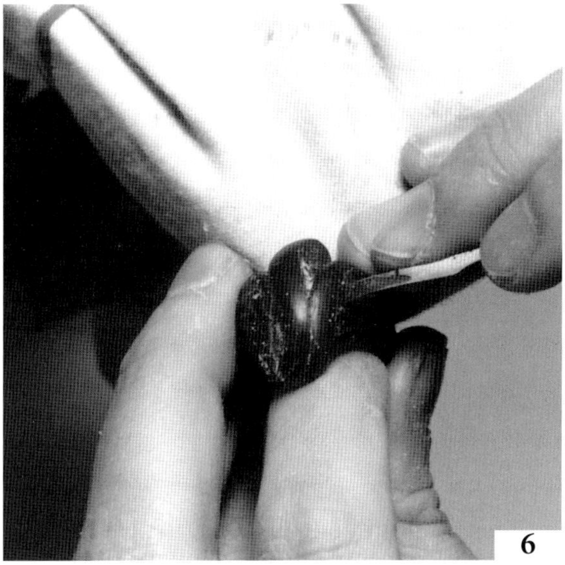

6

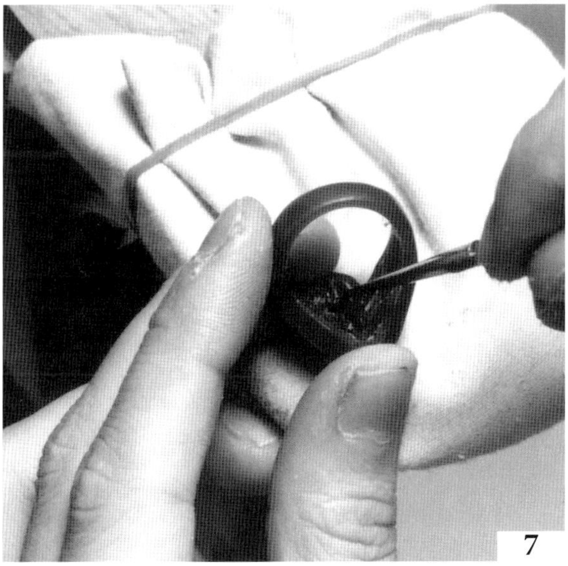

7

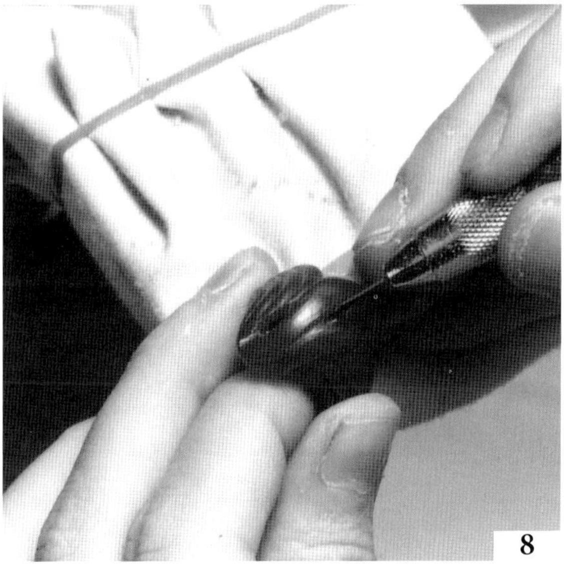

8

Remove material from the underside. The open work in the space is a step lower: penetrate it at the same time. With a gouge carver, whose width matches the waves, finish the underside uniformly to the smallest detail.

Patiently finish the contact joint and protruding area (floating twist) with a thin blade knife. Use small strips of abrasive paper and complete the ring accurately.

Open Tear Drop Shaped Ring with Stone.

Ring with Twisted Waves.

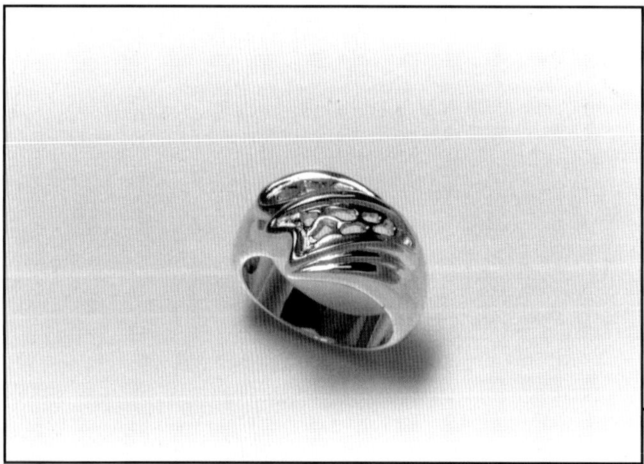

Ring with Pierced Patterns.

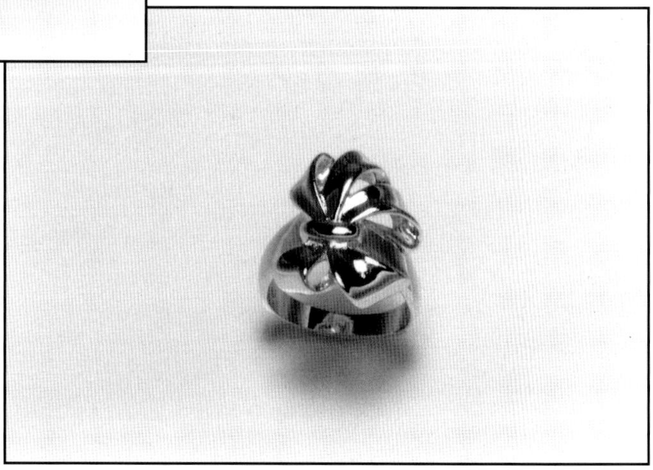

Ribbon Motif Ring.

BUILT-UP RING

GENERAL DESCRIPTION:

This ring is made up from heaped up bits of melted hard wax. After enough wax is built-up you will carve sharp lines in the wax and complete the ring with the removal of material from the underside.
Once the wax has been deposited the carving may begin but, depending on the melting temperature and method of build-up, various textures can be attained. Experiment with these to develop the practical skills of this technique.

WORK HINTS:

1. Be thoroughly familiar with the melting temperature of the wax you work with.
2. Learn the method of placing and shaping wax where carving is to occur.
3. Eliminate bubbles forming in build-up process.

MATERIALS:

Wax scraps	Tracing paper
Wax pen	Carvers
Files	*Kisage*
Spatulas	Wooden mandrel

Wrap a piece of tracing paper around a tapered rod at the desired size. Draw the design which will become the pattern in light lines. Make certain the shank is not askew.

Deposit melted wax from bits and pieces of hard wax onto the pattern. Do not allow bubbles to form in the wax. The tip of the wax pen should be pointed enough to deposit thin lines of wax.

1

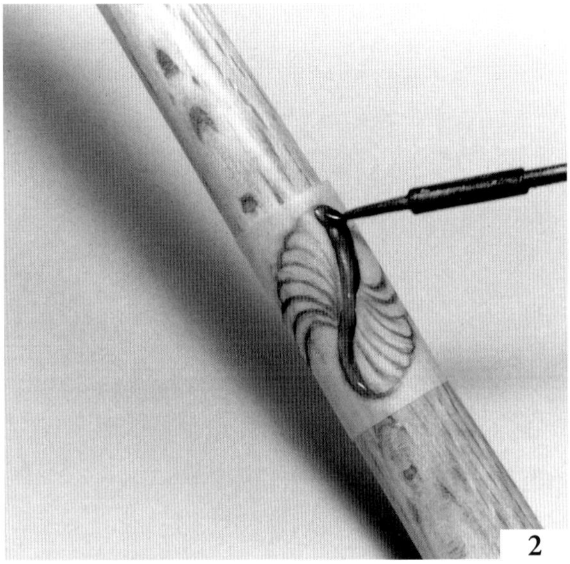
2

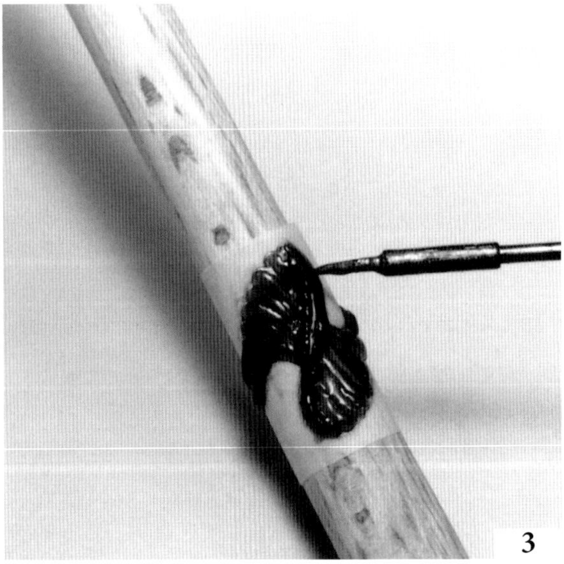
3

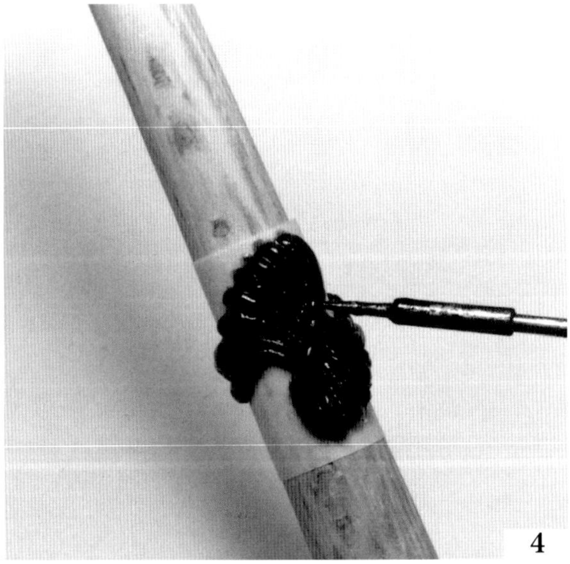
4

Deposit small amounts over the entire area. With the thickness/height requirement in mind, follow the outline with the wax. However, if too much is deposited at one time, it will be difficult to separate the model from the paper. It is best to apply the wax in a thin and uniform procedure.

As the main wave is the highest, deposit a sufficient amount of wax. Since it will later be shaped with a file, apply on the heavy side. The same consideration will be given to the shank as well.

Thickness is preferable. After you have built up enough to achieve a good balance, remove the model from the stick. Be patient: do not force or attempt to remove in a heavy-handed manner.

After separation, clean up the ragged edges around the perimeter with a wax pen or a heated spatula. Add wax wherever required.

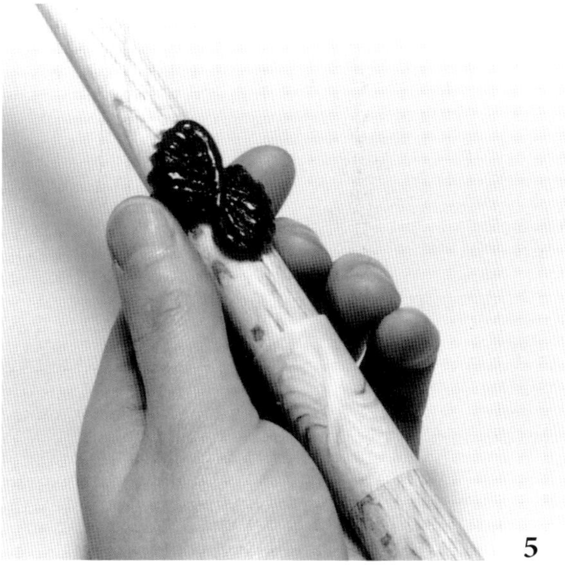

5

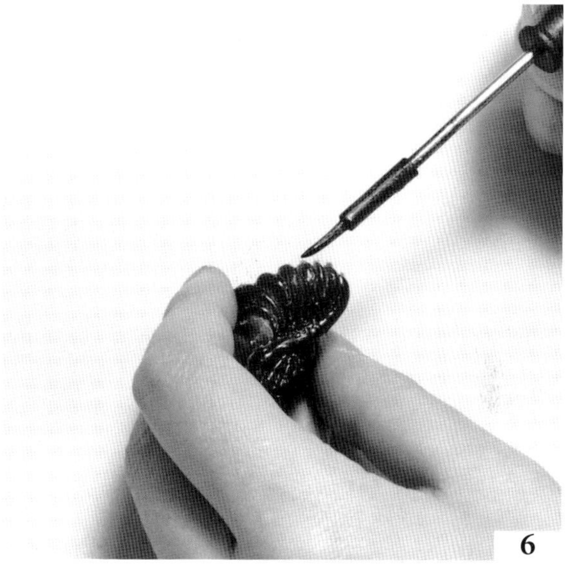

6

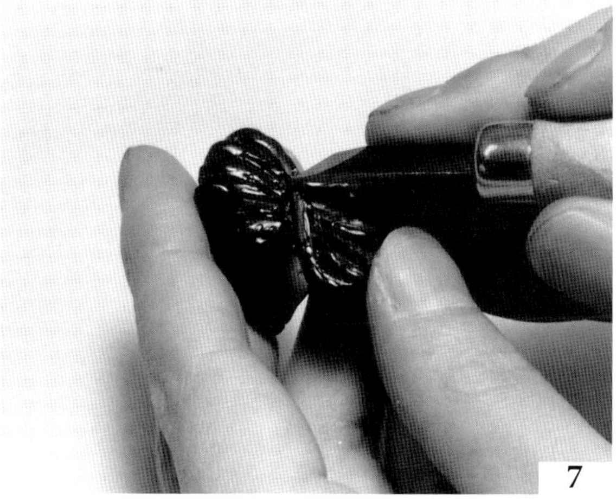

7

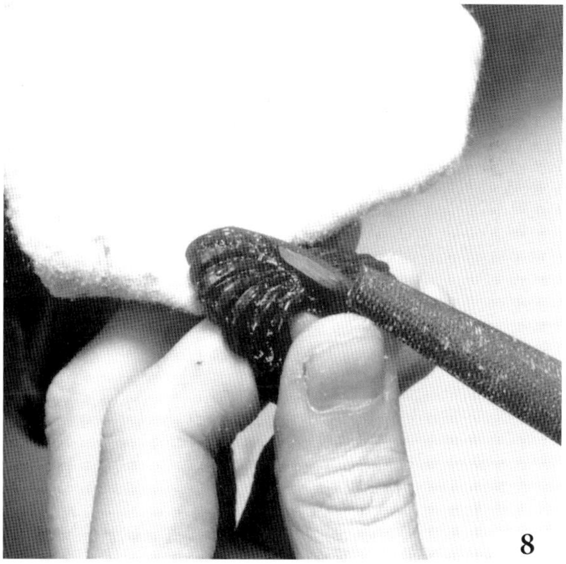

8

Use a knife carver to pare down areas with too much wax. Repair areas where the balance is bad or the grooves are buried.

As the large wave is the center of attraction use a file, from coarse to fine, to get a smooth shiny surface.

After the center portion has been tidied up use the *kisage,* abrasive papers and *takegushi* to finish up. Pay special attention to the grooves and edges. Use a *takegushi* shaped like a *kisage*.

In the event bubbles or cavities remain, repair them with wax again and refinish. The top surfaces other than the central wave will have an irregular, random texture as if created with the wax pen.

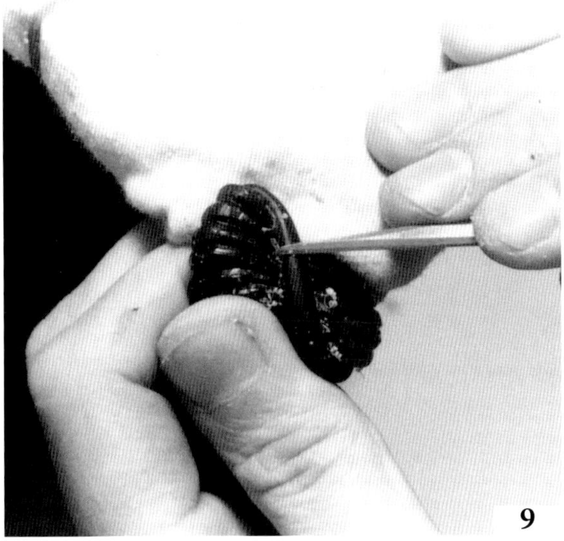

9

10

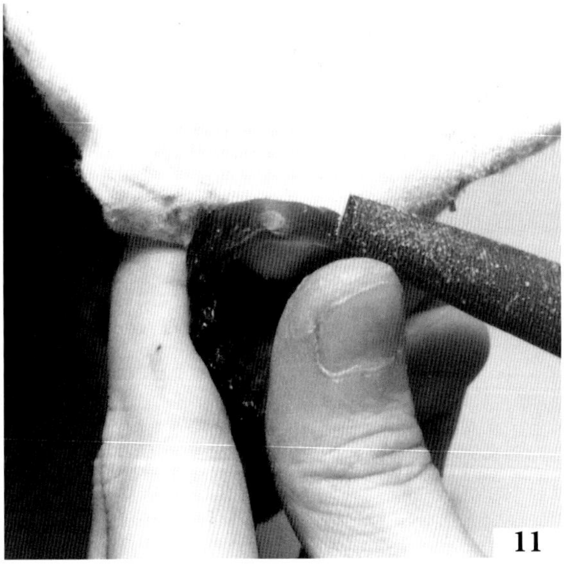

11

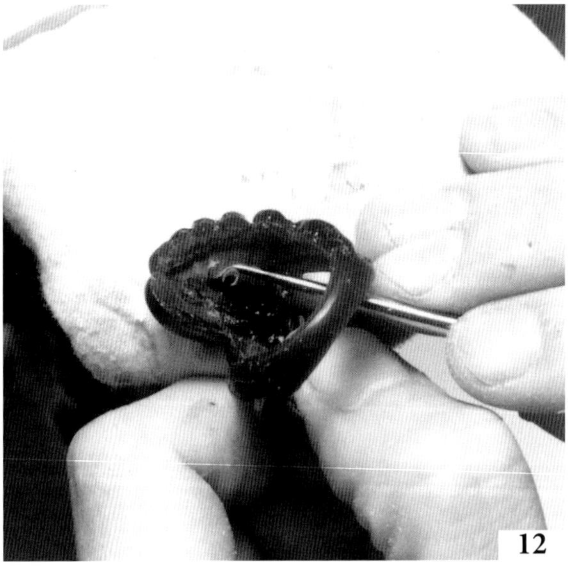

12

Shape the shank with a coarse file. Use the *kisage* and abrasive papers to finish. Finish the inner surfaces of the ring in a similar manner.

Last step — remove the excess material from the underside. Repair the bubbled areas with wax. Since the undersurface will be very uneven, hold it up to a light occasionally and remove small amounts at a time to prevent removing too much; use utmost care.

HOLLOW PENDANT

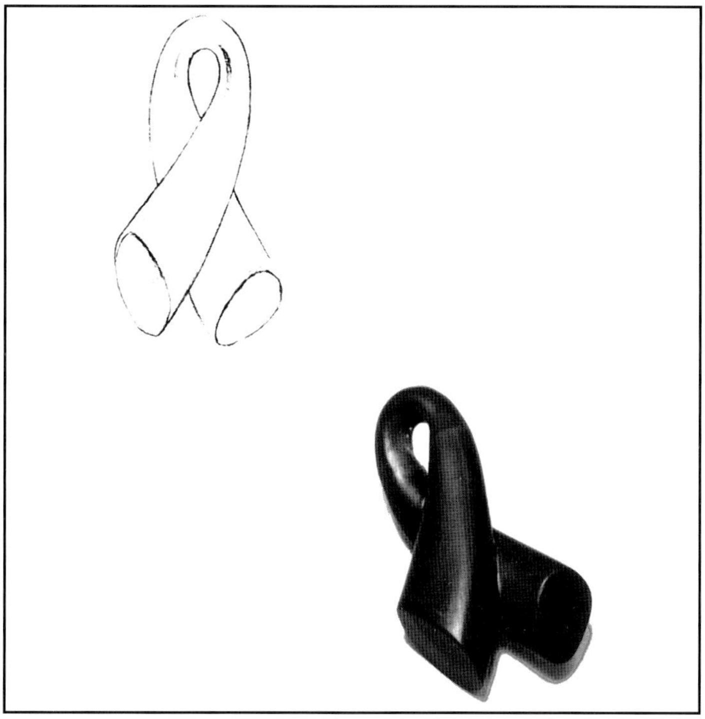

GENERAL DESCRIPTION:

In the case of a solid object, difficulties may be encountered in hollowing out the back or underside. By adapting the two part ring construction it will be possible to cut, hollow out and process each individual part and reassemble. This process of cutting off parts at the proper locations and hollowing out will be of great value in large weight reduction and cast metal economy.
Some thought will be required in reassembling the parts without altering or damaging the shape. Again, keep in mind the temperature requirement when wax build-up is needed and preventing bubbles in deposited wax.

WORK HINTS:

1. Determine the best locations to make the cuts.
2. Take precautions not to alter the shape.
3. Build up wax and finish to conceal the reassembled joints.

MATERIALS:

Slab of wax	Scriber
Jeweler's saw	Files
Abrasive papers	Spatulas
Carvers	Bur
Wax pen	

Use a piece of wax slightly larger than the design and draw the center lines in. Next, neatly reproduce the design about the center with a scriber. Keeping outside of the lines saw out the pendant. Do not cant the saw: hold it perpendicular to the piece.

1

File the sawn outline. At this time, file right up to the scribed lines. It may help to reproduce the design outline on the reverse face to keep from slanting off.

2

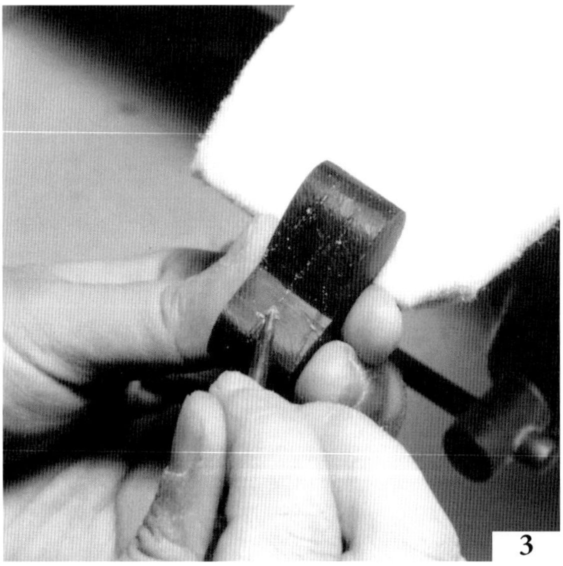

3

Next, scribe the center line. Also, add side views on both sides of the piece.

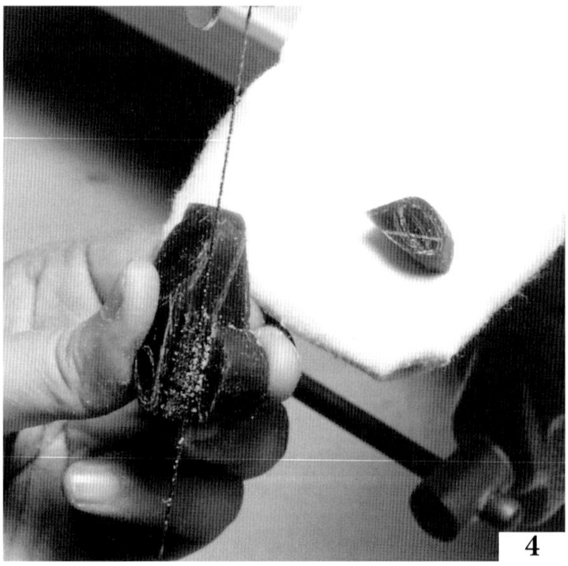

4

Cut the surplus material away. Cut in a manner to unite the front and back faces. Take care not to cut any more than necessary at this time.

Gradually shape the piece. From time to time mark corrections to be made with a scriber as you proceed. File the ends smoothly on an angle.

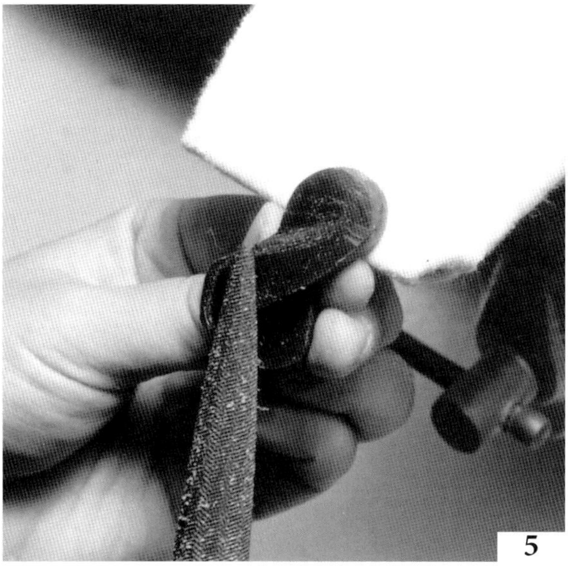

5

This design is like a twisted pipe. Bore a hole in the center of the crossover opening. Use a bud bur. A small hole will suffice as it will be shaped later with a file.

6

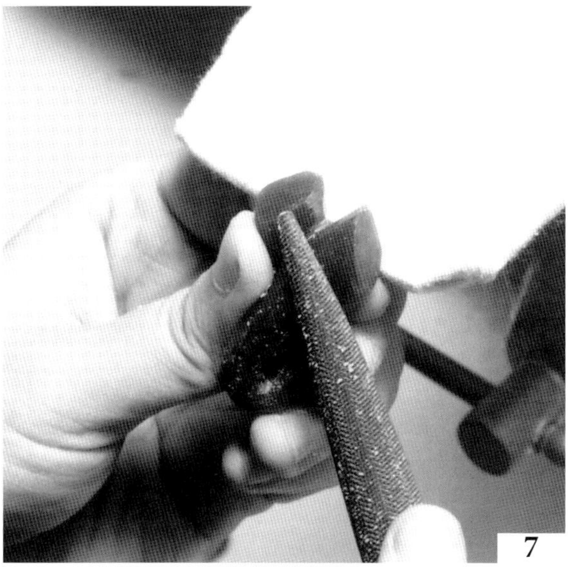

7

Round all the edges; the entire piece will have a round cross section. In places where access is difficult, use needle files.

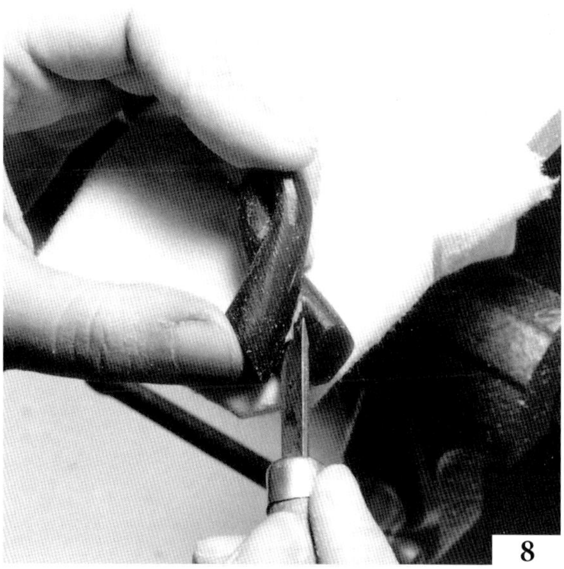

8

At the intersection, use a knife or *kisage* to get into the tight niches. Work on both sides together at the same time examining the progress.

Smoothly finish the opening with a small round file. Work on both sides at the same time to keep it balanced. Use the *kisage* to work on the tight portions.

Prepare the entire surface with a small file. Grip the file towards the end (short grip) for better control.

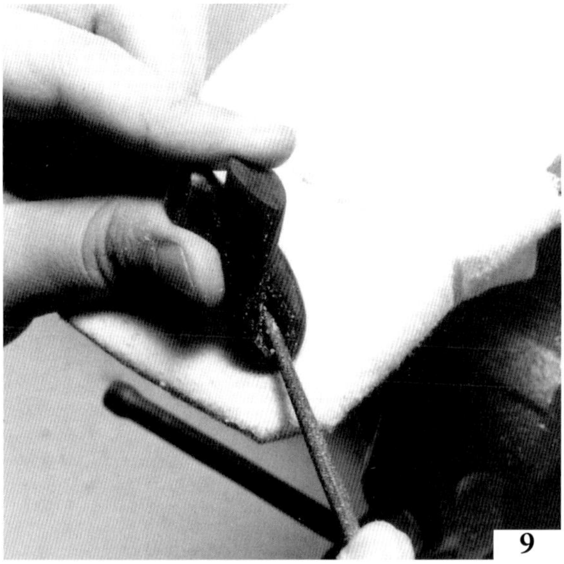

9

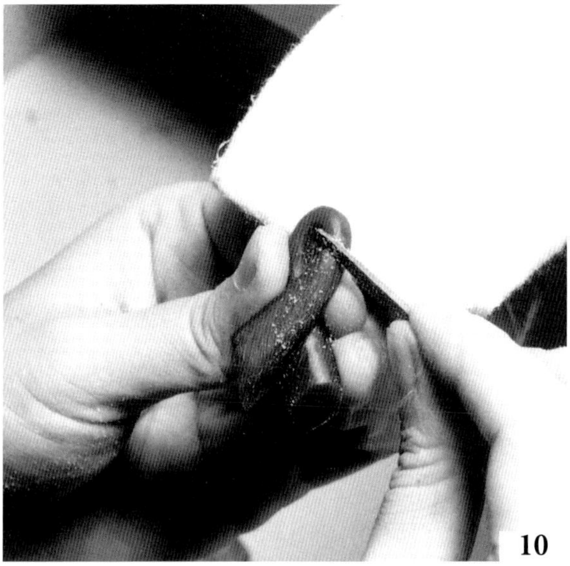

10

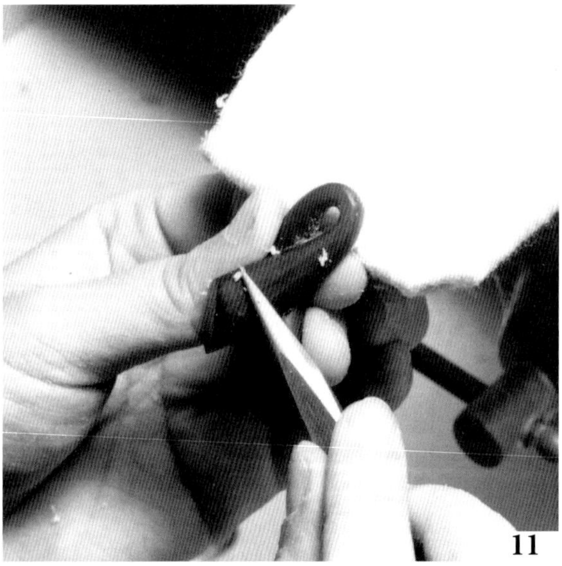

11

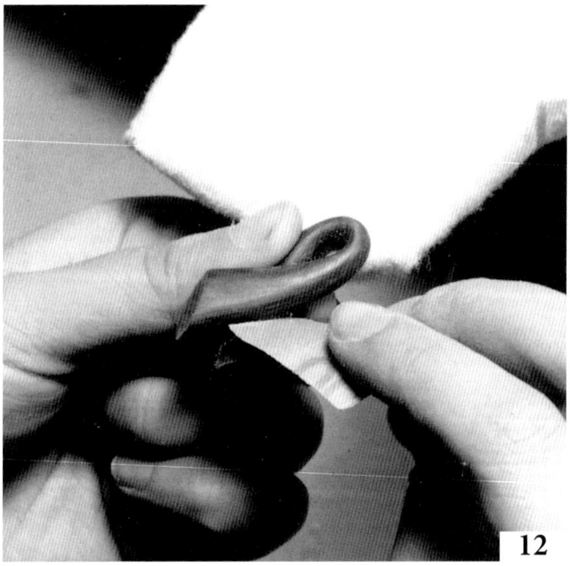

12

After the filing, follow up with the *kisage*. If the tool is difficult to manipulate, use abrasive papers. Finish the edges carefully.

Put the finishing touches on the entire piece with strips of abrasive paper, giving special attention to the tight areas.

Begin the material removal process. We will start from the ends, however, after the excess wax has been removed it will be covered. So first, scribe a line about 1 mm from the edges.

13

Cut off the end at the scribed line. At this time replace the wax blade with a finer metal cutting blade to keep the cut as fine and accurate as possible. Do not discard the cut off piece as it will be used as a cover.

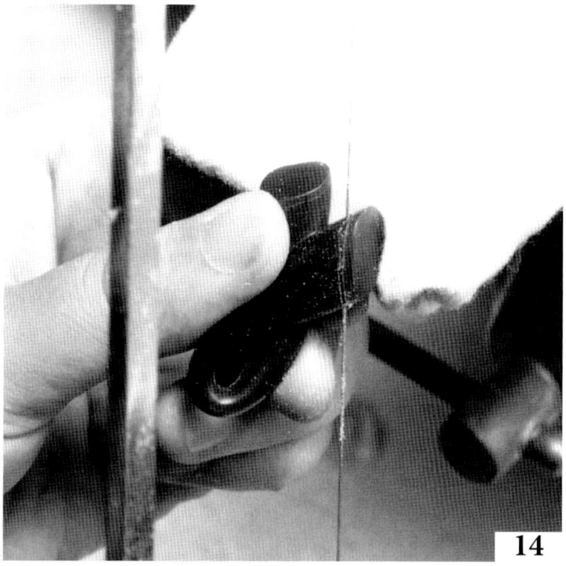

14

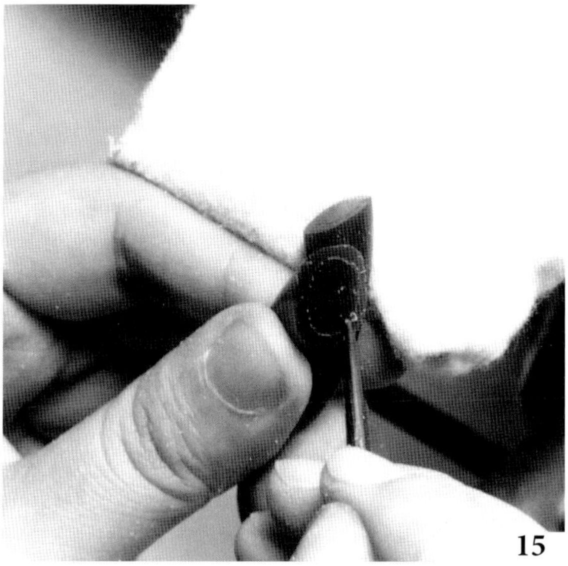

15

File the cut end lightly. Next, scribe a line about 1 mm from the edge. Material within that line will be removed with a bur and carvers.

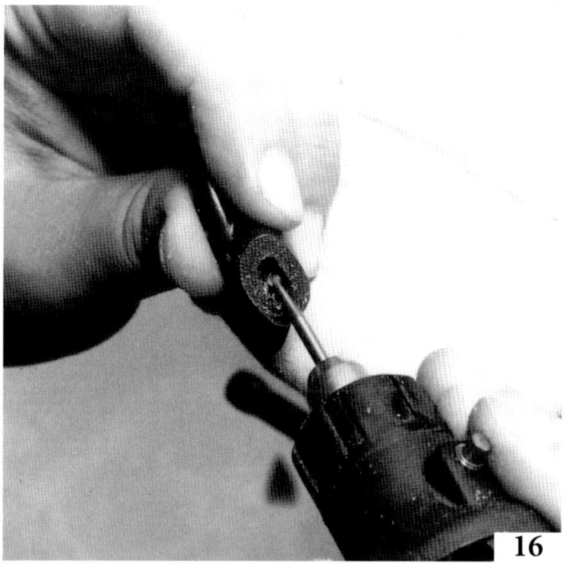

16

After removing the larger mass with a bur, use carvers to remove material as deeply as is feasible. Be watchful to stay within the limit set by the scriber and that the "wall" does not get overly thin.

To access the material which has not been removed, the pendant will be cut into parts which will be reassembled afterward. Determine where to place openings for investment entry and cut-off lines to sever the "U" part. Sketch with a marking pen and follow up with a scriber.

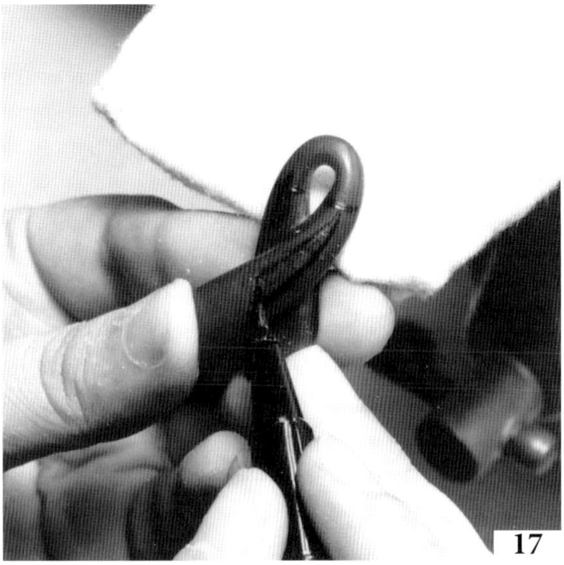
17

The placement of the "U" cut should be located where reassembly and material removal may be done expeditiously. When satisfied, cut the part off with a saw fitted with a metal cutting blade.

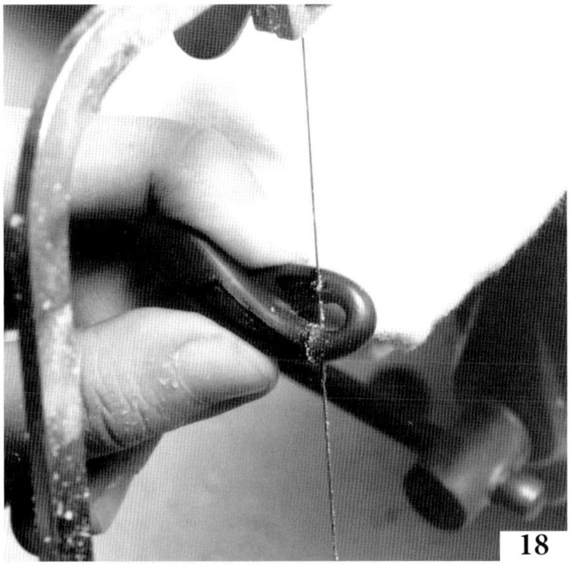
18

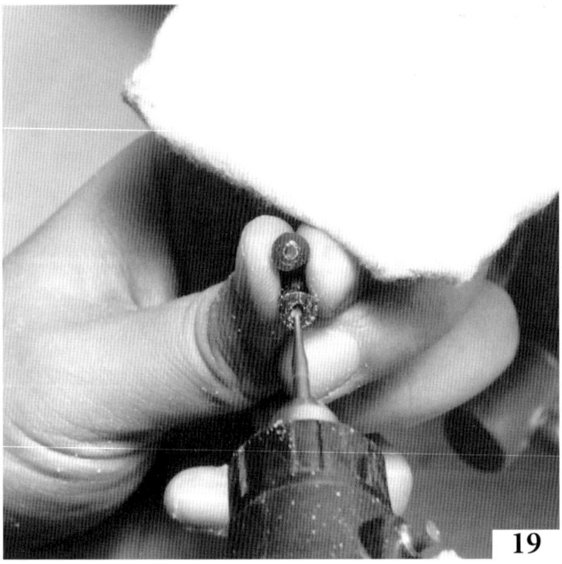
19

Remove material from the "U". Remove the excess wax with a bur and off-set carvers.

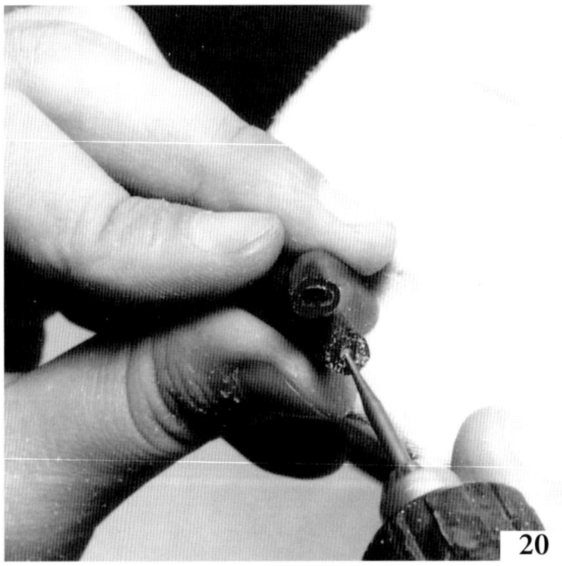
20

Remove material from the main body. Proceed as in the previous step. As the part is delicate, handle with care to prevent breakage.

Cut out the investment access opening with a carver. Through this opening remove any excess material. While removing, keep the wall thickness as uniform as possible.

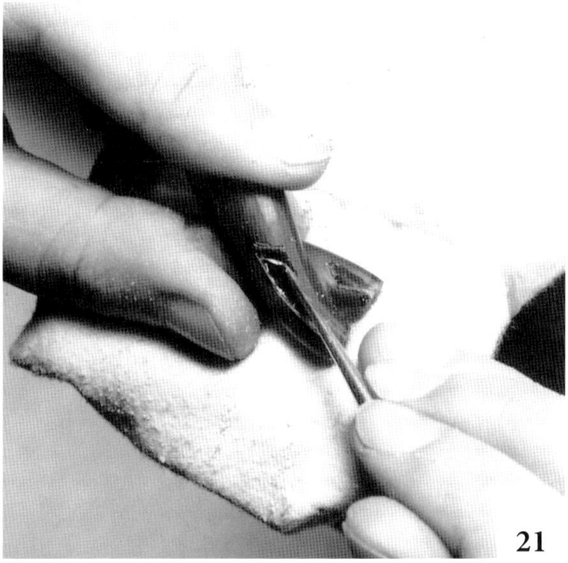

21

Finish the edges with the *kisage*. Give special attention to appearance, take added care to prevent any breakage.

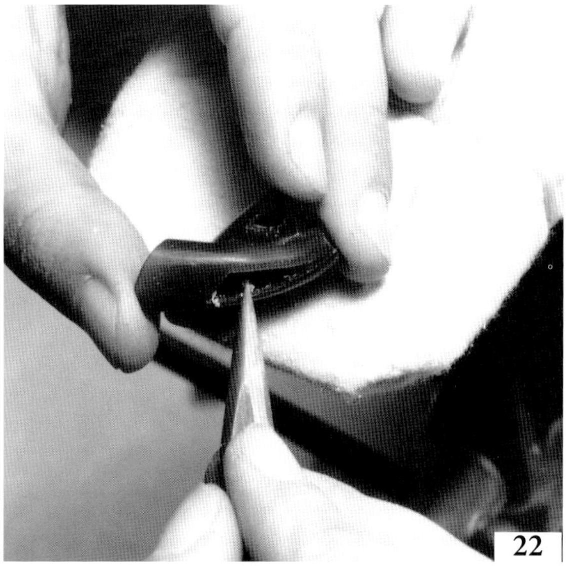

22

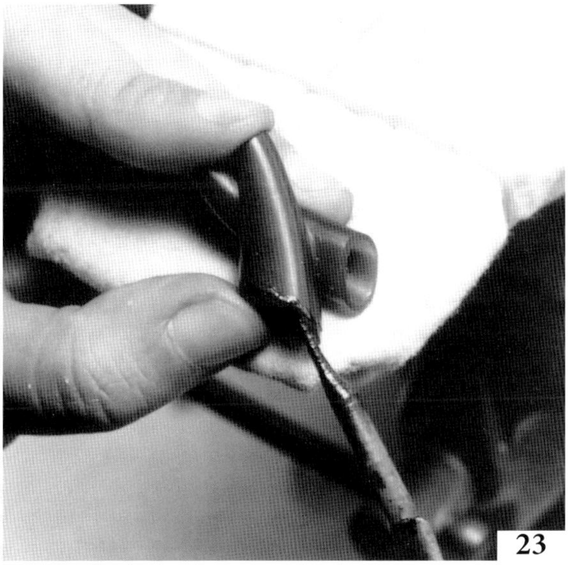

23

Reassemble the parts. Tack the cover with a hot needle and place additional wax along the seam with a wax pen. If cast separately this cover may be soldered on later.

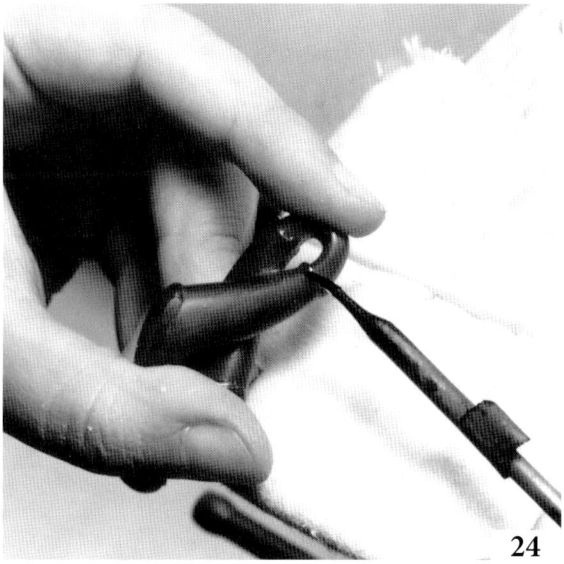

24

Refit the "U" joint. Proceed in the same manner as in Step 23 and apply wax to the seam. Because of its small size, excess heat may cause the wax to melt and distortion will occur; use care.

File the seam with a coarse file, then a finer file and finish up as explained in previous processes.

25

Repair wax bubbles and cavities. Use the wax pen and apply additional wax.

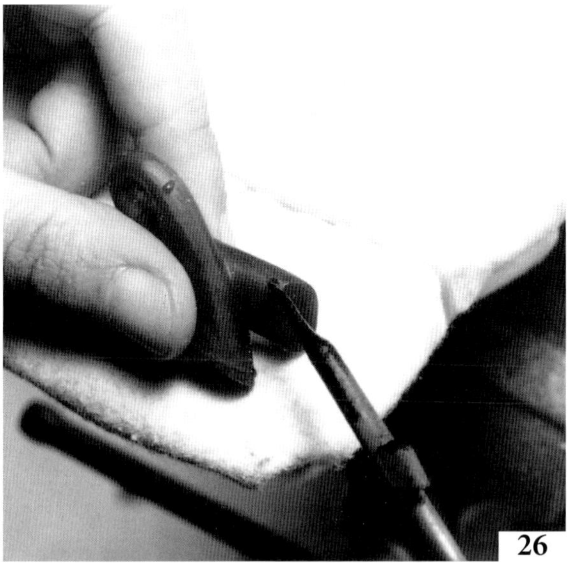

26

27

After you have finished shaping with the files, use abrasive papers to sand out small scratches. Use an abrasive eraser (ink or abrasive impregnated), *takegushi* and other tools, bring the surfaces to a polished finish.

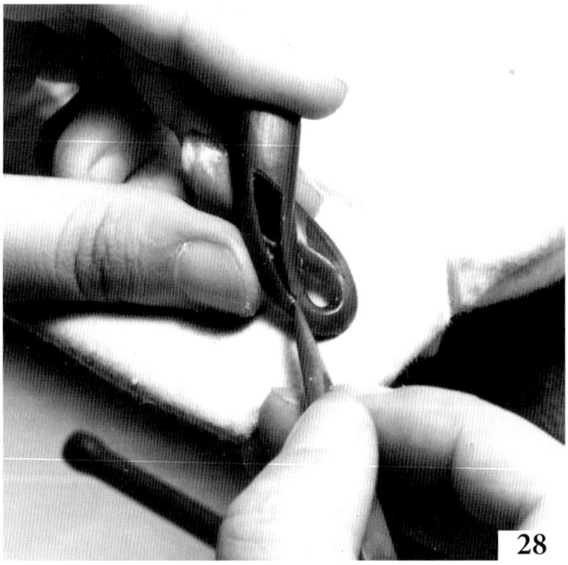

28

Use the *kisage* and go over the access openings again, leaving nice sharp edges.

BROOCH USING HARD AND SOFT WAX

GENERAL DESCRIPTION:

This brooch is constructed by melding the characteristics of hard and soft wax. After the main body is made from a block of wax with the underside hollowed out, wax wire pieces will be welded to it. The melting temperatures of the hard block wax and the soft wax wires are different so assemble with caution. Texture applied to the wax wires offers an effective contrast to the highly polished body.

WORK HINTS:

1. Learn the differences in the melting temperatures between hard and soft waxes.
2. Technique of applying texture to thin wax wires.
3. Welding hard and soft wax joints neatly.

MATERIALS:

Block of wax	Wax wires files
Scriber	Jeweler's saw
Abrasive papers	Welding needle
Carvers	

Determine from the design drawing the size of the wax slab which is required. Scribe the center lines and sketch the piece onto the wax. Cut the piece out: stay outside of the sketched lines.

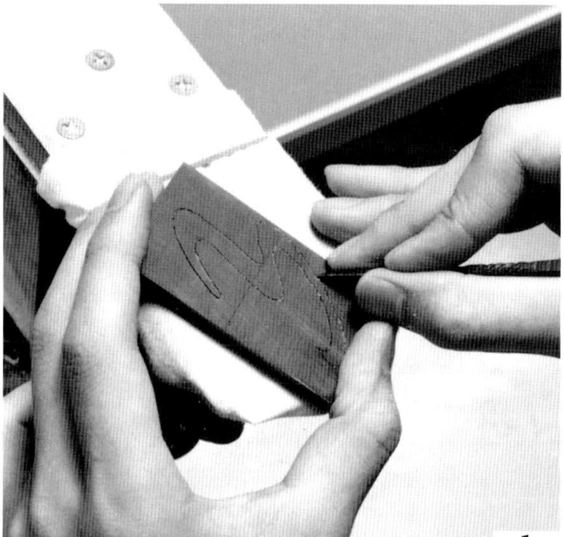

1

Trim the piece right up the outline with a wax file. Use a coarse file to produce a rounded profile.

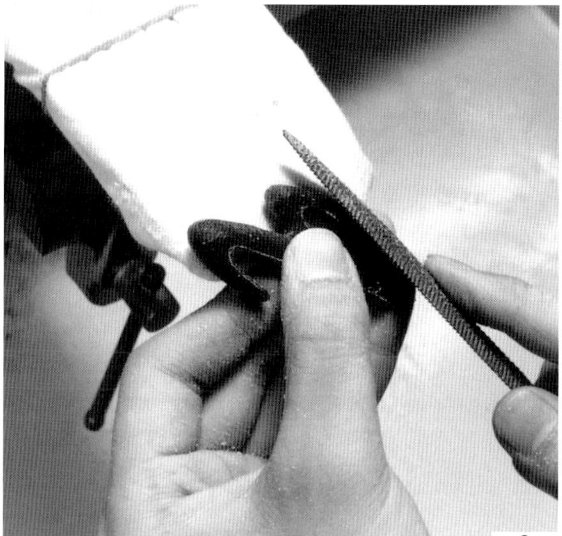

2

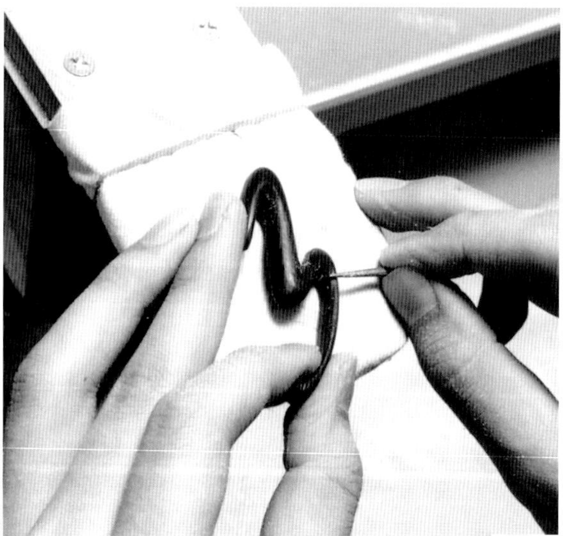

3

After the entire piece has been coarse filed, smoothen with a finer file. Use a round needle file to clean up the inner portions of the curves. Run a file over the entire surface, creating sleek irregular curves.

4

Use abrasive papers, in order, from coarse to fine. Where access is difficult for papers, use the *takegushi* and abrasive erasers to achieve a nice finish.

Use the bur and carvers to remove wax from the underside. Slender carvers will clean the material from the ends. Finish the piece with a thickness of about 0.8 mm.

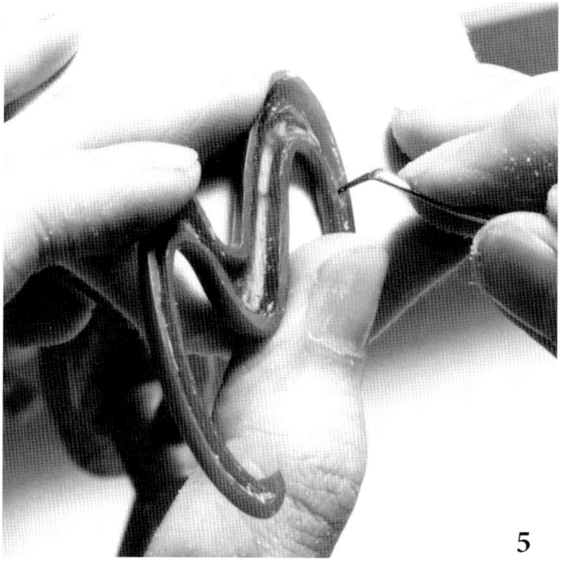

5

As you melt the main piece with a hot needle, weld the wax wires on, one-by-one. Melt the wax sufficiently as you insert the wires. By heating the immediate area near melt temperature again, the wire will blend in smoothly.

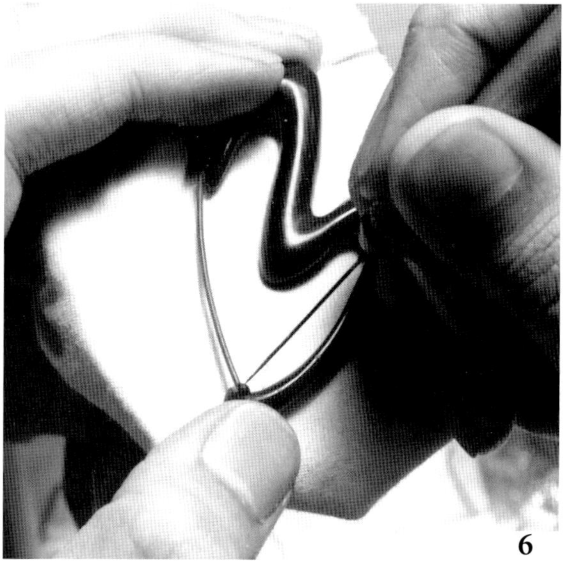

6

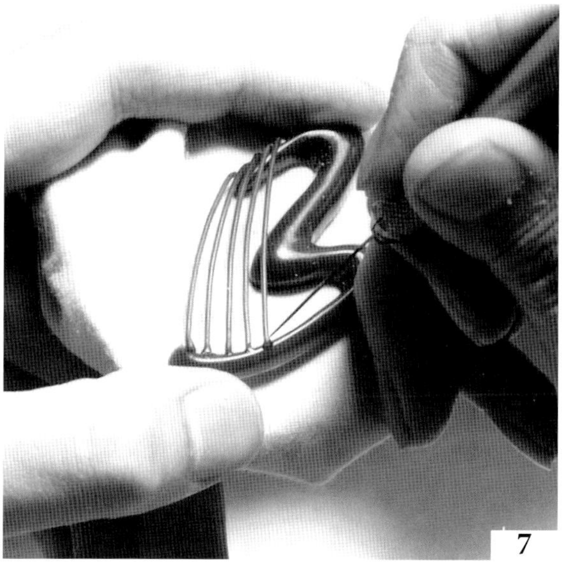

7

With appearance in mind, neatly insert wires one at a time equally spaced. At this time put a slight upward bow to the wires which will create a floating three dimensional effect.

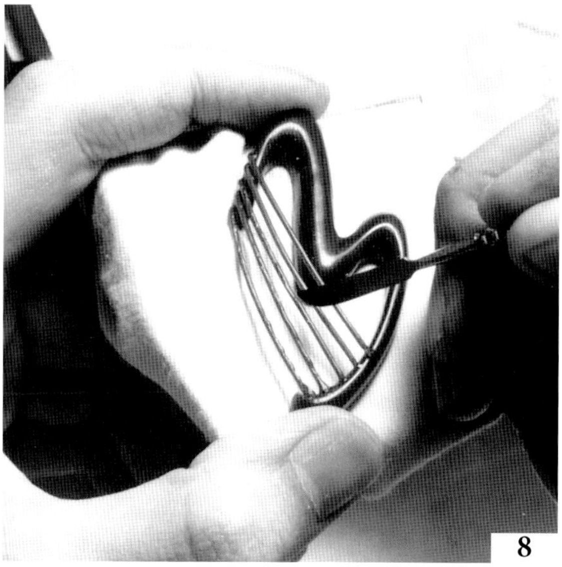

8

Apply texture to the wires with a warm spatula which will impart a unique, soft impression.

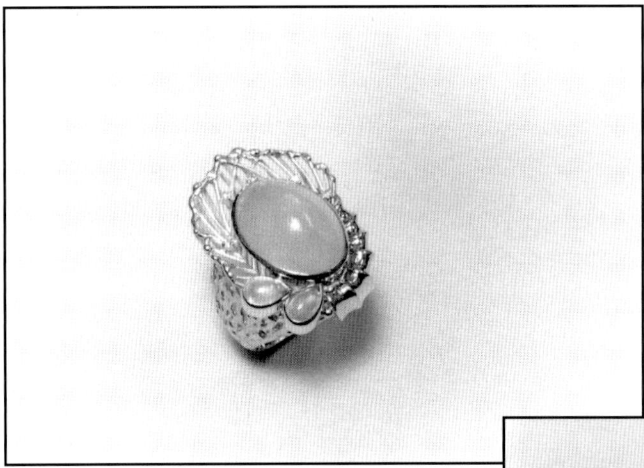

Ring with Wire Ornamentation.

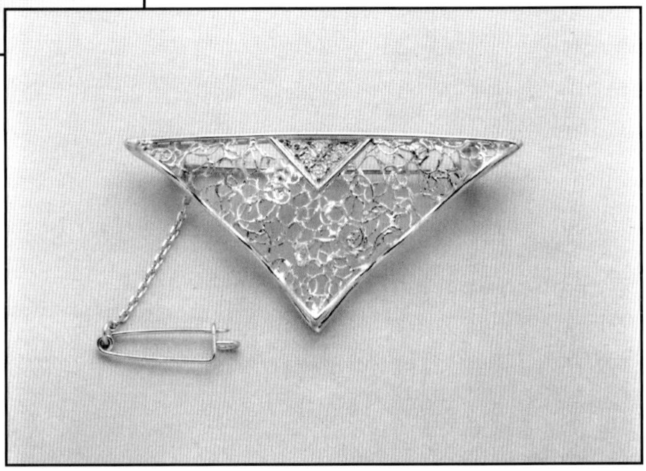

Wire Brooch in Mesh (Filigree Style).

Bent Wire Creation Adds Liveliness to a Brooch.

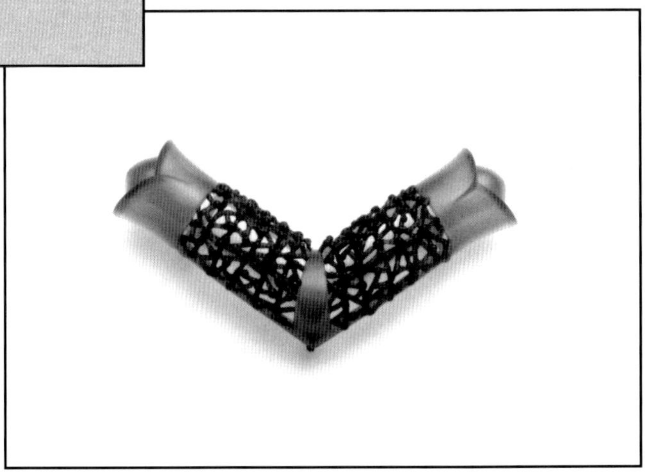

Brooch Constructed of Small Bits of Wire.

BROOCH WITH REALISTIC MODELING

GENERAL DESCRIPTION:

One characteristic of hard wax is that it can be carved. To express the embodiment of people, animals and plants in wax form, hard wax is most suitable. Materials and the art of carving are found in wood-carving, sculpturing in clay, metal-carving, etc. Methods of carving precious metals with gravers can be found in the jewelry world as well, but extensive experience is necessary. Compared to precious metals, one might say that wax is a very easy material to manage and convenient to carve or add on.

Here, you will carve a girl's head in relief, however, her face and hair will be made in two parts and assembled afterward. It is possible to construct it in one piece but it is easier to bring out the 3 dimensional features using this method. This construction method of assembling and fusing with heat brings out the special characteristics of the wax.

WORK HINTS:

1. As you construct the model, bear in mind that the facial expression and the flow of the hair are integral to the whole.
2. Avoid making the model look "flat".
3. Fit the face and hair exactly.

MATERIALS:

Blocks of wax	Spring gauge	Bur
Jeweler's saw	Toothbrush	*Kisage*
Abrasive papers	Scriber	Tracing paper
Knives	Files	Abrasive impregnated eraser
Wax pen	Carvers	

Here, we will construct the face and the hair separately. Trace the outlines of these two parts from the design drawing onto tracing paper.

Tape or use rubber cement to secure each tracing on separate blocks of wax and transfer the outline with a series of piercing dots made with a scriber (connect the dots on the wax with the scriber afterward). Use blocks of ample thickness, especially for the face.

1

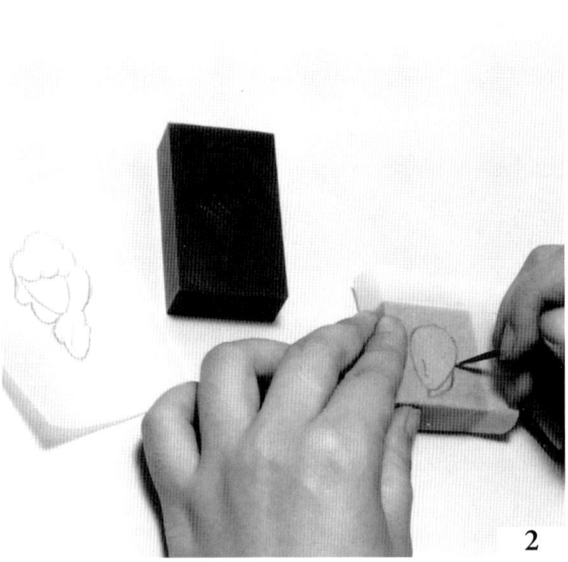

2

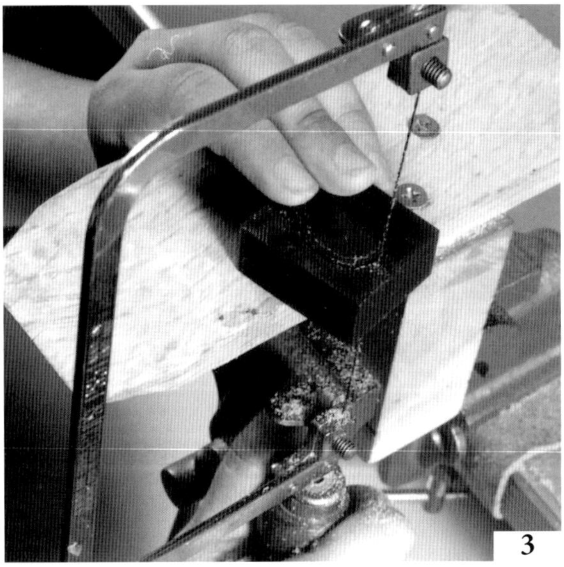

3

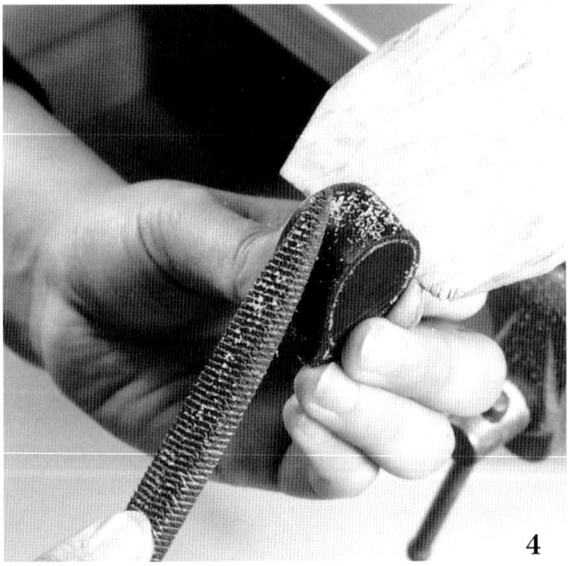

4

Start first with the face. Cut slightly outside of the scribed lines. As the piece is quite thick, keep the saw in a vertical position. There is less chance for error if the piece is copied on both sides.

File to the scribed lines. Afterward, check the different heights between the face and neck, scribe this difference on both sides of the piece with a scriber.

Following the scribed lines, file the neck portion down. At this time, take care not to over cut. From time to time, check the appearance and patiently proceed with the work.

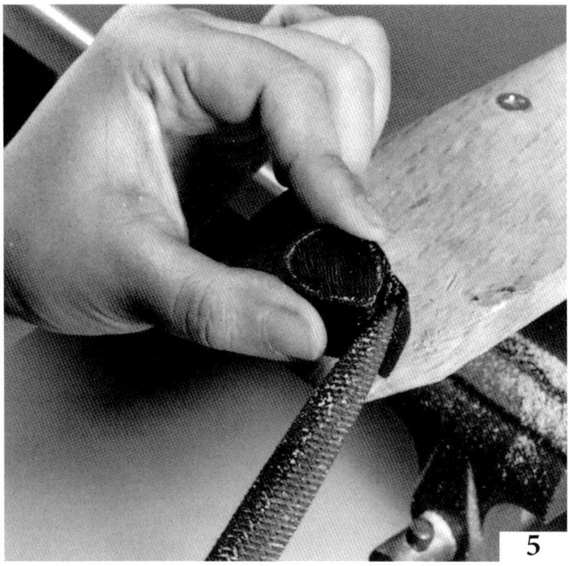

5

Round the head and face. File in a stroking manner as you break the edges. Do the same for the neck.

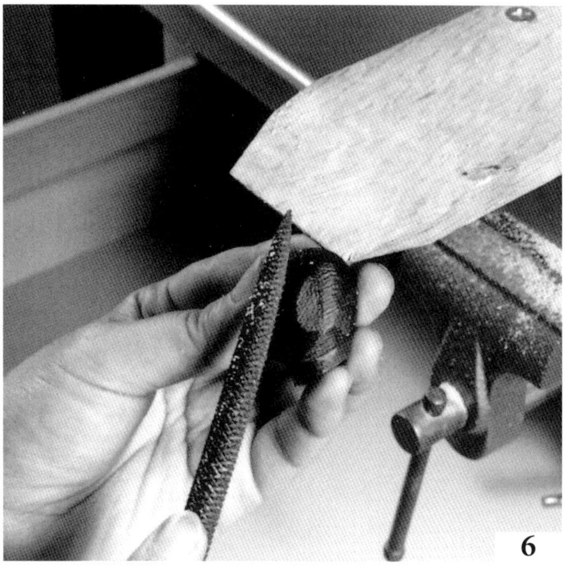

6

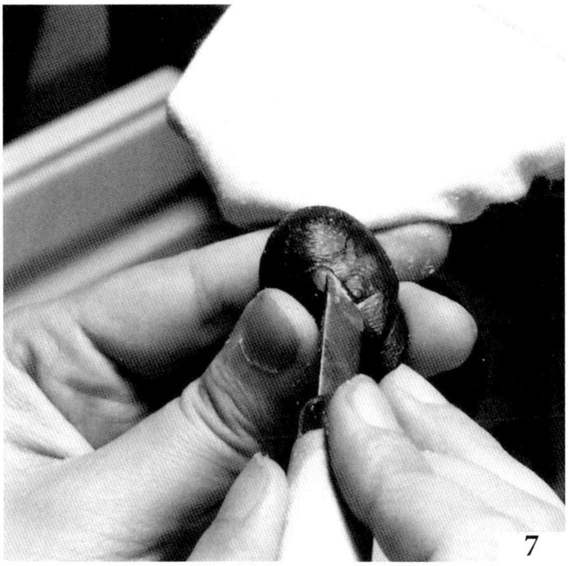

7

After rounding, first cut out the nose. Work on both sides of the nose: although there may not be enough material to reach the top of the nose, it may be built up with wax later.

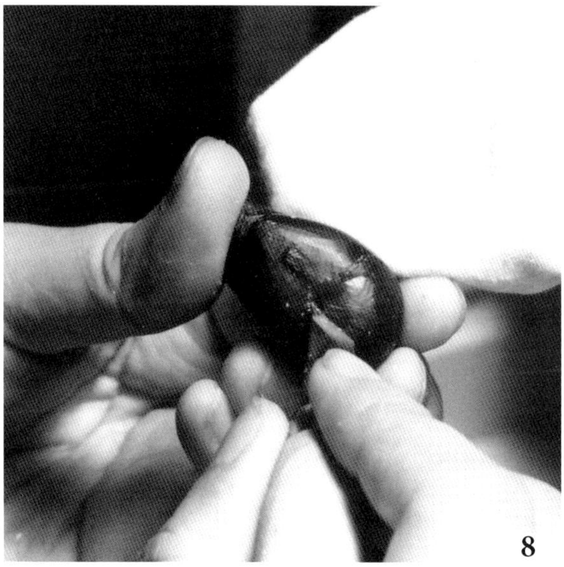

8

Work the eye area. First lower the area under the eyebrows. Leave a slight protrusion between the eyebrows. Next, determine the location of the eyes: draw them in with a marking pen. If the eyes are set too deep the expression will be severe. Work carefully to maintain balance.

Remove as much material as you can with a knife carver; use a small round carver to deepen the upper eye area. Contour the face. Use the carver to develop the slight swelling of the eyelids of the model's closed eyes.

Next carve the lips. Since the lips, along with the nose, protrude the most, it's possible to build up wax for them. First carve the level line which separates the lips, then trim both sides slightly to bring out the contour of the lips.

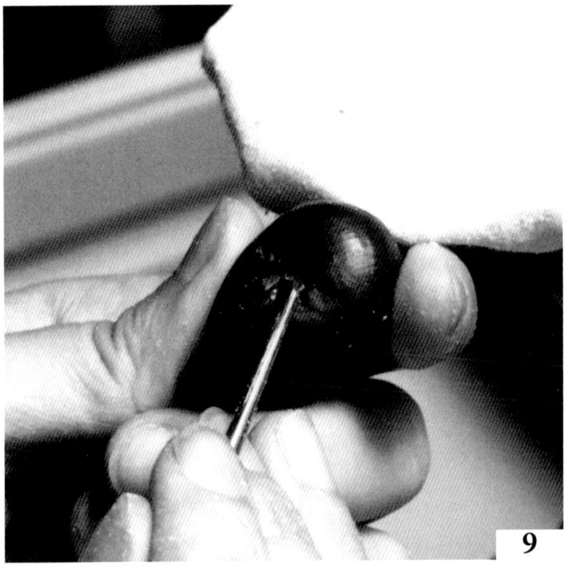

9

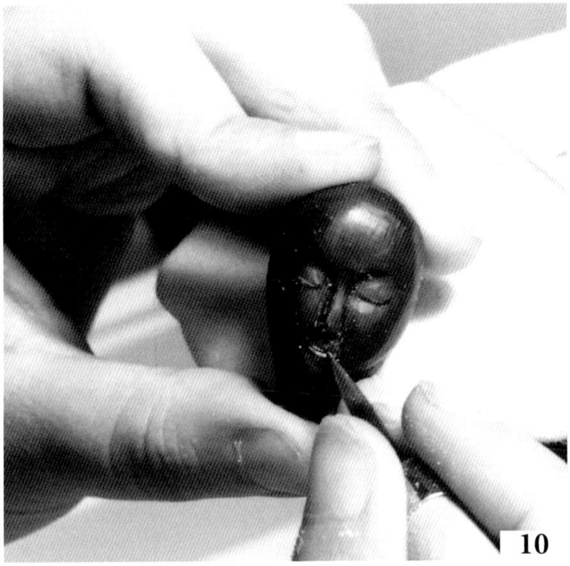

10

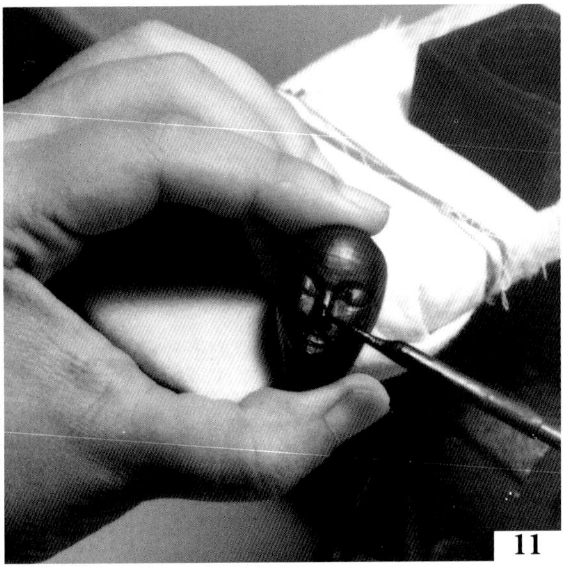

11

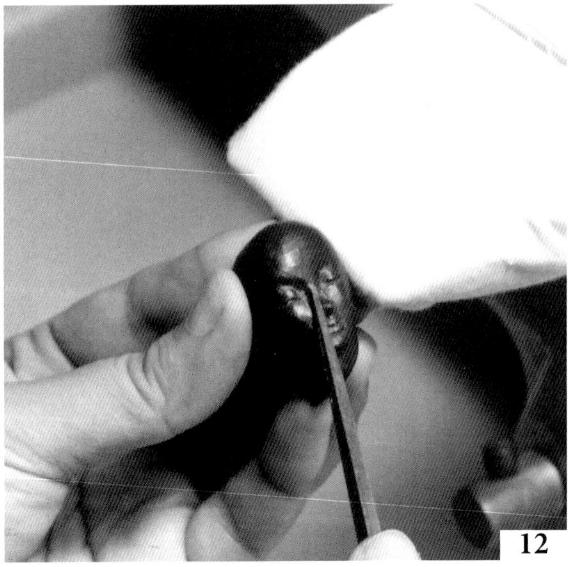

12

After the model is roughed in, build up the tip of the nose and the nostrils with a heated spatula or a wax pen. However, check from front to side to establish the height.

Now, shape the nose. With a small file finish up neatly, with special attention to its shape.

After the nose is finished, turn the figure upside down and create the nostrils with a pointed spatula or needle. Make holes about 2 or 3 mm deep. There is no need to go deep.

Build up the lips with small amounts of wax. Too much lip will cause the model to lose its daintiness. The groove line separating the lips will be filled if too much wax is applied: add wax moderately.

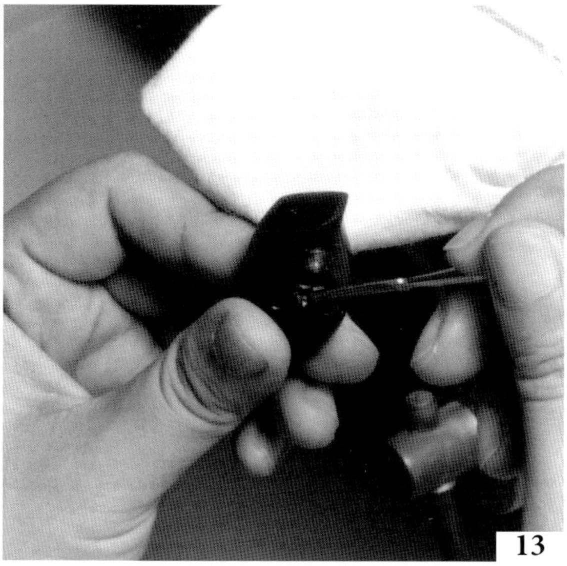

13

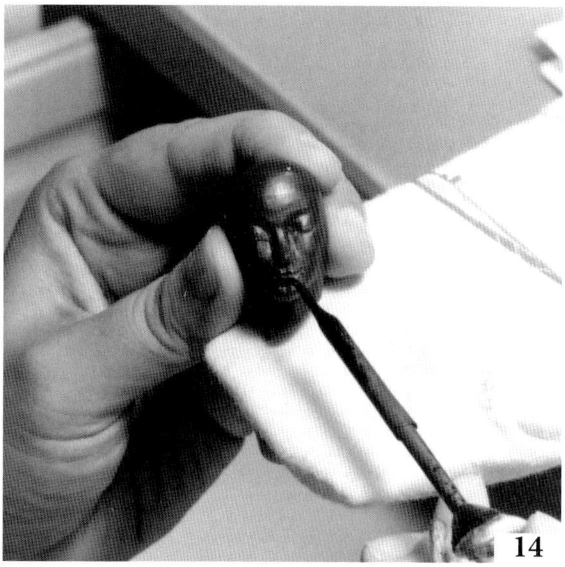

14

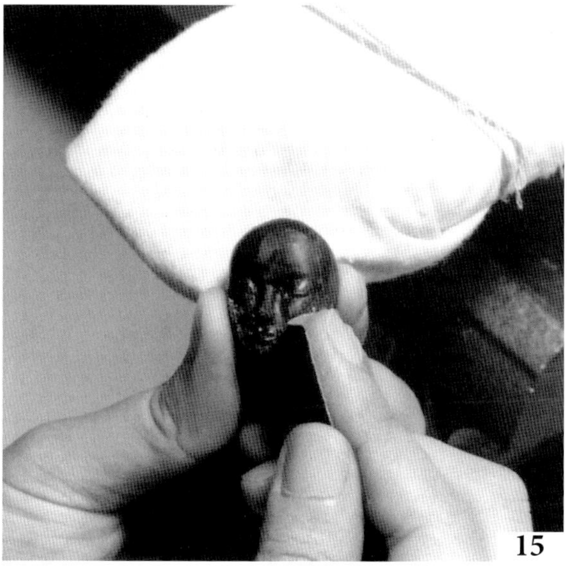

15

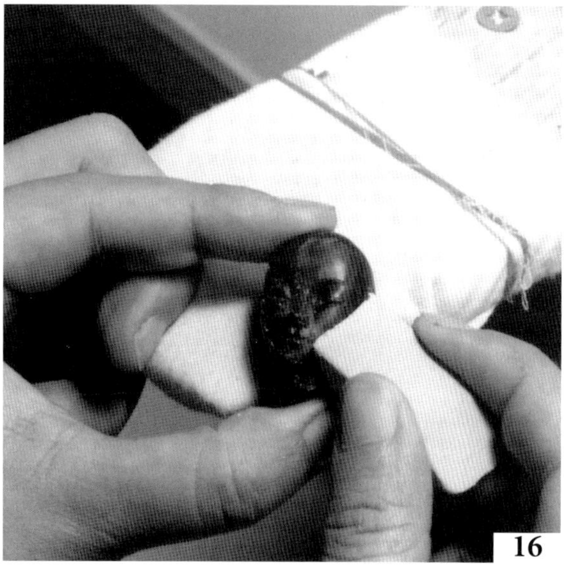

16

After you've carved the nose and lips, polish the entire piece with abrasive papers. Where access is tight, use a pointed *takegushi.*

To round out the cheek and forehead, use an abrasive impregnated eraser to polish out small scratches. To smoothen small areas around the eyes and mouth, etc., the *takegushi* is convenient. Completely finish the neck and forehead in a similar manner.

To bring out the sheen, use a tooth brush or piece of nylon. Take pains to eradicate small bothersome scratches. The work on the face is put aside for now.

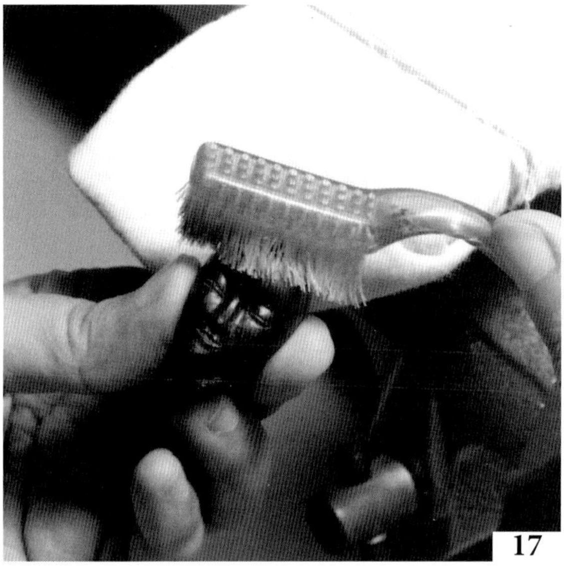

17

Make the hair next. Transfer the pattern onto the block of wax; cut larger than the sketch. Clean up the cut surfaces with a file. Carve out the portion for the face.

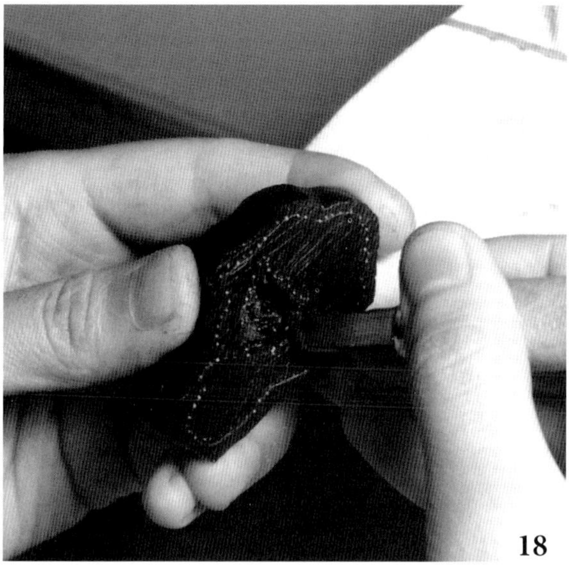

18

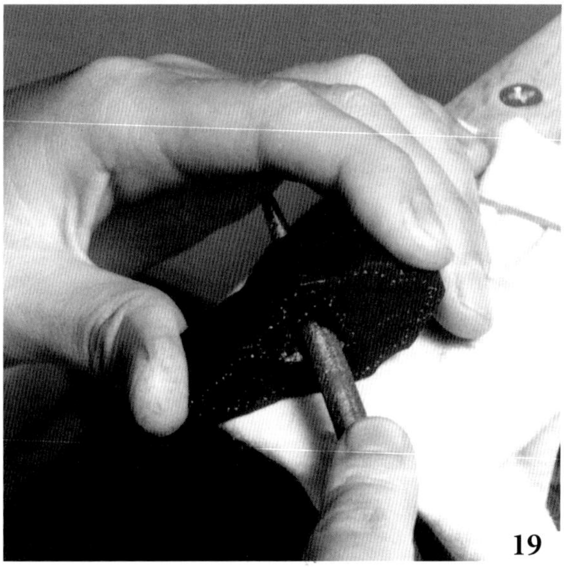

19

As you carve into the opening use a carver, enlarge the hole with a file. However, the hole should be smaller than the final opening for the face at this time.

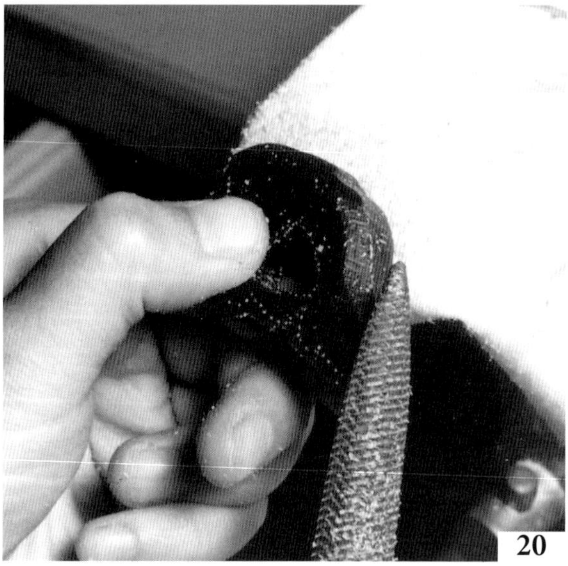

20

After the opening has been completed, round out the entire front portion with a file, conscious of the billowing effect required for the hair. Use a coarse wax file; the main purpose is to reduce the excess material.

Establish the high and low areas with the file, referring to the design drawing as you proceed. Now and again scribe control lines to conform with the design.

21

After the rough filing is done, cut in the grooves (demarcating the parts in the hair). Visualize the hair as a large cascade as you cut to represent this flow.

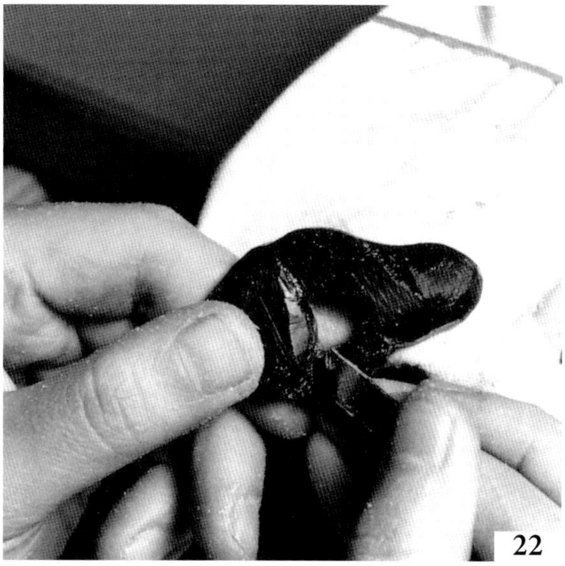

22

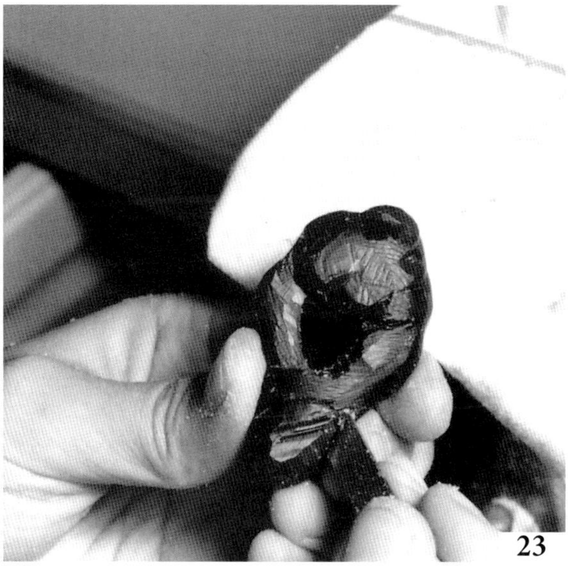

23

Carve the hollow for the face and other small areas a little at a time. You can use a knife and carvers but, a knife with a reduced size cutting point will work better.

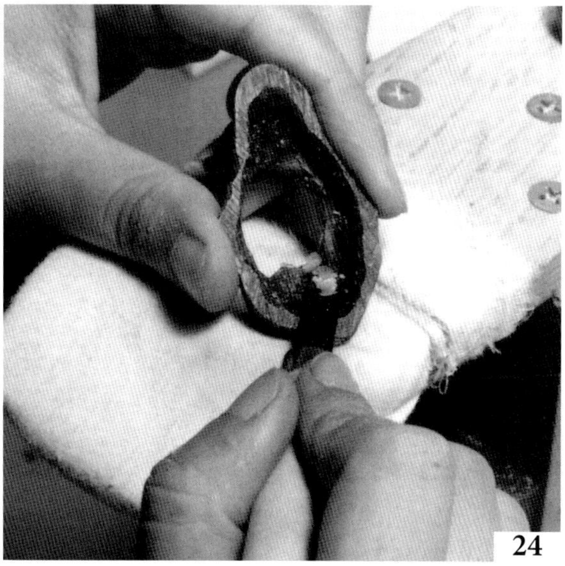

24

When the front portion is 60-70 percent complete, begin removal of excess wax from the back. In as much as the face must fit in from the reverse side give its size some thought as you rough out.

After the rough carving is finished, make a trial fit of the parts. Pare down the areas of interference with the bur and carvers until you arrive at an exact fit. Take care not to over cut or leave cuts undone.

Examine the front. To get the hair over the face as per the design, carefully widen the opening as required with a file. Make slight adjustments to the hair part. Where it is slightly high, trim down with a file. If the face is hidden too much, widen the opening.

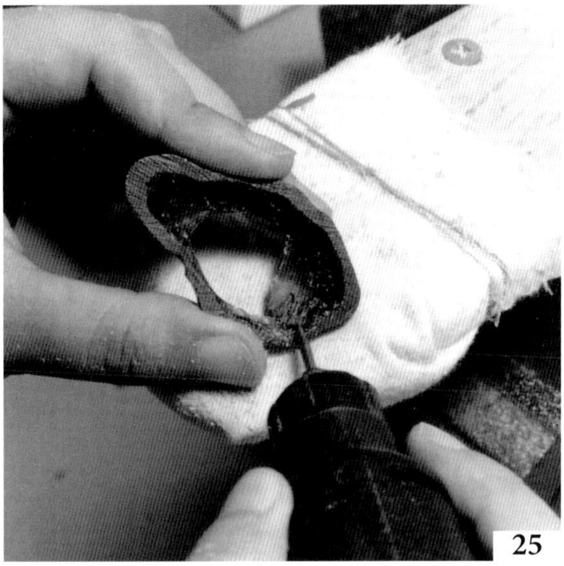
25

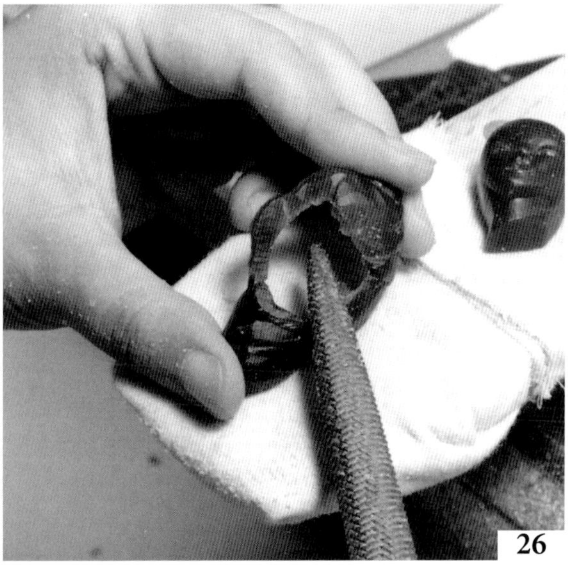
26

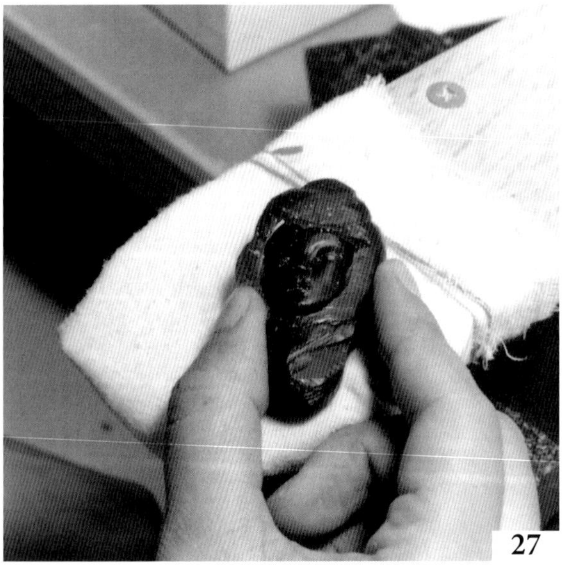
27

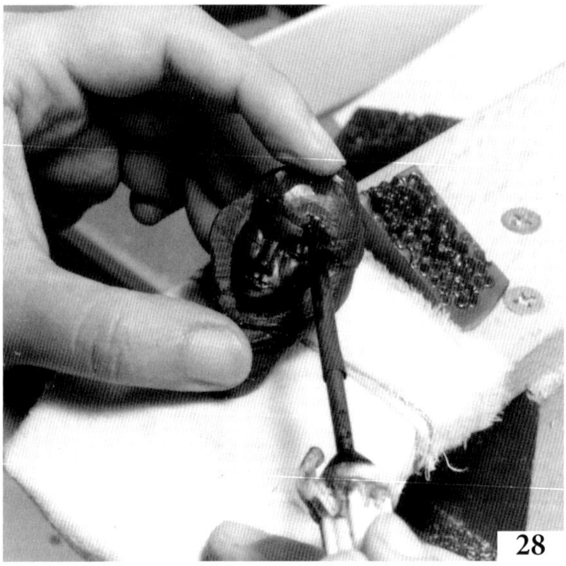
28

Fit the parts together. While checking for overall balance, look for gaps. In the event of a gap, patch it up with wax; shave down projections etc., making adjustments as necessary.

Once the face and hair fit exactly, use a heated spatula or a wax pen with a small tip and join the two together. Adding wax if it is needed, unite the parts accurately.

Weld the contact seams together from the rear. Unite the pieces into one body by melting the wax from the face and hair at the same time. At this time, take care not to allow air bubbles to form.

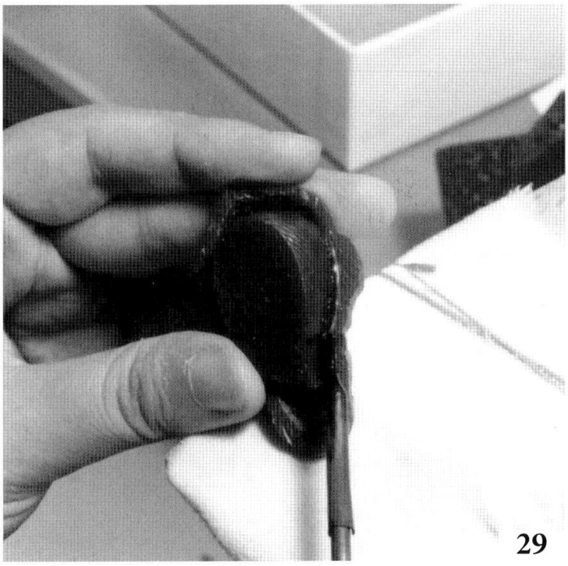
29

Cut away all excess material from the head. File the sawed surface flush and smooth.

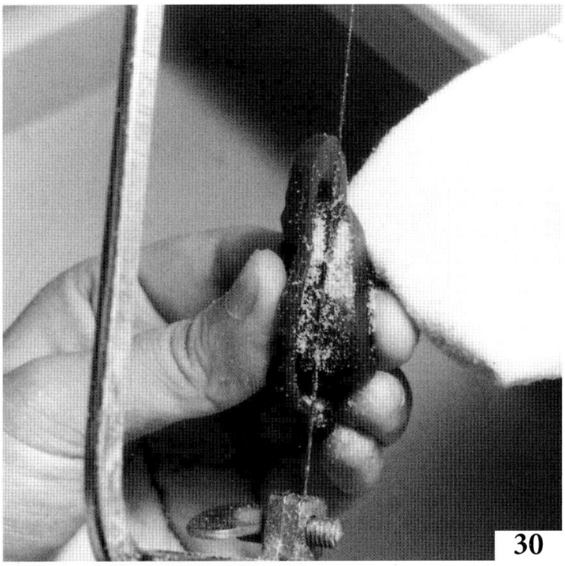
30

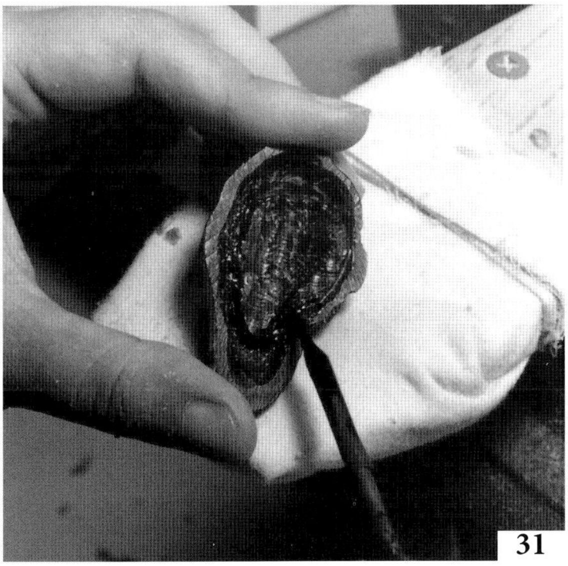
31

In this step a large amount of material from the backside will be removed. Remove material from the head portion with carvers; carve up to the edge of the hair part. While removing, if you come across a gap, fill it with wax. Carve to a thickness of about 3 mm.

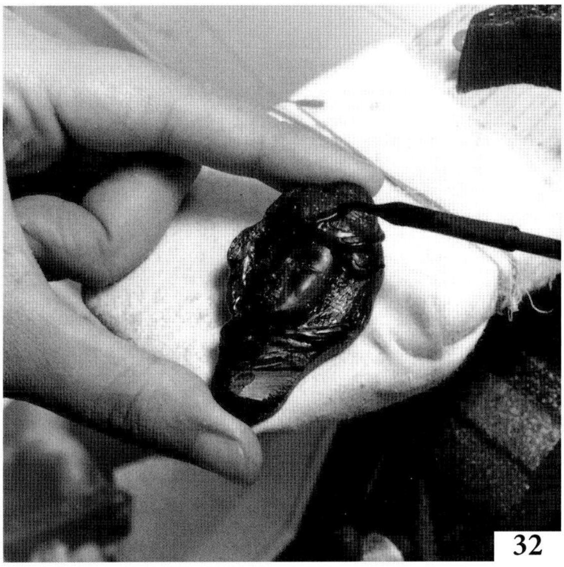
32

Return to the front. As you build up the wax with a wax pen for the large wave, apply it in a flowing manner. You may also build up wax to simulate hair in a curly arrangement.

Shape and style the hair. The details of the flow of hair strands will be incised with a knife carver. Clean up the junction of the face and hair with the same carver.

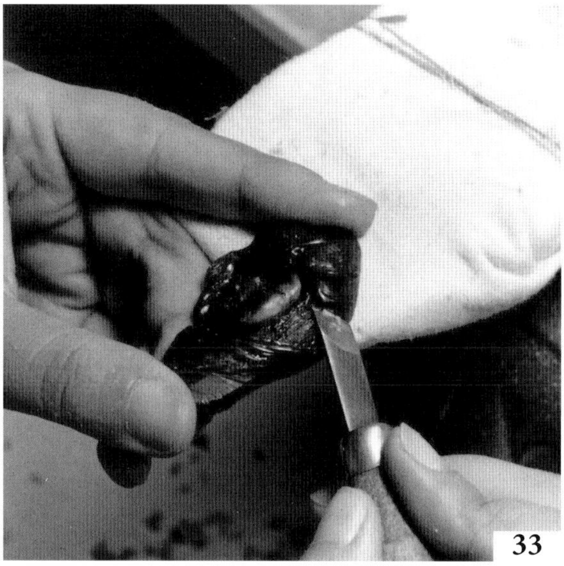

33

There are openings where the hair passes over the neck portion. Create these openings with a bur. Widen the openings with small files and a slender knife and cut the hair to shape.

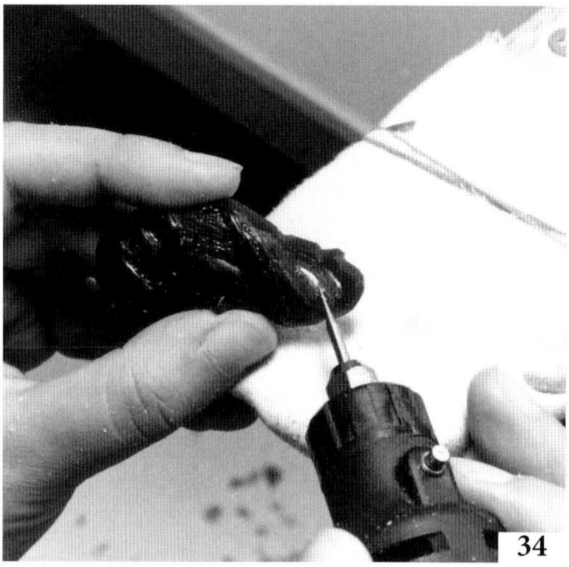

34

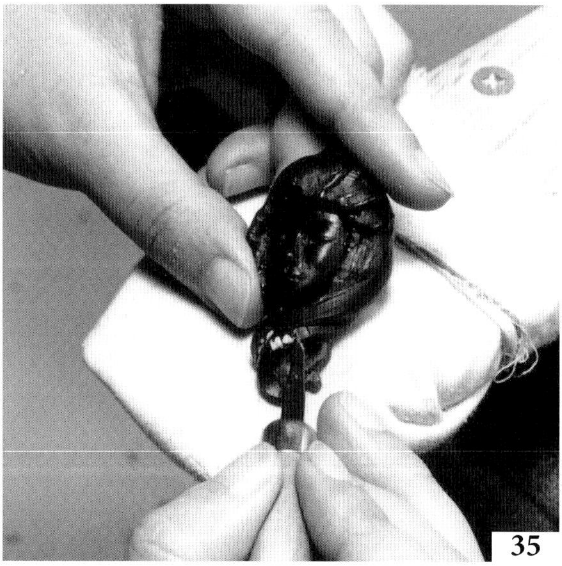

35

After the openings have been created, follow the flow and add contour and "motion" to the waves with small carvers.

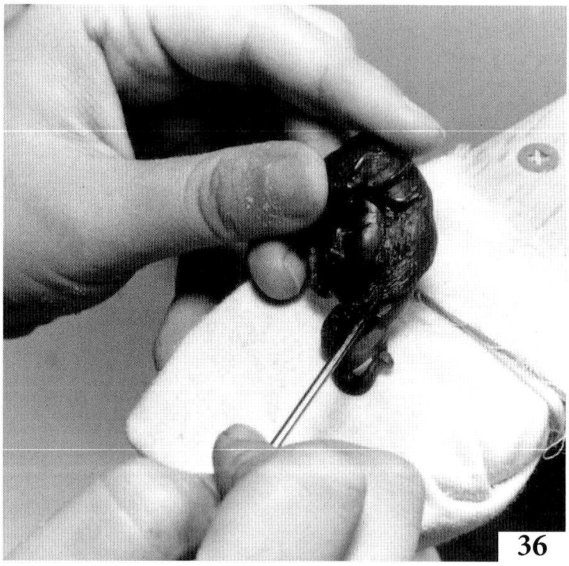

36

After the hair has been styled, add texture. Use a warm sharp pointed spatula and neatly incise minute lines simulating strands of hair.

It is preferable to put in many lines at the base of the hair, fewer at the top. Try to impart the feeling of softness and volume to the hair.

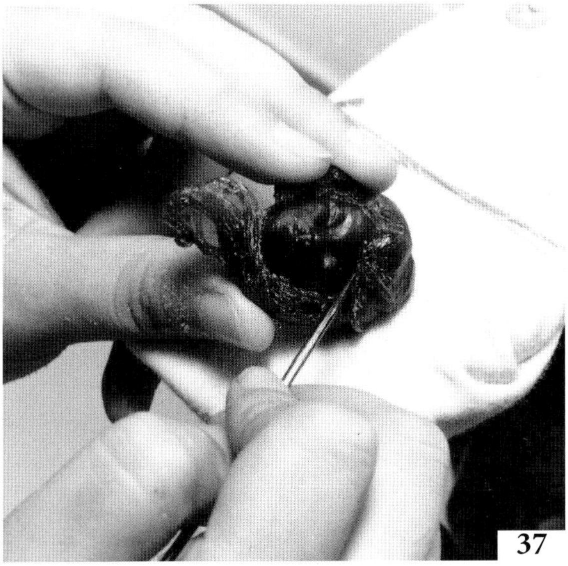
37

Use spatula and abrasive papers to repair scratches which were made inadvertently on the face. As the base of the hair will draw attention, finish to produce an especially neat appearance here.

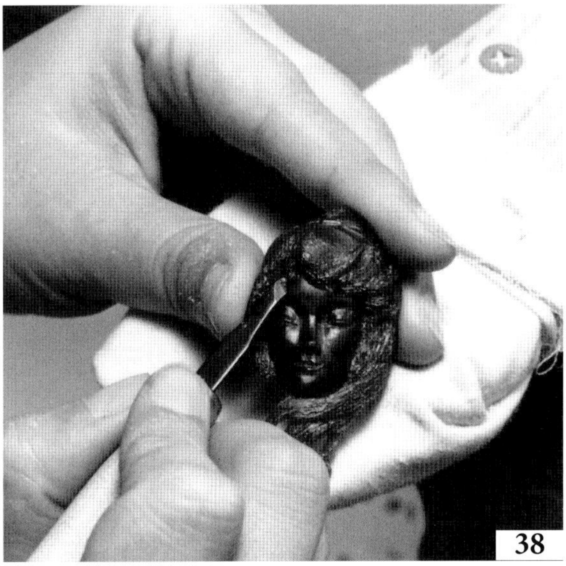
38

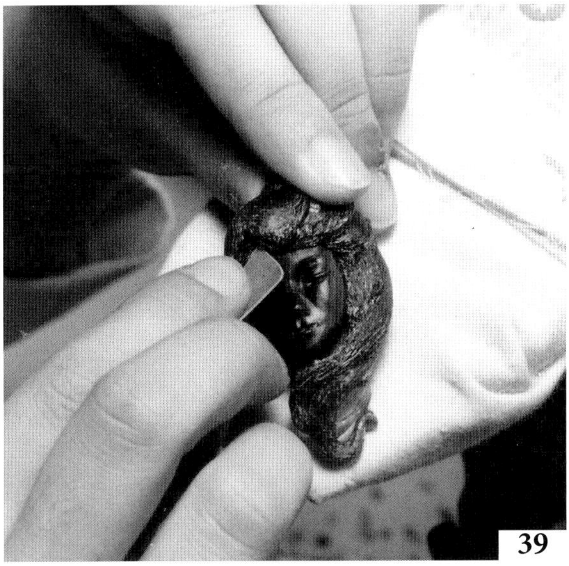
39

Finalize work on the front. Use abrasive papers and *takegushi* along the edges, polish out small scratches, etc, and finish up neatly. When cast, tight areas will be difficult to polish so to avoid any oversight, work carefully from edge to edge, corner to corner.

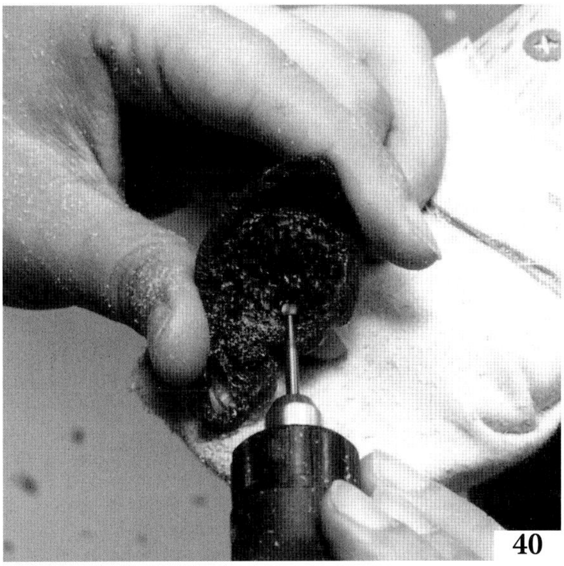
40

As you have roughed out the backside, use the bur to finish up. Since the face and hair are extremely contoured, hold the model up to the light from time to time, taking care not to go through. If some bubbles have formed, add wax and repair.

Brooch - Figure with Hair Created from a Free Form.

Brooch - Stylized Dress.

Brooch - Owl.

Brooch - Pegasus.

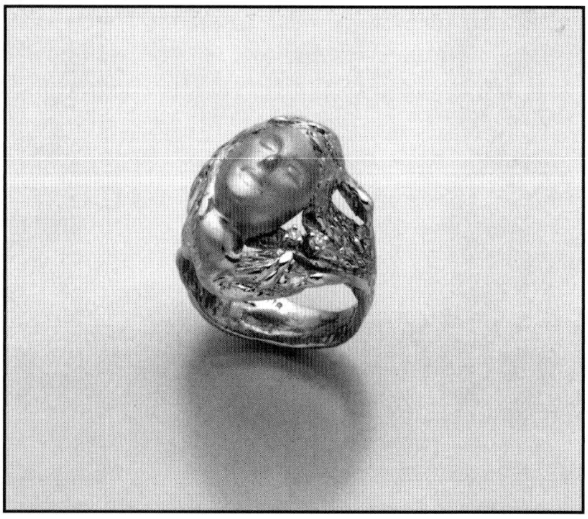

Brooch - Portrait in Relief.

II

SOFT WAX MODELING TECHNIQUES

EMBOSSED FIGURE BROOCH

GENERAL DESCRIPTION:

We will make a model of clay, on top of which will be placed a sheet of wax, and give it form. As I reminisce on my adolescent days of clay modeling, we will make a model in relief. Whether abstract or concrete, where the contour is moderate, any shape is possible. Put into use after the clay mold has dried out, any number of duplicates may be made. This method is very useful where the project is in relief.

WORK HINTS:

1. Finish the clay model down to the smallest detail.
2. Work with shallow contoured models as it is difficult to form wax over deep contours.
3. Use a dryer to form the wax over the mold.

MATERIALS:

Soft sheet wax (18-20 gauge)	Paper clay
Sheet of glass	Knife
Takebera	Dryer (hair dryer or similar)
Abrasive eraser	

Place a glass plate on the design drawing and build the model on top of the glass. Build the body first and then the wings. Use a small amount of water to paste the joints together.

Remove the plate from the drawing and while looking at the drawing, shape the model with a *takegushi* and carvers. As the body/wing joints are fragile, fit the joints well. At this time, put in the grooves in the wings one by one.

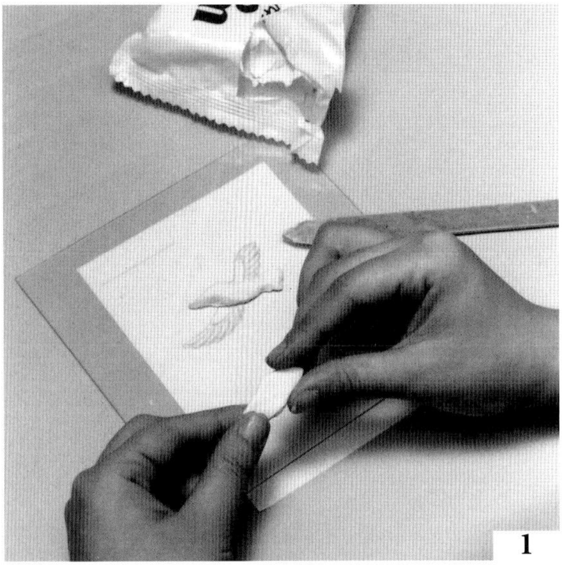

1

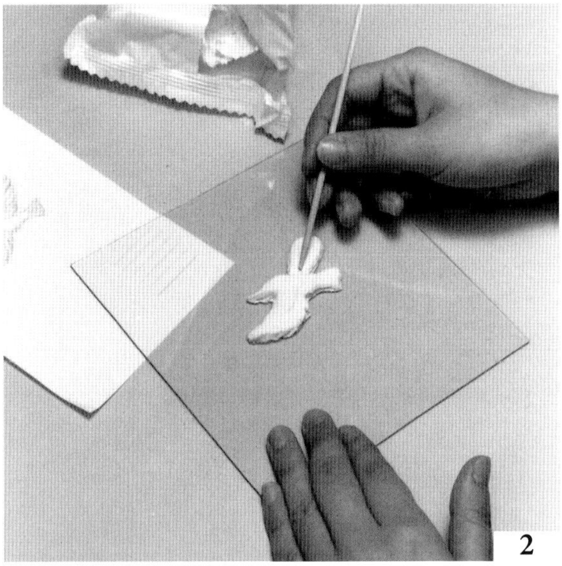

2

3

Allow a day for the mold to dry out. Separate the mold from the glass carefully. Finish the top surfaces with abrasive paper (240 grit).

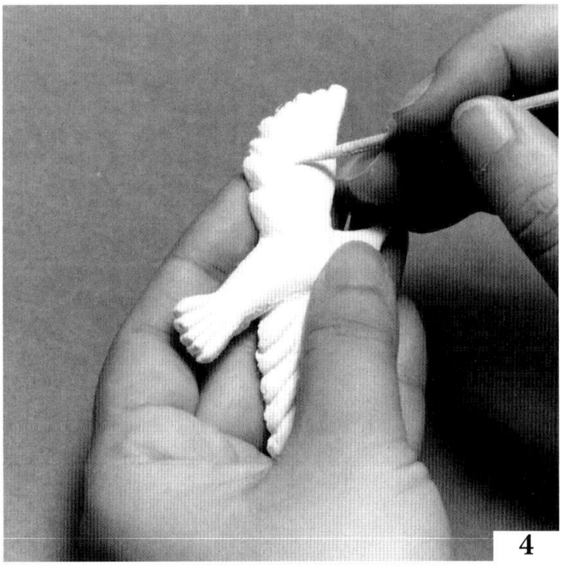

4

Use the *takegushi* or similar and cut the grooves deeper and completely smooth otherwise it will be difficult to bring out the curves later. Carve the beak and other small areas slightly smaller than shown on the drawing.

Look at the assembly from the reverse side to confirm that there are no gaps. Use a knife to trim the excess. Use a small pointed knife to cut around the tight areas.

Remove the assembly from the glass; use your fingers to shape the wax to the mold. Trim the excess wax with a knife.

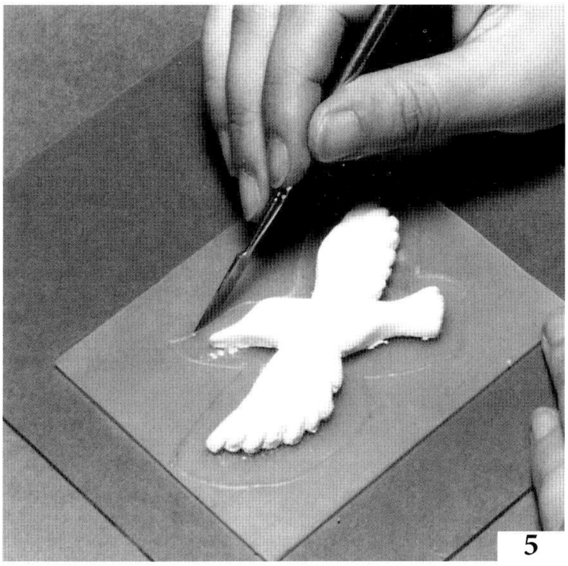
5

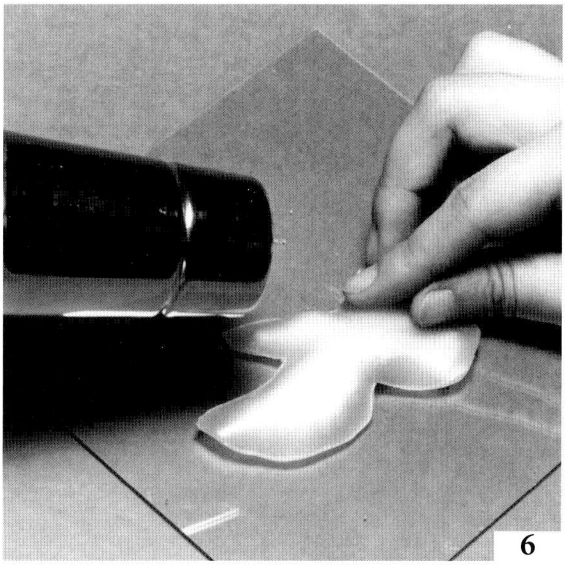
6

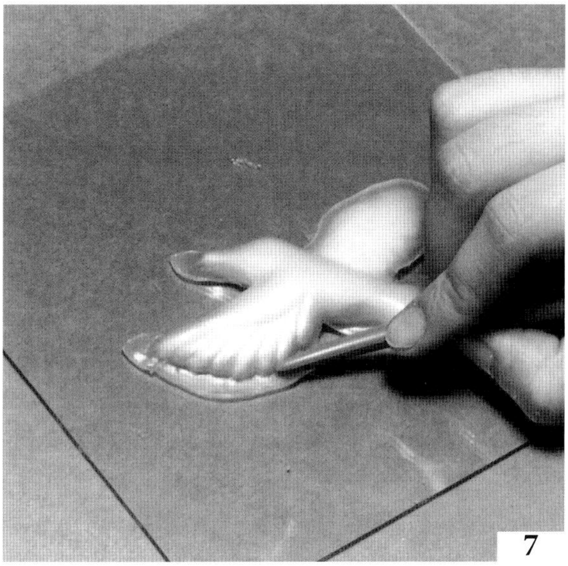
7

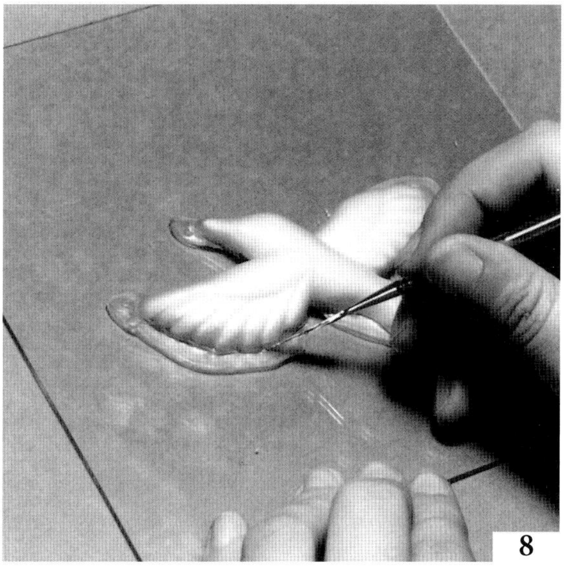
8

Work along the grooves and edges with a spatula. If you have overly softened the wax through overheating, wait a moment and press the area with a spatula.

Look at the assembly from the reverse side to confirm that there are no gaps. Use a knife to trim the excess. Use a small pointed knife to cut around the tight areas.

Remove the assembly from the glass: use your fingers to shape the wax to the mold. Trim the excess wax with a knife.

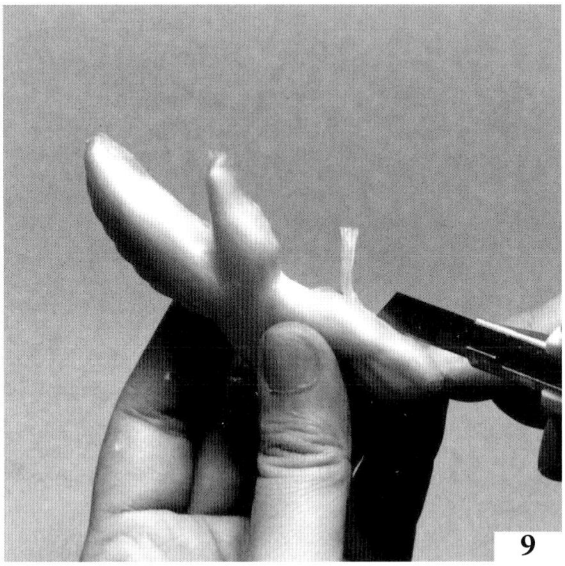

9

Where difficulty is encountered in pressing the wax into the grooves and other areas, use an eraser or other material with "give" to coax the wax down. If you use rigid materials you may leave scratches.

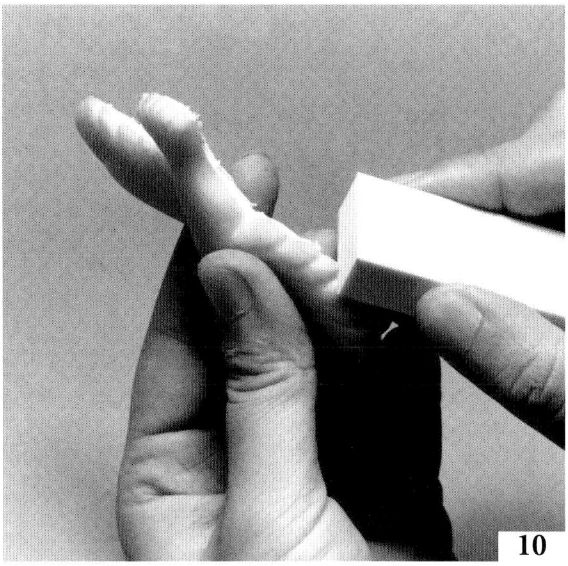

10

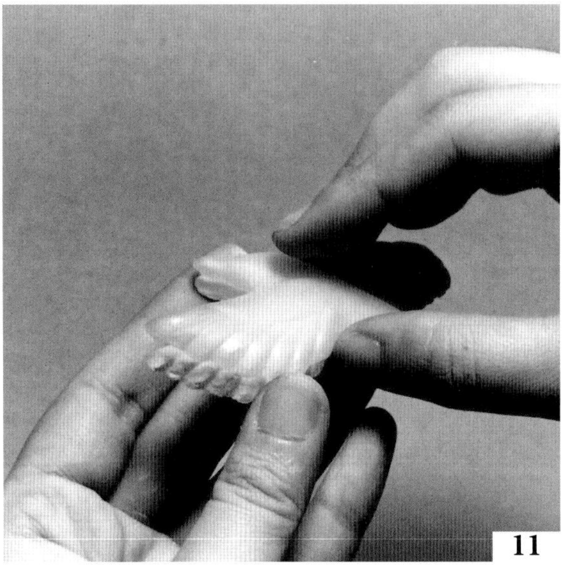

11

Gently remove the wax from the mold. If there is resistance, place a thin knife in the gap to aid removal.

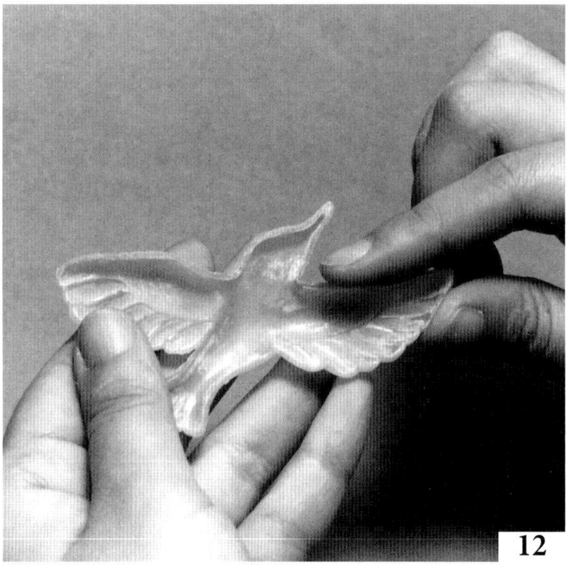

12

As you warm the trailing edges of the wings with your finger, gently persuade them inward. Break the sharp edges with a file or by rubbing with your fingers.

FLORAL PATTERNED RING

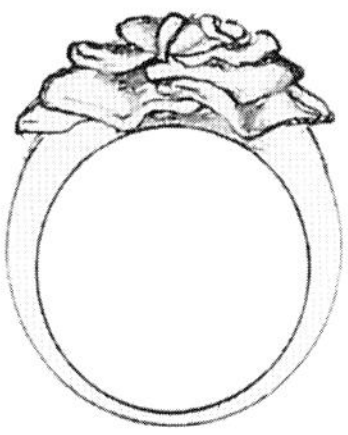

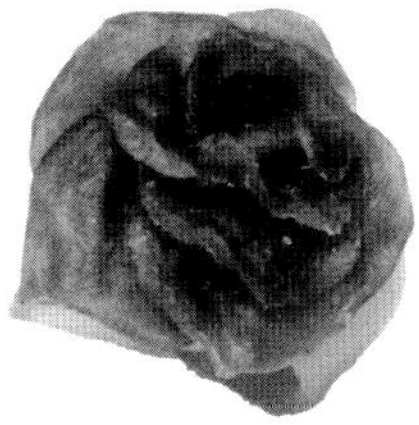

GENERAL DESCRIPTION:

As petals are added, a flower will be fashioned on a formed wax ring. As delicate petals will be formed by the warmth of your hands, perceive the feeling of reality while putting them together. A domed shaped bulge will be put into the sheet wax which will be the base on which the flower will sit. Using sheet wax with its uniform thickness is an easy method to use when making a simple ring. Utilize the two types of wax together and try a variety of designs.

WORK HINTS:

1. Learn how to work with sheet wax.
2. Create representations of flower petals by sense of feel in the tips of your fingers.
3. Develop care in handling these fragile forms.

MATERIALS:

Soft sheet wax (20 gauge)	Pliable wax (utility grade)
Sheet of glass	Knife
Dapping punches	Alcohol lamp
Wooden mandrel	Ring mandrel
Takebera	Bamboo

Draw the ring, which will become the base, in its developed length. Place a glass sheet on top of the drawing and lay the 20 ga. sheet wax on top of the glass. Cut the sheet to the outline with a narrow blade knife. Avoid leaving any jagged edges.

Create a hump in the center (flower bed and shank) of the strip with a dapping punch or like. Warm the wax uniformly over the entire area; use the punch in a slight pushing motion to create the hump.

1

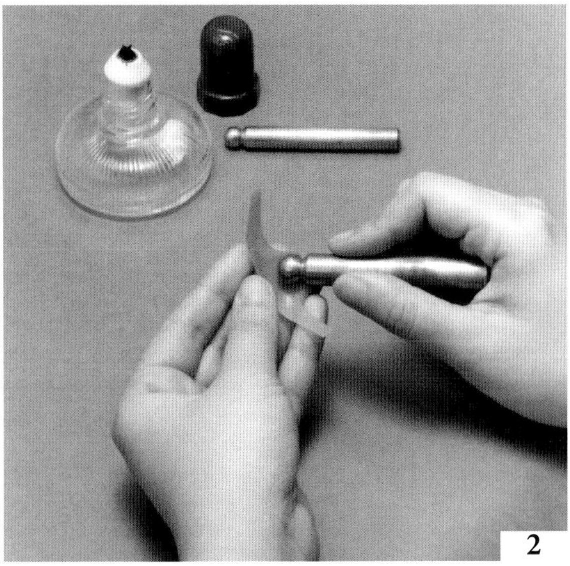

2

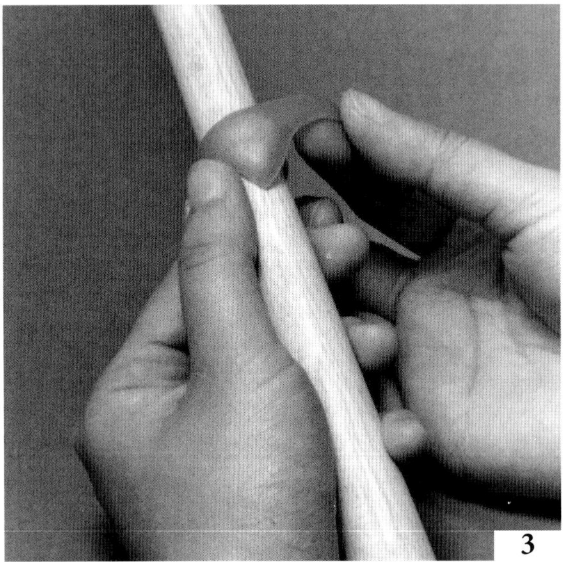

3

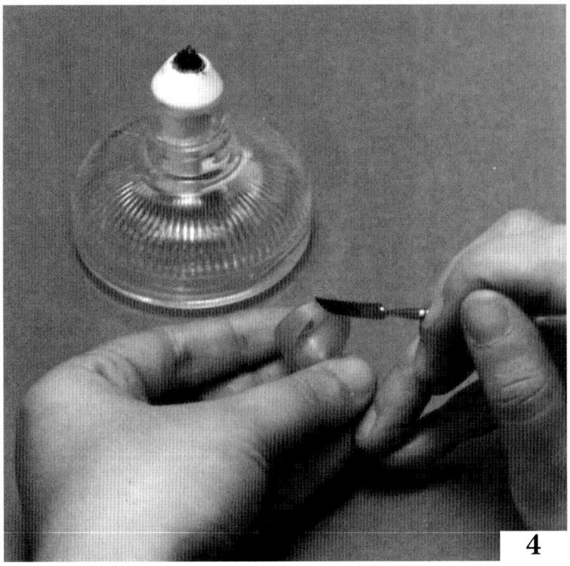

4

After the hump is made, place the strip on a wooden mandrel. Starting from the top, press the strip lightly around the stick. Be certain that the wax fits the stick closely. Cut the excess from the shank ends and form the shank perfectly round.

Determine the size. Add wax to the joint with a heated spatula. Any excess may be trimmed off with a knife.

After the base has been completed, place it into a slit put into a piece of foam sponge. In this manner soft pieces may be picked up and replaced without breakage.

After the base has been taken care of make the petals. The petals will be made from soft wax, one at a time. As this wax is very soft, it tends to stick to the fingers, therefore, keep your fingers moistened with water during construction.

5

6

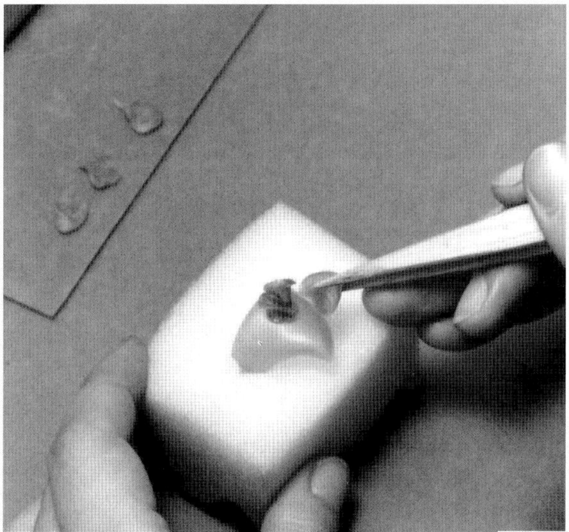

7

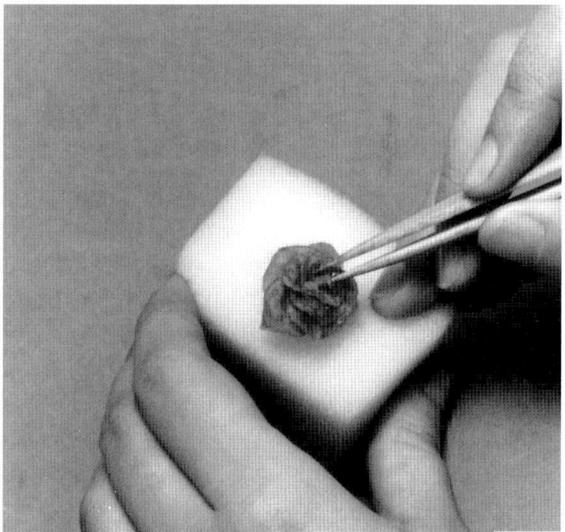

8

The petals will be placed on the base carefully with a pair of tweezers. As you put each petal into position, attach the base of the petal to the ring securely. Also, be aware that too many petals will add weight to the ring.

After the petals have been placed, arrange them neatly with tweezers. Arrange them slightly horizontal. The reason for this is that otherwise the finished ring may catch on things.

Sunflower Ring.

Leaf Motif Ring.

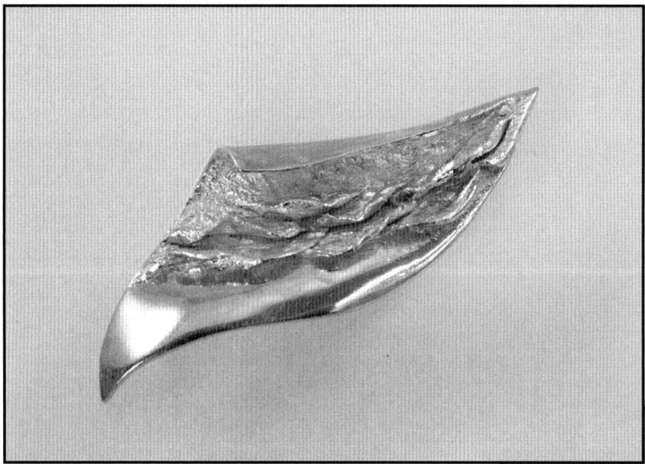

Pendant with Texture and Waves.

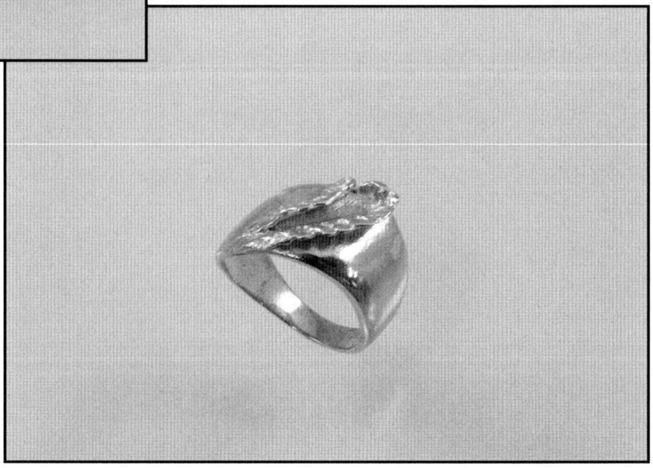

Ring with a Simple Arrangement of Waves.

RING OF WAX WIRE CONSTRUCTION

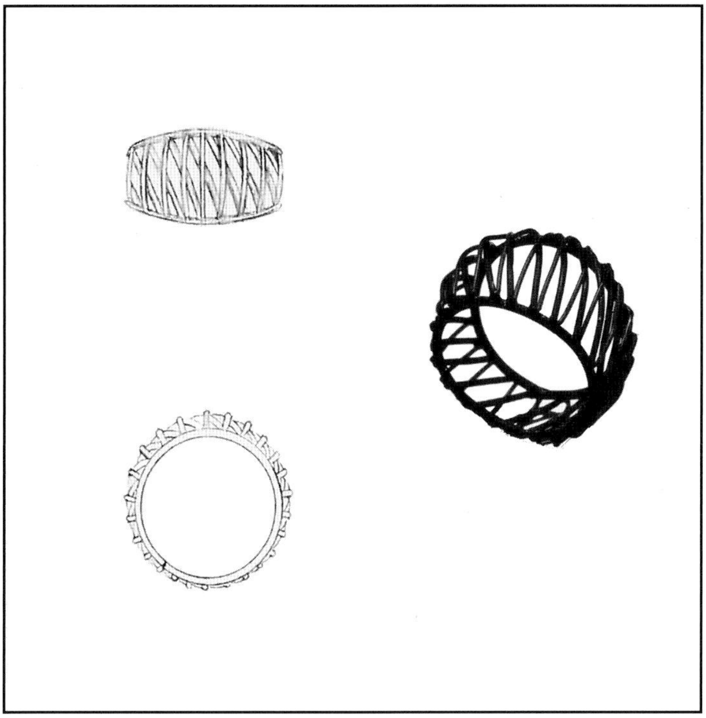

GENERAL DESCRIPTION:

Construct a light, delicate ring from tiny, intricately connected, wax wires. Laid against a clay form, wax wires are made stable and construction becomes simplified as well. As the ring is put together with a needle, a great deal of care must be exercised in keeping the tip of the needle at just the right temperature.

WORK HINTS:

1. Become adept in fitting the curved wires.
2. Provide for the easy removal of the paper clay form.
3. Take care not to overly melt the wax wires.

MATERIALS:

Wax wires	Paper clay
Wooden mandrel	*Takebera*
Needle	Bamboo spatula
Bamboo tweezers	

At the proper finger size on the wooden mandrel, wrap a 1.0 - 1.5 mm diameter wax wire. Cut the wire and weld the ends together. In the same manner install another one.

Spread the wax wires about the center of the size selected (looking directly at the "top"): make the spread narrower at the "bottom" of the shank. Be careful not to scratch the wires with your finger nails.

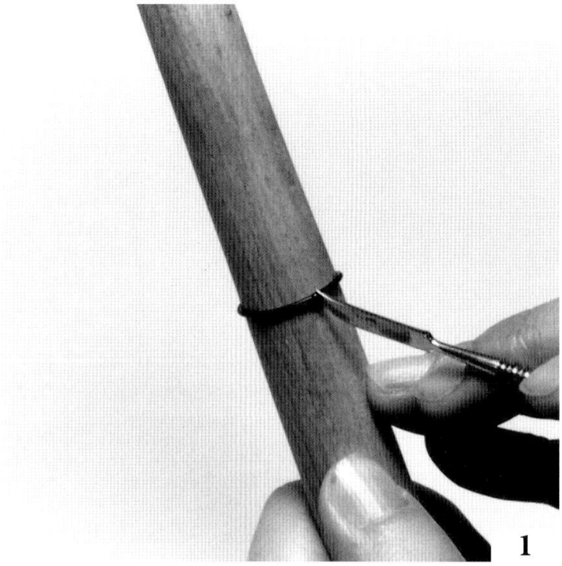

1

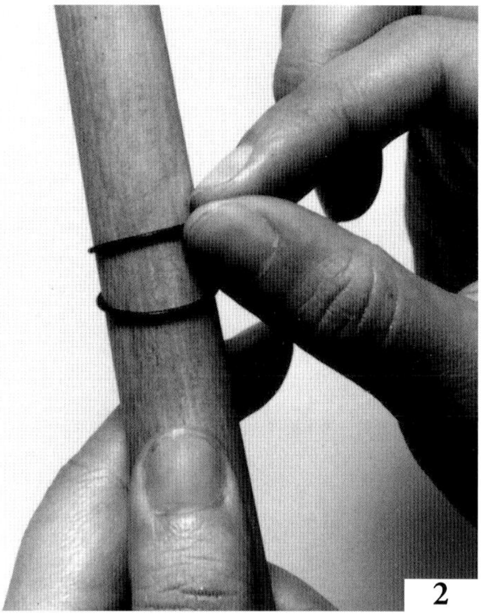

2

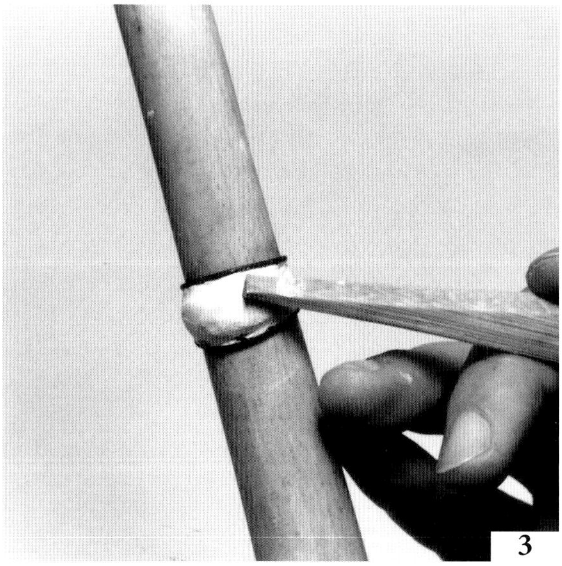

3

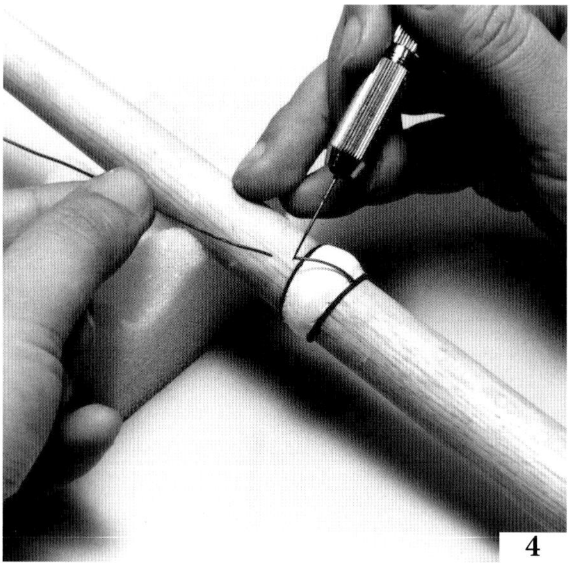

4

Deposit paper clay between the wires for height only (use of tracing paper as a base on which to place the clay, allowing easier removal of the assembly is omitted here).

Span wax wires (0.6 - 0.8 mm) across the opening one at a time. When attaching, with the wires just touching the clay, melt just a touch and attach with a heated needle.

Attach the wires diagonally at equally spaced intervals. Do not allow the mandrel to touch the work table; stabilize it by propping up one end on a sponge or something similar.

Next, neatly install wires crossing the diagonals one at a time. Changing the size of wires will add to the three dimensional appearance.

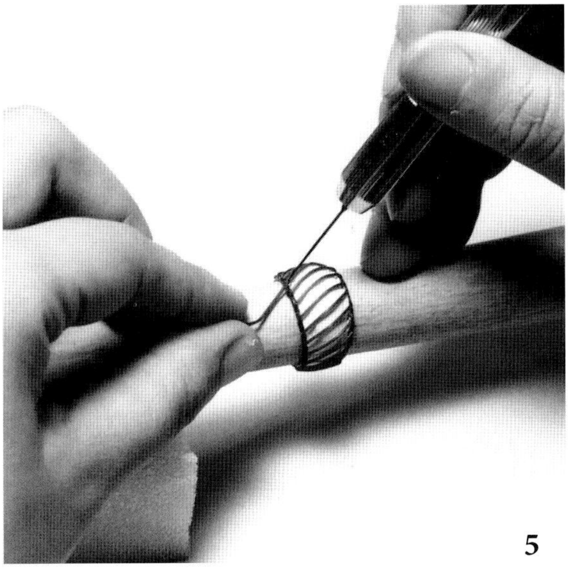

5

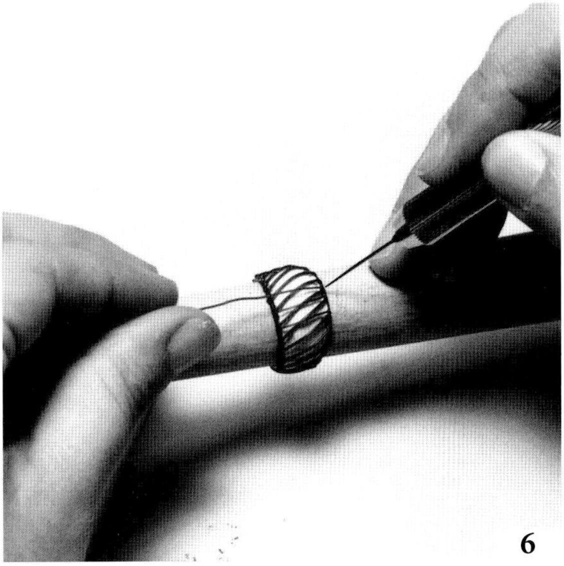

6

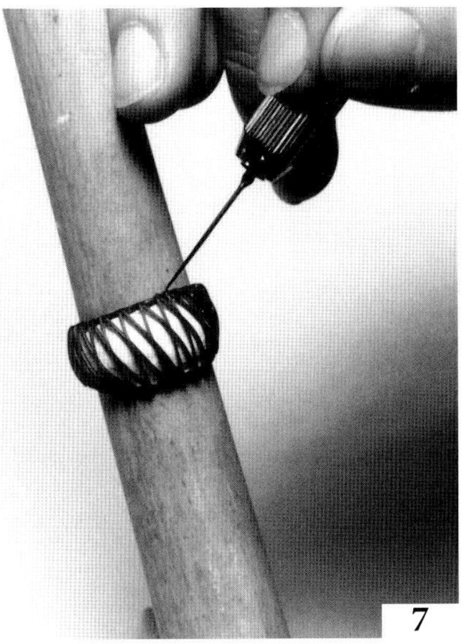

7

8

When that is completed, lightly touch a heated needle to the intersections of the wires. Inspect to see that they will not come apart later. Reinforce spots with wax where the attachment is weak.

Remove the ring from the mandrel. Place the ring in water and the paper clay will be extracted with a tweezer. At this time do not apply excessive pressure as it may damage the ring.

Ring - Wire Filigree Added for Volume.

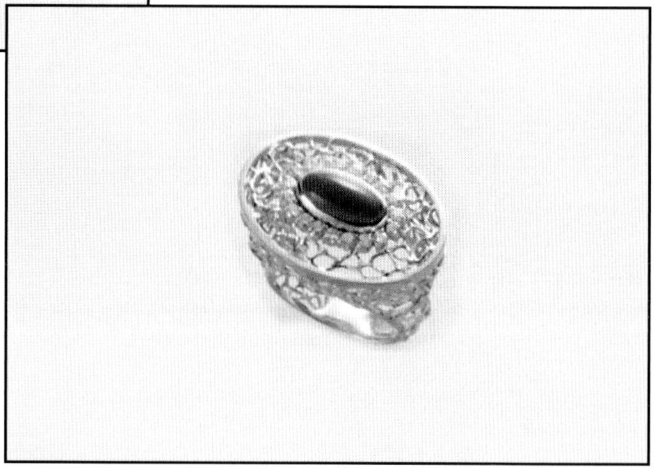

Ring - Wire Added within the Frame.

Ring in Thick "Melted Wire" Motif.

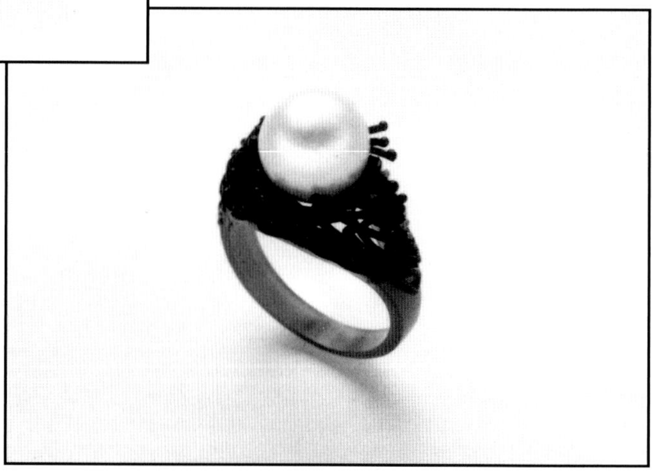

Ring - Pearl Wrapped in Wire.

PENDANT CONSTRUCTED OF WAX WIRE

GENERAL DESCRIPTION:

This pendant will be structured in a similar manner to the previous ring. Let us plan an out-of-the-ordinary presentation by adding texture to wax wires and adding decorative beads. It is important to advise you to concentrate on the precise placement of each curved wax wire to maintain good balance. Try to bring out the three-dimensional effect in the bowing of wax wires and balance as well.

WORK HINTS:

1. Master the method of applying wax wire.
2. Attention to sense of balance and arrangement.
3. Try adding texture and beads effectively to show your own expression.

MATERIALS:

Wax wire	Knife
Needle	*Takebera*
Sponge	

Make the central stem from a half round wax wire about 1.2 - 1.5 mm in diameter. Start with a length about 10 cm; form a bail (flat side down) on one end using a dowel.

Warm the wax with your fingers as you slowly form a loop (curved side up) as per the drawing. Work carefully; do not scratch the front side with your finger nails.

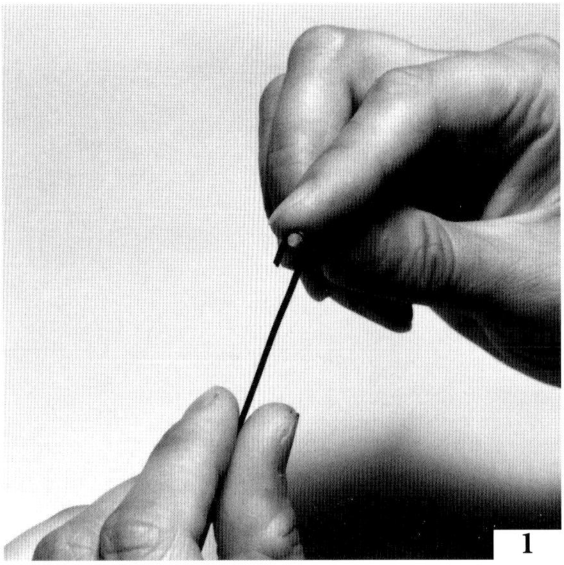

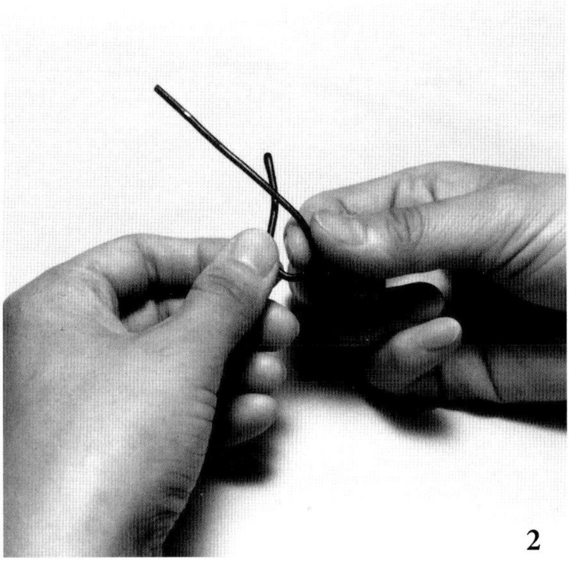

Cut off the excess wire neatly with a thin blade knife (recommended: a razor blade).

Weld the bail and loop joints securely. Add wax if necessary.

Apply wax wires (0.7 - 0.8 mm) to the stem. Put the stem on a sponge and melt the stem with the point of a hot needle, then insert the smaller wire.

Shape the wire as you warm it with your fingers. Use the tip of a heated needle to cut the wire off at the proper length; in this manner the shape will not be spoiled.

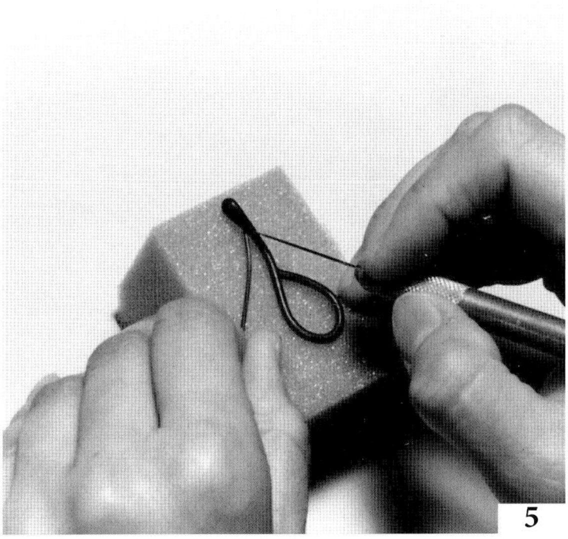

5

6

7

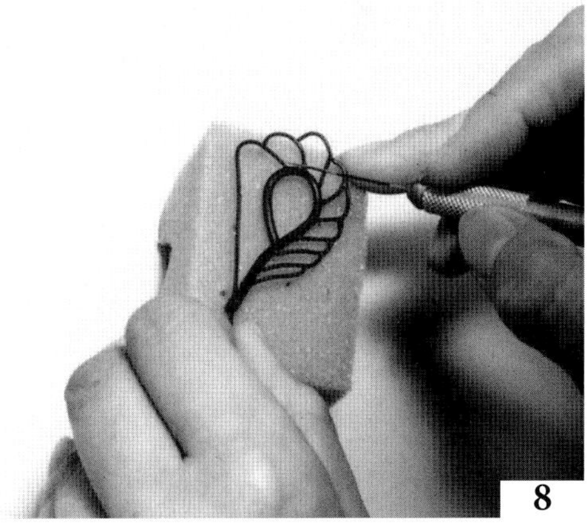

8

Install the second piece in the same manner. At this time, weld the pieces together. As the wires are thin take ample care not to over melt (just a touch of the needle will do).

Refer to the design; apply each segment neatly as you proceed. Pay attention to the balance and avoid any unnatural bends in the wires.

When this layer has been completed, weld each joint from the reverse side. Again add extra wax where required.

Moving on, add another layer of wax wires in the same manner as Step 9. A nice appearance will be produced by putting a slight curve in the wire before you weld it.

9

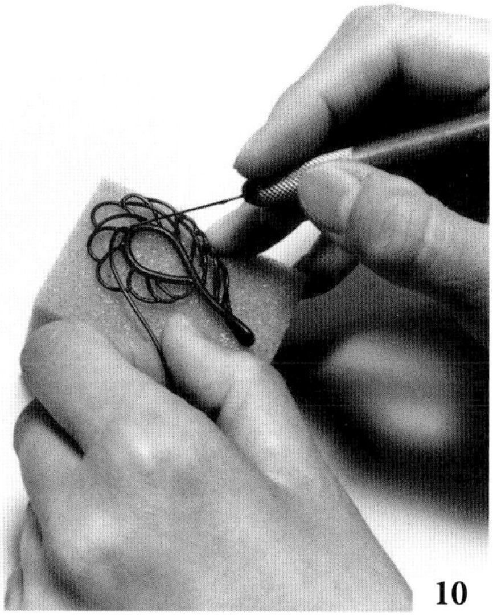

10

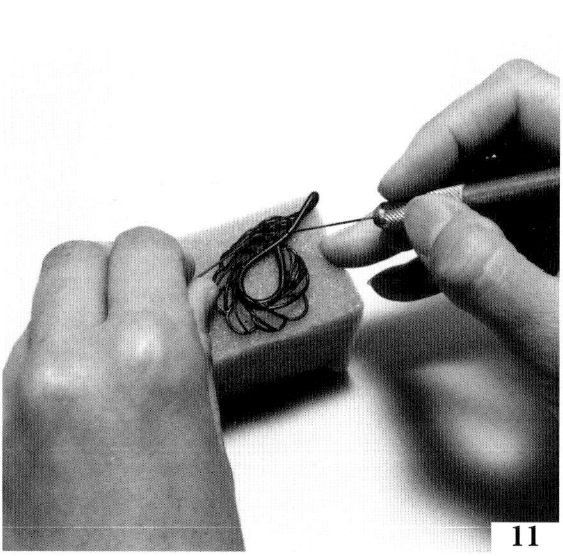

11

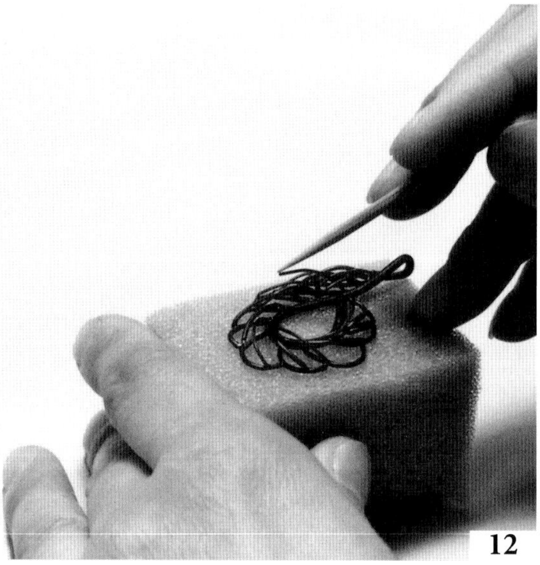

12

After you have completed the round, yet another layer of wax wires will be added at the midpoints of the other layers. Gradually things will become crowded: be very careful not to melt the other wires in the process.

As you will not be able to use your fingers to install the wires due to crowding, shape the wires with a pointed *takegushi* or dowel. If the ambient temperature is cool, breathe on the wires to make them pliable.

Check over the entire assembly and make certain that each part is nicely welded. Re-weld joints that appear weak.

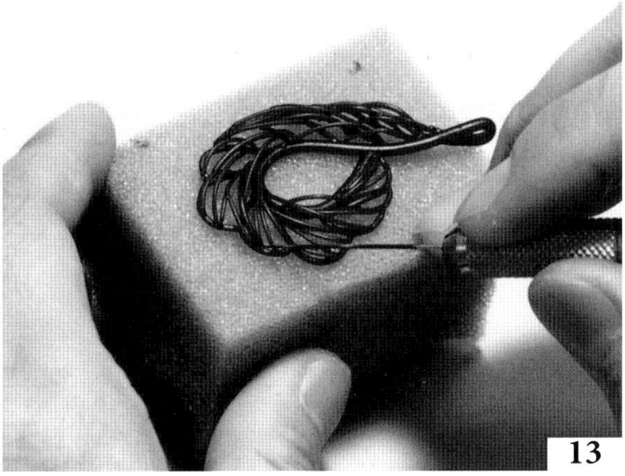

13

Add texture to the wires. To impart a slight roughened appearance, dot the wires with the point of a warm needle. Patiently dot each wire.

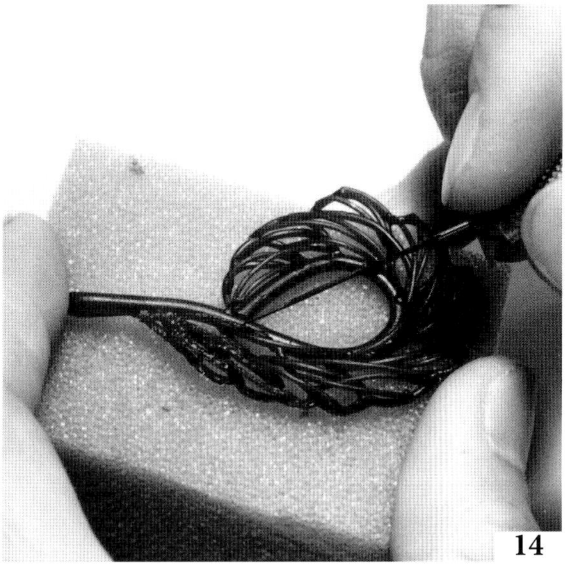

14

15

Apply texture to the junction of the wires as well. Do not over-heat the needle.

16

Place beads over the entire assembly uniformly. Try to keep the beads all the same size. Pick up a tiny amount of wax on the tip of the hot needle. The trick is to place the bead quickly and gently.

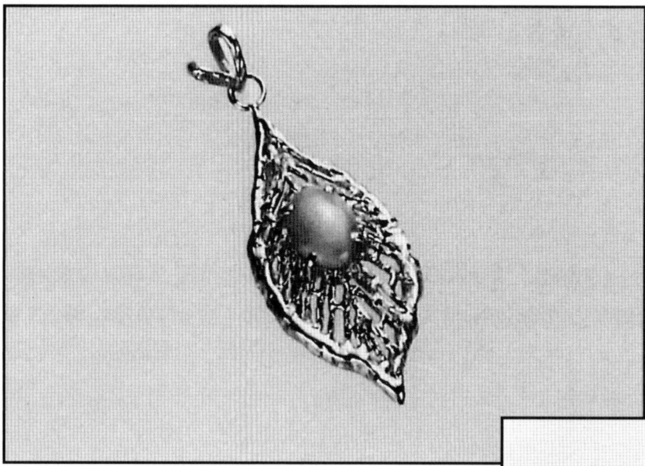

Pendant with Textured Wires.

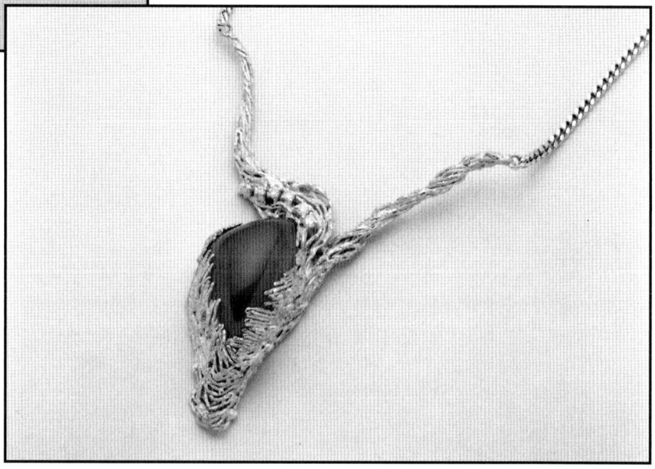

Pendant with Wire, Beads and Melle.

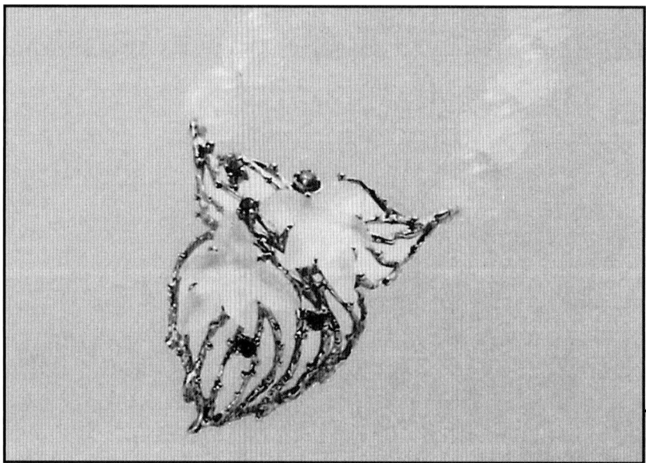

Pendant with Stone Encased in Wires.

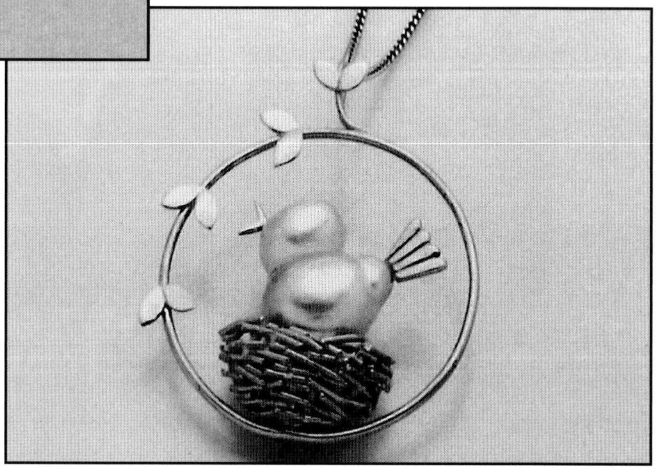

Pendant with a Realistic Nest Made with Bits of Wire.

MAKING "*MITSURO*", TRADITIONAL WAX FORMULA

GENERAL DESCRIPTION:

Mitsuro has been Japan's traditional material of use for centuries. It was used in the lost wax process construction of the Great Buddha during the Nara Era (746 AD). The technique in the use of *mitsuro* to create striated texture may be seen in the design of many products. As *mitsuro* is not sold in stores, you will have to prepare the product yourself. *Mitsuro* is weakened by heat; proportional adjustments will be necessary to suit the temperature of your work place, the time of year, etc. Work out a composition suitable for you after you have familiarized yourself with basic *mitsuro* production.

WORK HINTS:

1. Master the method of applying wax wire.
2. Attention to sense of balance and arrangement.
3. Try adding texture and beads effectively to show your own expression.

MATERIALS:

Yellow impression wax	Pine resin	Flat pan
Soft wax	Scale	
Stove	Perforated metal pad	
Spoon	Bowl	
Scissors	Gauze	

Assemble equal weights of yellow impression wax and pine resin, add soft wax to equal 5 - 7% of the total weight of the resin and yellow impression wax.

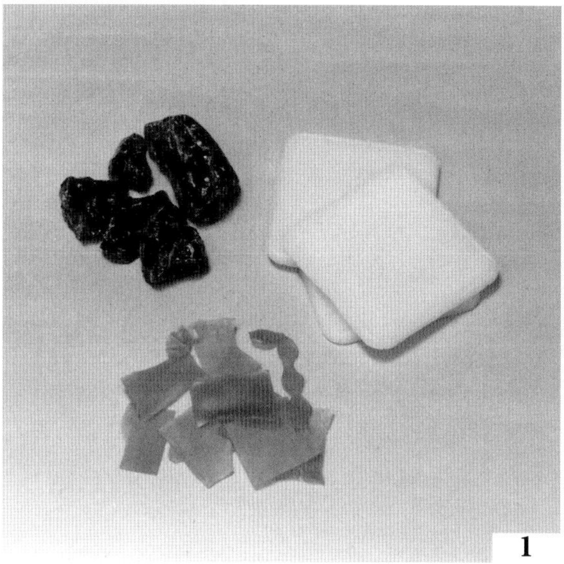

1

Weigh equal amounts of impression wax and pine resin. In summer use more resin and less in winter to adjust the hardness.

2

3

Melt the impression wax and resin in a flat pan. It is imperative that the heat be kept down; place a perforated metal pad/ grill under the pan.

4

Warm the mixture slowly, waiting for it to melt naturally. If it is over-heated, it will be ruined. By all means, be patient.

As the mixture begins to melt, stir slowly; used *mitsuro* may be mixed in at this time if you have any. Used *mitsuro* will contain air; recooking will renew it and add to the total.

5

After the impression wax and pine resin have melted together, stir in the soft wax. Check the mixture. If the *mitsuro* sticks to your fingers, add more soft wax.

6

7

After the *mitsuro* has been completely mixed, allow it to "cook" for 30 minutes to one hour. To test the *mitsuro* for hardness and stretchability, pour a spoonful into a pan containing water.

8

The mixture will set in water, test it for hardness, etc. If it is too hard, add more impression wax: if it is too soft, add more pine resin.

Stretch it a little and if you notice small lines and furrows, the mixture is okay. If it appears as in the photo, this represents line texture brought to life in *hikime* (see next page).

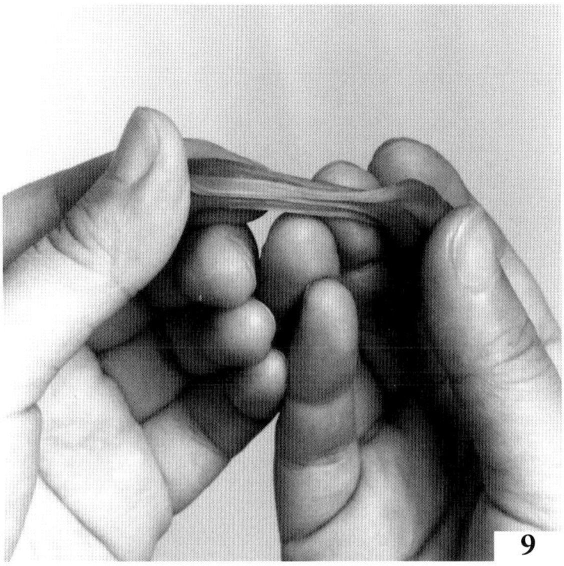

9

Strain the *mitsuro* through several layers of gauze into a pan containing water. The floating *mitsuro* will spread out into a sheet. It is possible to pour the mixture onto a sheet of aluminum foil as an alternative method.

10

11

Wait until the mixture has solidified. If a large amount of *mitsuro* is made and the mixture is poured at one time, it will be difficult to remove. On such occasions, divide the pour into small quantities.

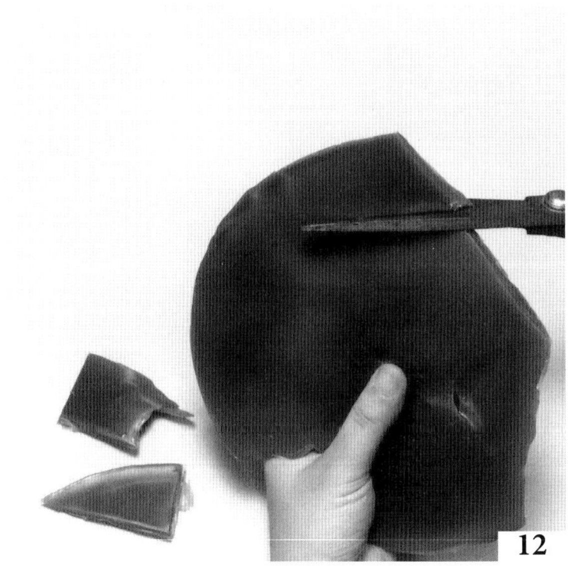

12

Remove the solidified *mitsuro* from the water and while it is in the soft state, cut it up into small pieces; they will be easier to handle and store.

MITSURO RING

GENERAL DESCRIPTION:

Mitsuro, when warmed with your hands, may be elongated producing a striated texture. This texture is referred to as *hikime* (stretch texture), resembling the texture found on the leaves of some plants and bamboo trees.
As this is a soft wax and you can stretch it by warming the wax with your hands, it can also stick to your fingers, or break because you stretched it beyond its elastic limits. Accordingly, skill in working with the material is required. Until you learn the "know-how", practice, practice, practice.

WORK HINTS:

1. Stretch the *mitsuro* only after you've warmed it up completely to uniform temperature.
2. Learn the trick of stretching the *mitsuro* a number of times to arrive at the right uniform thickness.
3. Exercise care not to flatten the *hikime.*

MATERIALS:

Mitsuro	Wooden mandrel
Spatula	Alcohol lamp

Warm the *mitsuro*. Grasp it in your hand for about 10 minutes and it should soften enough to mold into an elongated shape.

Stretch the *mitsuro* into a stick. Tidy up the ends and stretch it again into a long slender strip. If you exert too much pressure with your finger tips, the surface will become wavy, therefore, work slowly as you make it thinner.

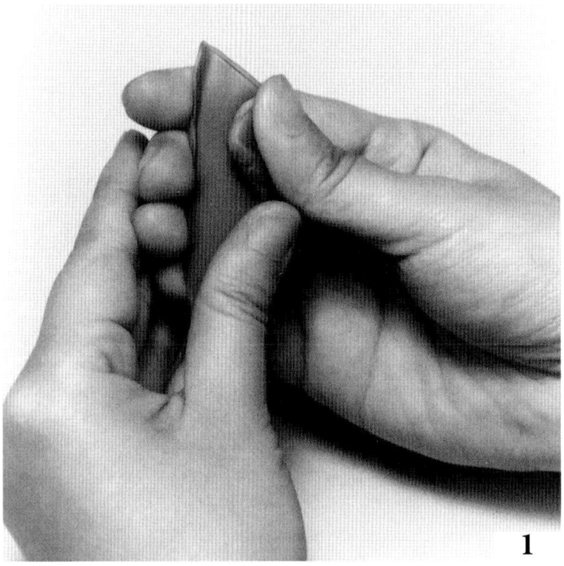

1

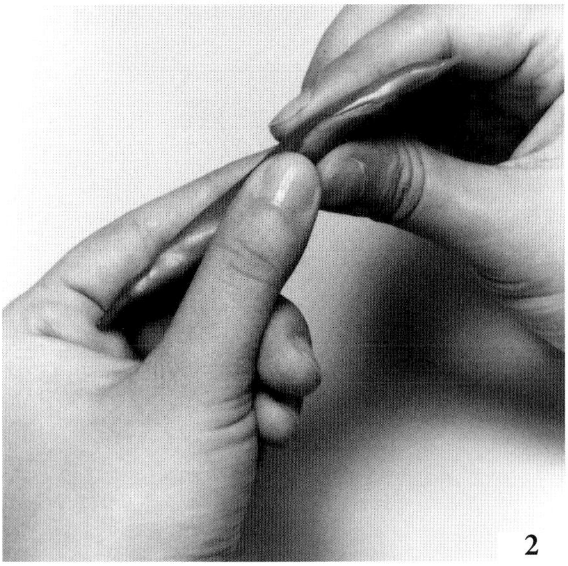

2

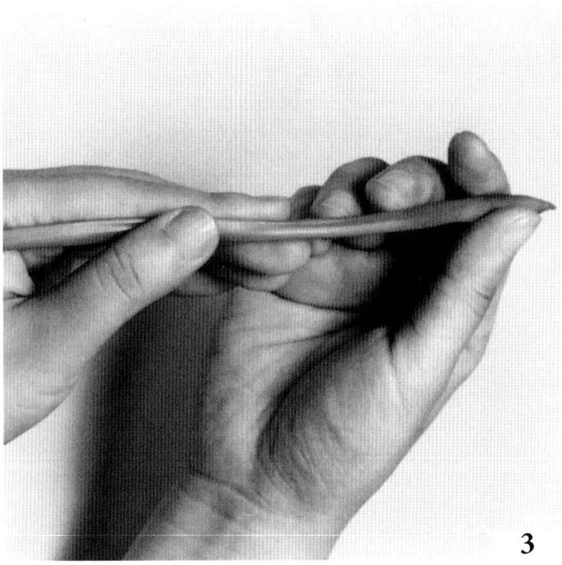

3

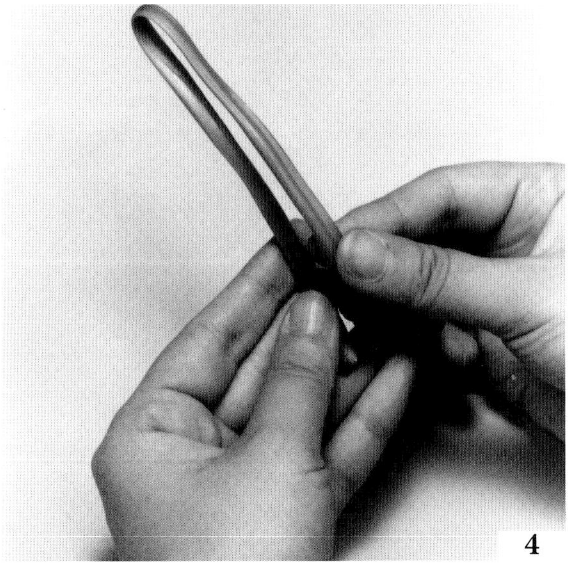

4

Using the warmth of your hands, stretch the entire piece; maintain a uniform thickness. To keep the *mitsuro* thoroughly warm, keep your fingers moving constantly. Where the material is too thick, warm up that portion only with your fingers and then pulling will make it thinner and longer.

After the *mitsuro* has a uniform thickness of 1.5 - 2.0 mm fold it in two. Shift the ends about 2 mm to either side and fold. This way it will be easier to produce deep lines. When shifting, fold so that the lines become parallel.

Press the folded parts together with your fingers. As in Step 3 slowly stretch the piece. Do not cause the lines to disappear due to excessive force.

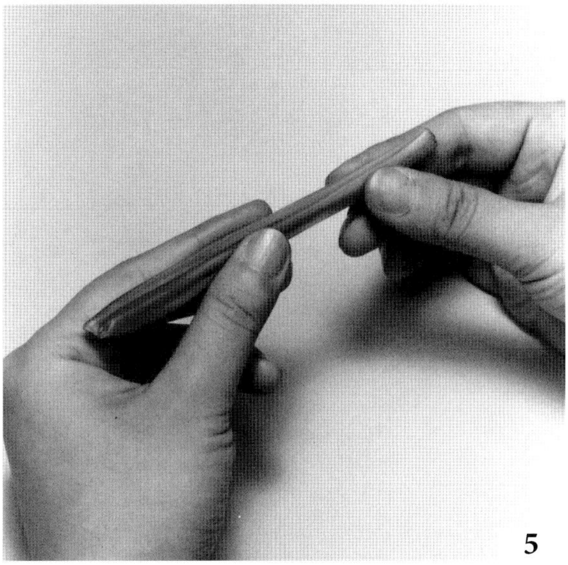

5

Double the length of the piece. For uniform thickness warm the piece with your hands and gradually lengthen. If the *hikime* appears you should stop here.

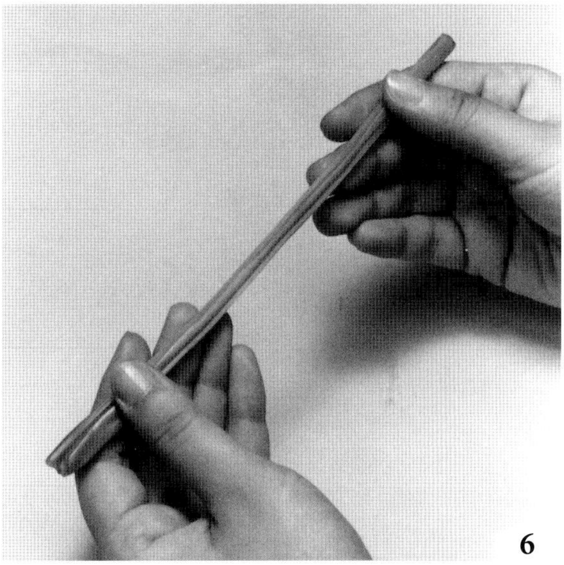

6

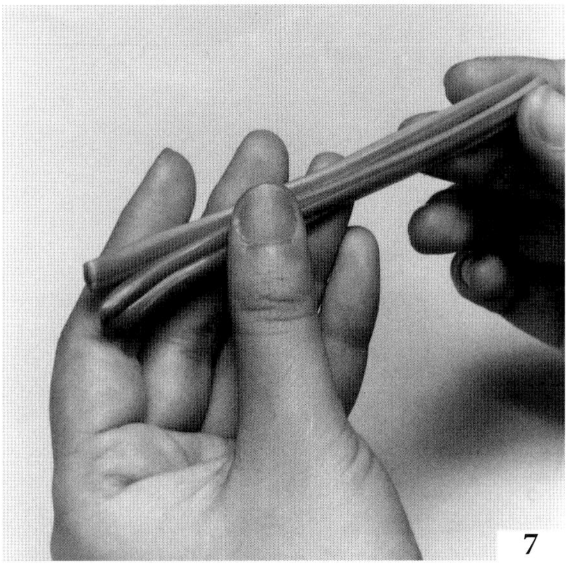

7

If enough lines do not appear, repeat the process. The limit of repetition is 5 or 6 times. Folding too many times will allow too much air to mix into the material. Failure to produce lines will require the *mitsuro* to be reheated to make it useable.

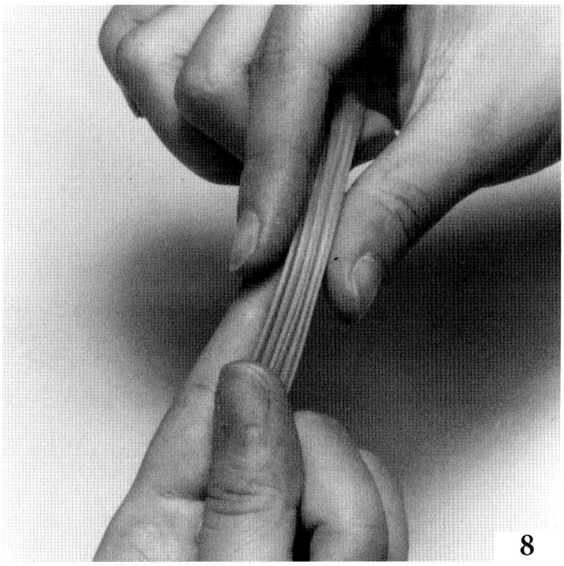

8

When the lines come out beautifully it is called *hikime*. To make certain the material does not get overly thin, stroke your fingers along both edges, raising them. The *hikime* portion should have a thickness of 1.0 mm, ideally.

To produce pointed ends like that of a bamboo leaf, hold the end until the *mitsuro* is reasonably warm and slowly pull apart. It will require the proper knack to get results.

Make this "bamboo leaf" about 8.0 cm long and wrap it around a wooden mandrel. At this time, grasp only with the finger tips; do not press it against the mandrel; wrap it lightly and carefully.

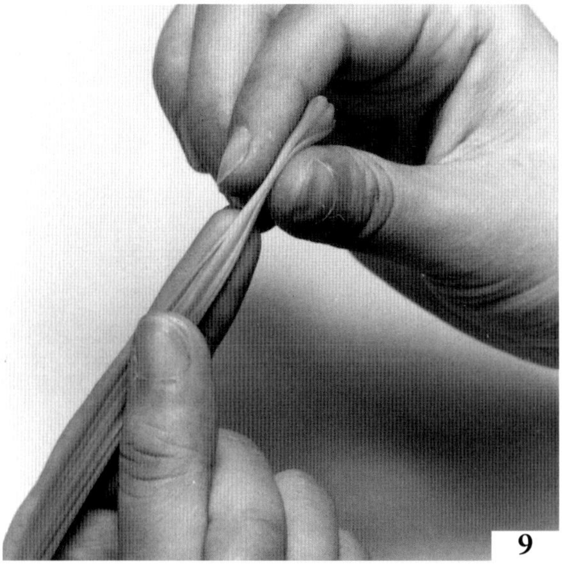

9

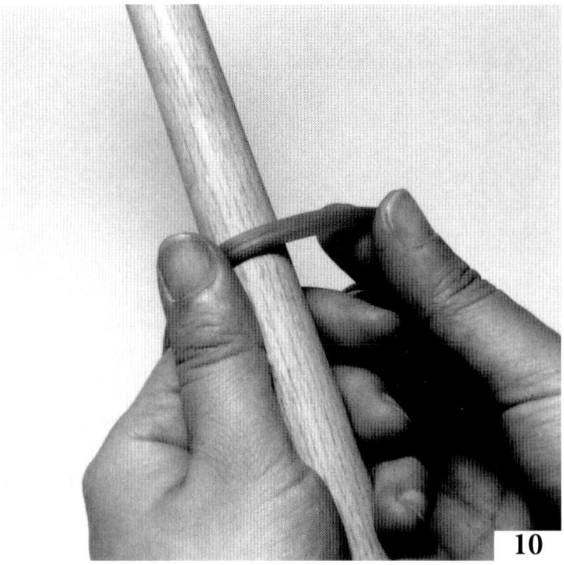

10

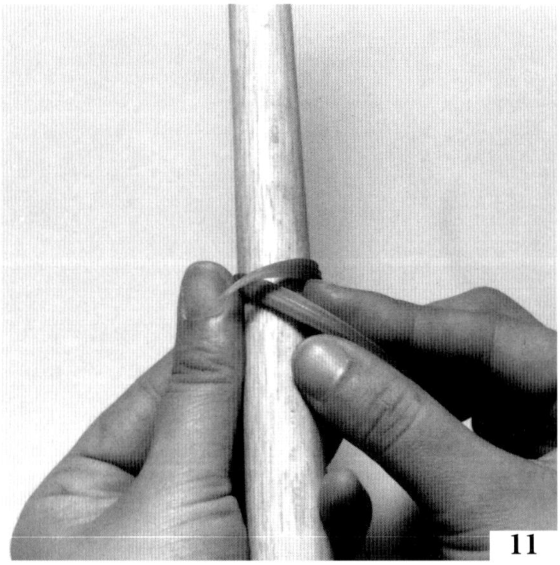

11

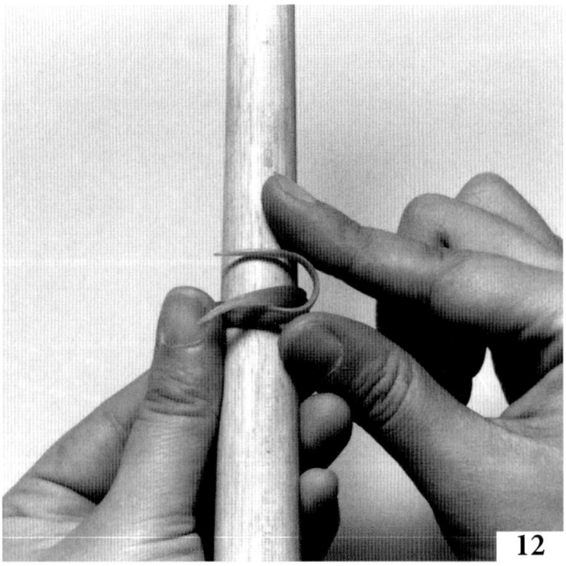

12

Locate the required size on the mandrel: wrap the central portion of the piece at this location. In the event the strip appears to be too long, remove it from the mandrel and make the adjustment and re-wrap.

The design of the ring will have the appearance of 2 leaves. When shaping, use the flat of the fingers and as you warm the piece, bend into a spontaneous moving curve.

The curved end will unite with the shank in a "natural" manner. As in Step 12 use the flat of your finger to stroke it into place. Do not forcibly push or bend.

The other end will gently cross over and wrap into the ring shank.

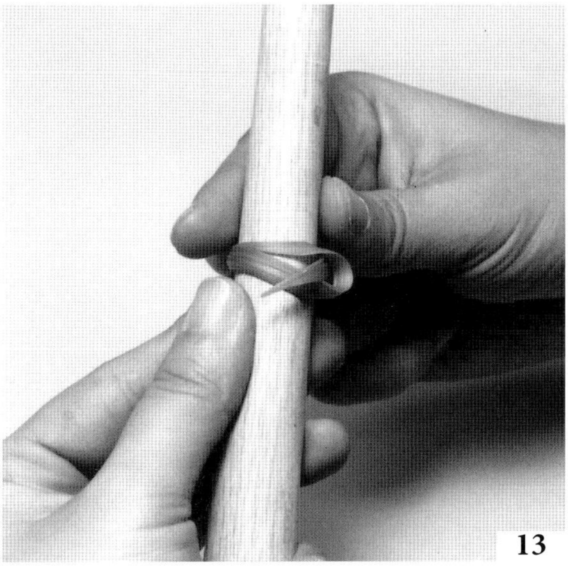

13

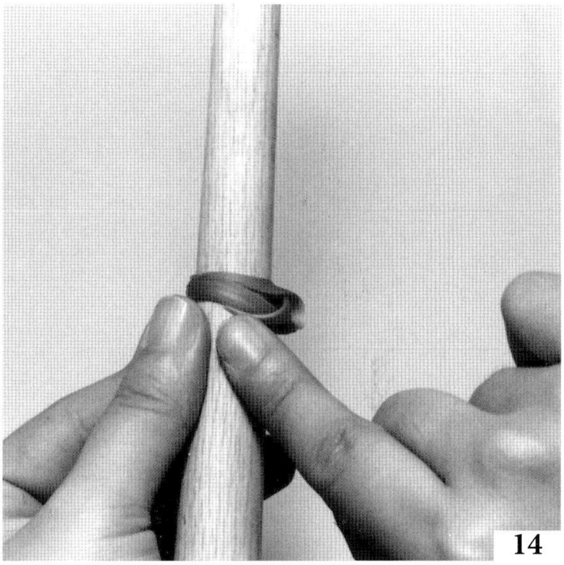

14

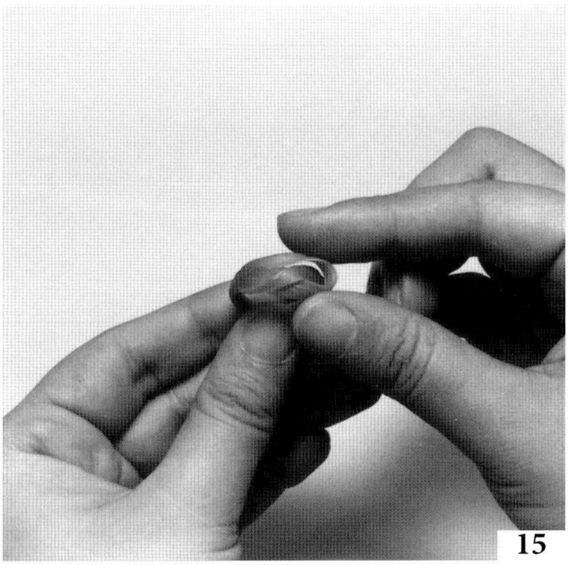

15

Remove the ring from the mandrel. Do not force its removal. Arrange portions of the ring as needed.

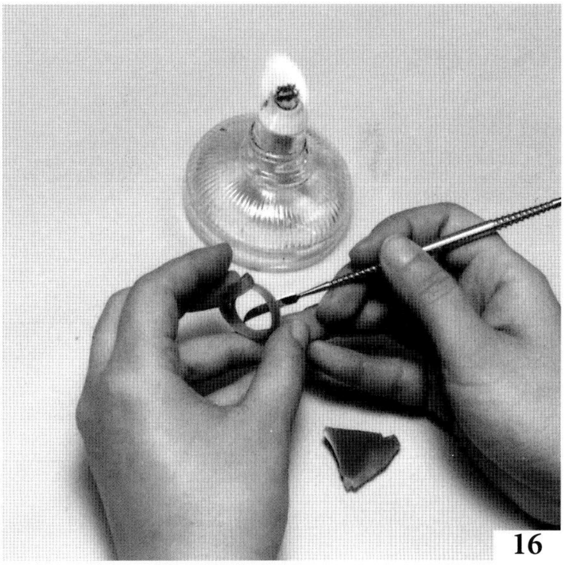

16

The ends will be anchored with a weld from the underside. Use additional wax as required.

Ring Fashioned around
a Stone Producing a Solid
Appearence.

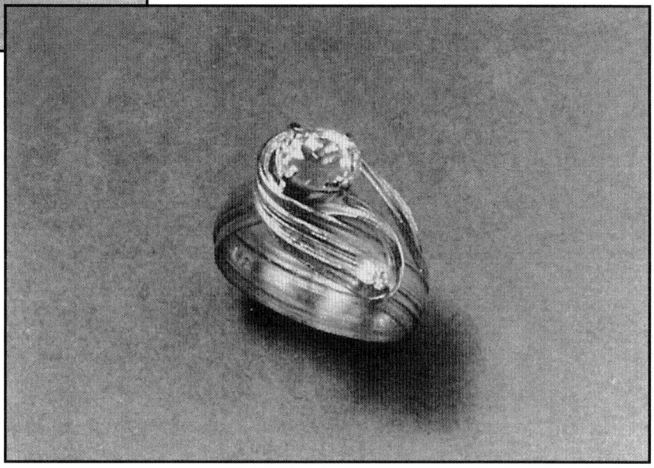

Ring with Melle Stone
Accenting the End of
the *Mitsuro*.

Ring in a Simple Arrangement
with a Single Center Stone.

Ring in a Flat Casual Motif.

MITSURO BROOCH

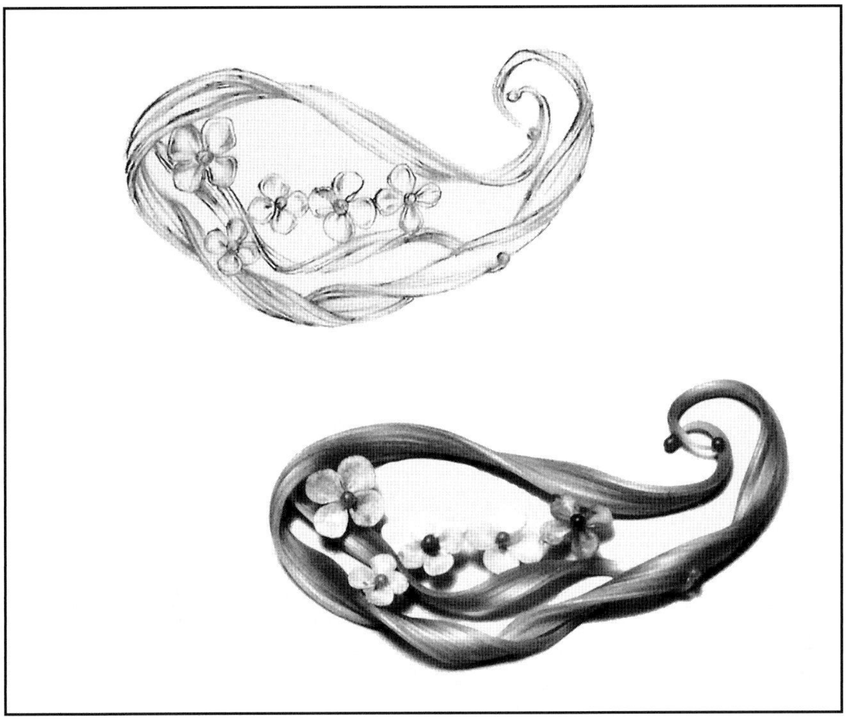

GENERAL DESCRIPTION:

We will make a brooch accenting the lively flow of *hikime* in the *mitsuro.* A pleasing atmosphere is created in the form of an arrangement of twisted slender leaves brought together with small flowers in the center.
In order to grasp the handling of *mitsuro* and the natural flow, experiment with various designs. Try a change in motif, so that you will be able to make small flowers as well as petals of the same size; small and charming.

WORK HINTS:

1. Work at the method of producing a natural flow of *hikime* in the *mitsuro.*
2. Make the four small flowers of the same thickness.
3. Follow the design concept and maintain good balance throughout.

MATERIALS:

Mitsuro	Spatula
Sheet of glass	Talcum powder
Pliers	Tweezers
Needle	

Produce *hikime* on a slender piece of *mitsuro,* with about 1 mm of uniform thickness. As both sides of this *mitsuro* will be seen, *hikime* must appear on both sides as well.

1

In producing *hikime,* the knack is to refrain from undue force; let it form spontaneously as it is stretched. Here, you will add twists to the *mitsuro.* After the length has been determined, the ends will be tapered off by controlled squeezing.

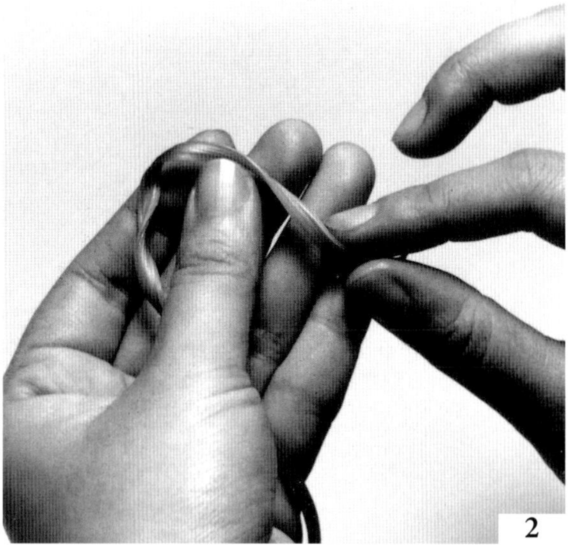

2

3

Next make the shorter piece. The ends of the slender *mitsuro* will be prepared as in Step 2.

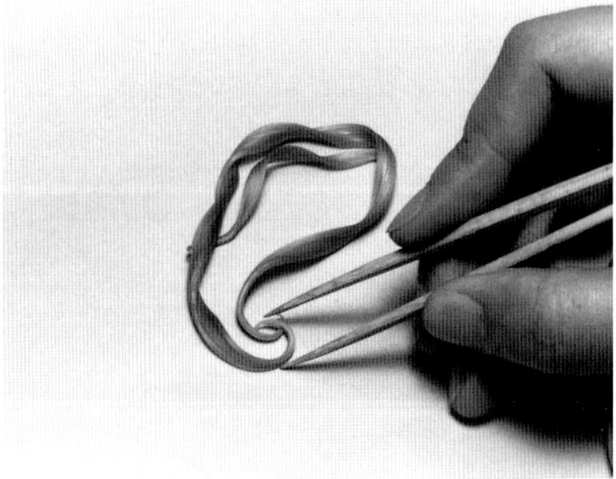

4

With balance in mind, assemble the *mitsuro* pieces. Entwine the ends "arabesque" style. Make certain that no sharp ends will appear in the casting.

Weld the ends of the *mitsuro* where they touch each other with a smidge of *mitsuro* applied with a heated needle. Do this where it can not be seen from the front.

5

Make the small flowers. First, form small balls of *mitsuro* with a heated, small, rounded-end spatula. Make the balls as uniform as you can. Line them up on a glass or metal plate.

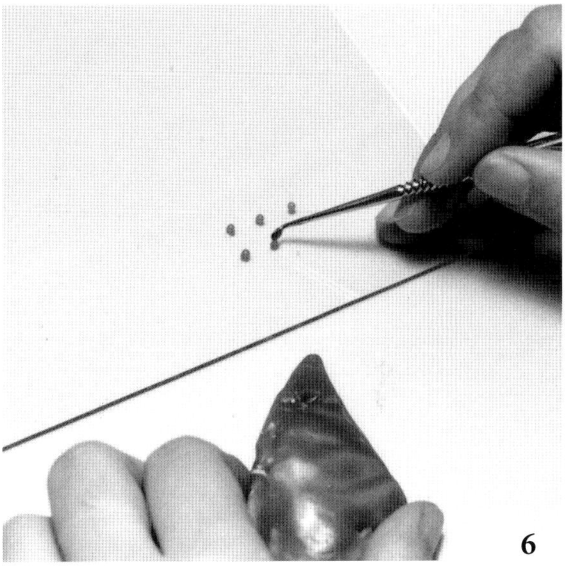

6

7

Flatten the balls with a pair of pliers. Dust talcum powder on the nibs so that the balls will not stick. Flatten them down to about 0.8 mm thick. These will made into petals.

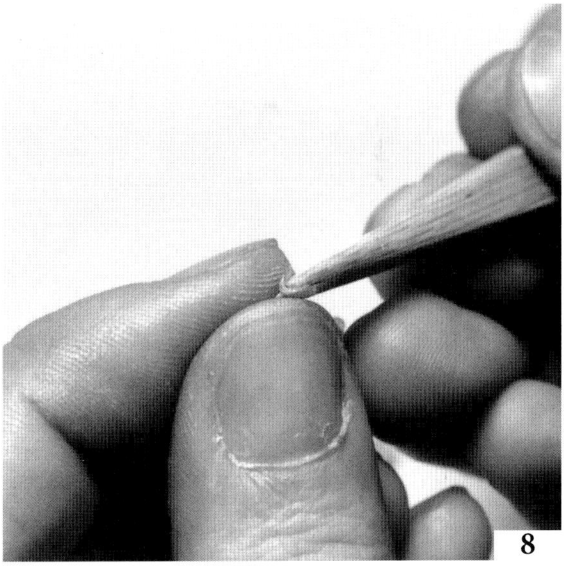

8

Hold a petal on the end of the tweezers and as if to envelope the end of the tweezers slowly collapse the exposed *mitsuro* upwards with your fingers and pinch the end slightly. Make the heart of the petal resemble a tear drop.

Assemble four petals reverse side up to form a flower. As it is delicate task use a pair of tweezers.

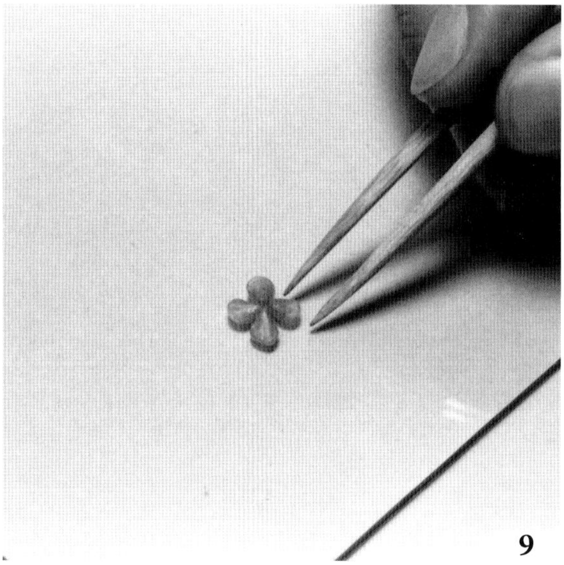

9

Turn the flower over and add a bead in the center of the flower. Do not overheat the needle; pick up a tiny bit of wax. Make five flowers of varying sizes.

11

Place a heated needle in the center and weld the petals together. Welding 2 petals at a time will produce good results. Adding a small bit of wax in the center will strengthen the bond.

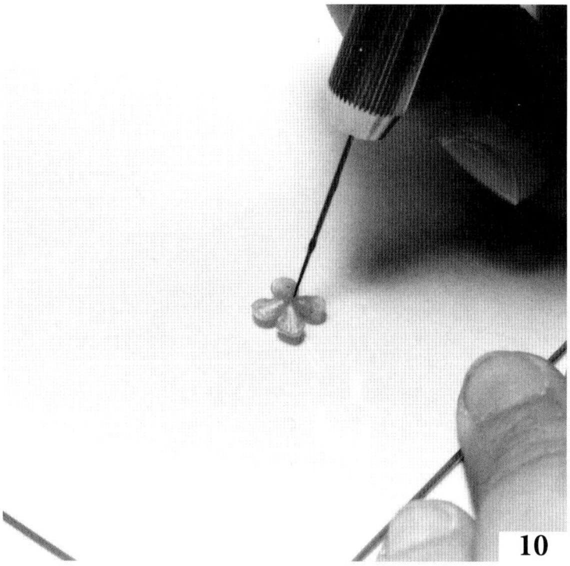

10

12

With balance in mind lay out the flowers. Place the flowers so that they touch the main brooch in more than two places. In the casting process the molten metal may not reach the flowers or may break off later if there is contact in only one spot.

When the placements are determined, each flower will be welded in place. They will be tacked into place from the front to be certain of their locations. Do this with a heated needle and touch lightly with the point of the needle.

13

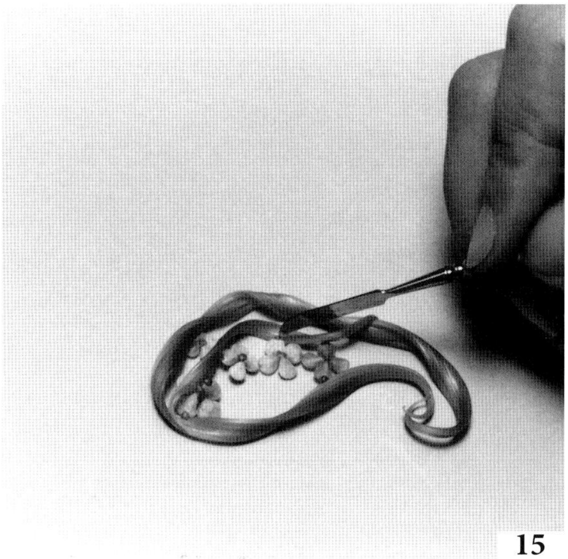

15

Weld the balance of the flowers using the same technique. Weld with added wax from the reverse side so that they will not move. Placing the assembly on top of a sponge may be more convenient.

Next, weld the flower from the reverse side with a small amount of wax. As the petals are very thin, using waxes with high melting temperatures for welding will affect the front side; work at low temperatures.

14

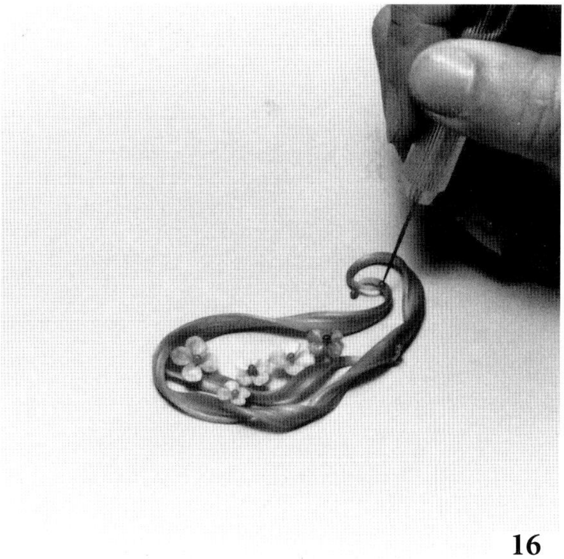

16

After the flowers have been completed, place a bead at the ends of the *hikime*. After casting, pin fittings will be soldered; provide a place for them.

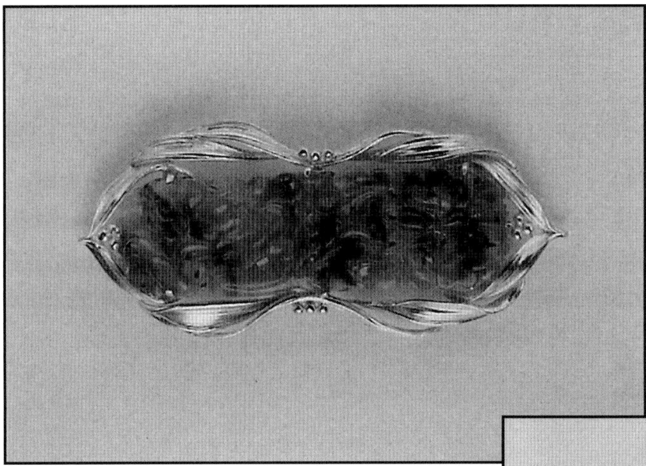

Obi Brooch with Effective Use of Beads.

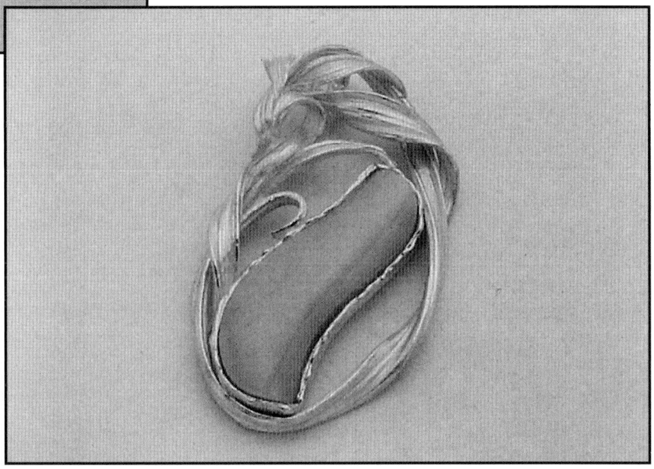

Pendant Made with Wide *Mitsuro* to Create Volume.

Brooch Made with Narrow *Mitsuro* and a Carved Flower in the Center.

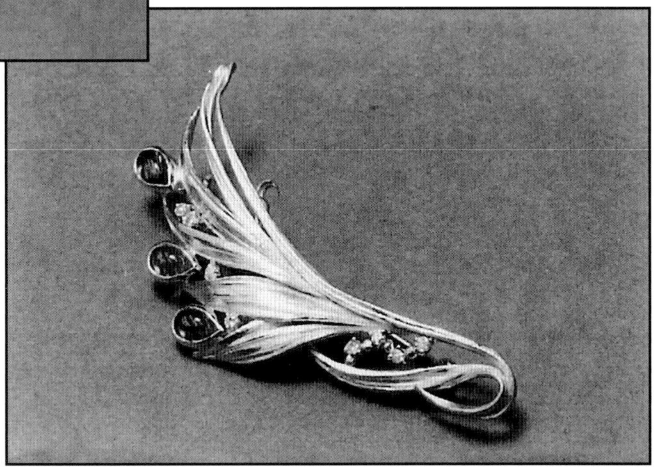

Vibrant *Mitsuro* Brooch.

MITSURO PENDANT

GENERAL DESCRIPTION:

Flowers are popular as a design motif. Various expressions of flowers may be created by the use of sheet wax or *mitsuro*. Here, small flowers resembling lilies will be made. Create these flowers, carefully preserving the ambience of the lovely flower petals.

WORK HINTS:

1. Pay attention to the size of the flower petals.
2. Produce a natural unfurled look to the flower.
3. Secure the base of the flower.

MATERIALS:

Mitsuro	Spatula
Needle	

Stretch the *mitsuro* flat and slender. It is not necessary to produce *hikime* here but, make a piece about 15 - 20 cm long.

Fold the piece into a "U" at a point about 2 cm from the end. Make the bend slowly with no excessive force.

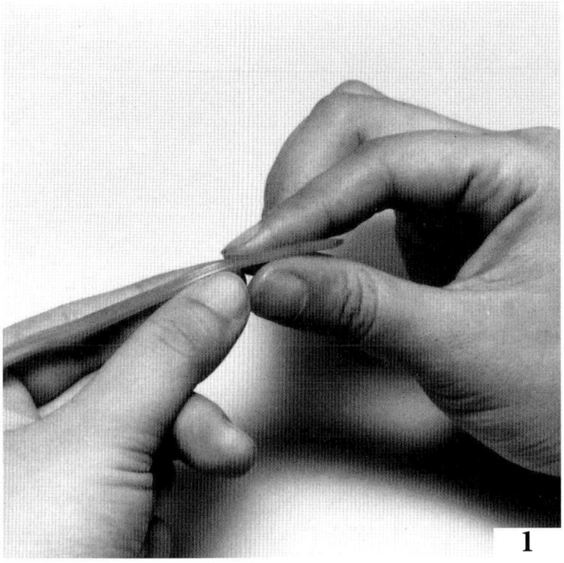

1

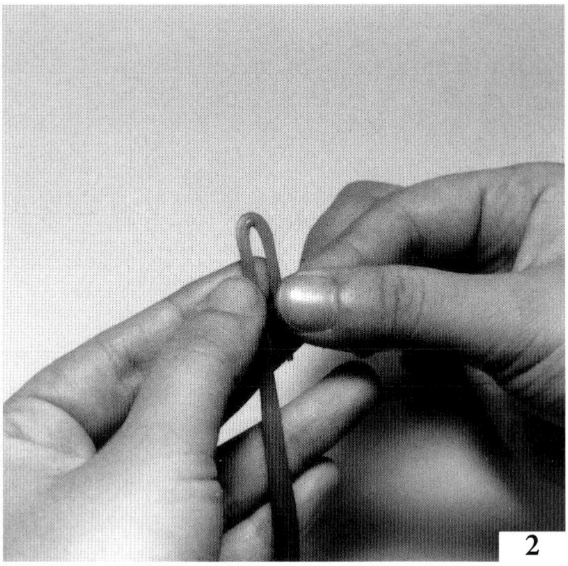

2

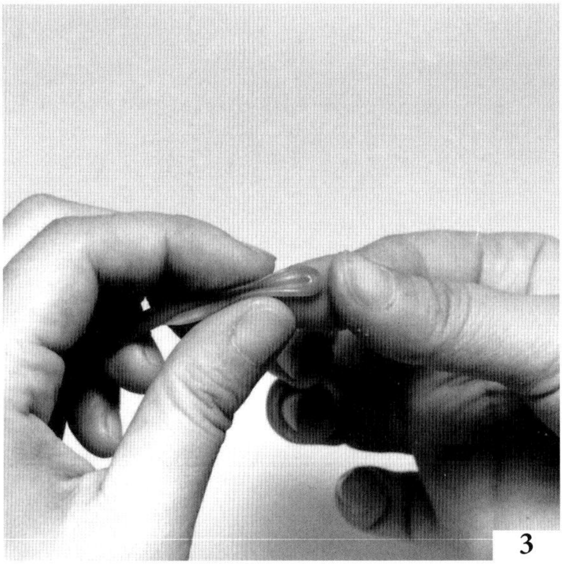

3

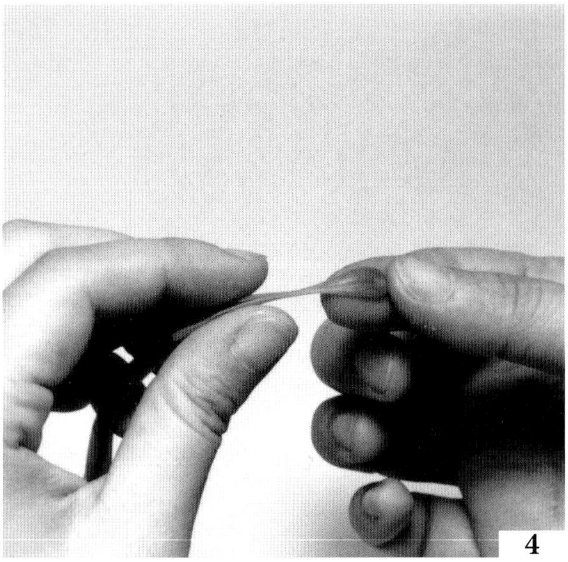

4

Lightly pinch the parts together against the thumb smoothly, about 5 mm below the loop. Slide your fingers so as not to leave fingerprints.

While warming the *mitsuro* with your fingers, grasp the end and pull apart. The tear drop shape will become a petal. Do not allow the end to get too thick. In the same manner make 5 petals of the same size.

As soon as five petals have been prepared, assemble them one at a time. While keeping the pointed parts warm, stick them together neatly. Flaring out the outer edges of the petals will add balance.

Assemble the petals in twos and threes first. It will go smoother to make them in this manner than to do the five petals at one time. It may be convenient to use a piece of wax wire to assemble the petals around.

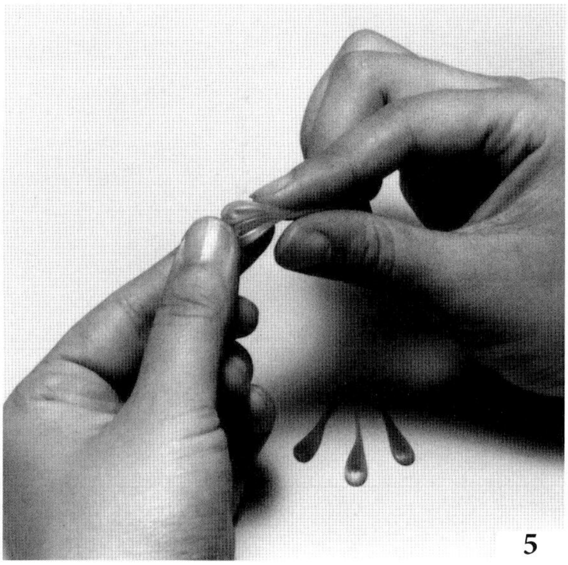

5

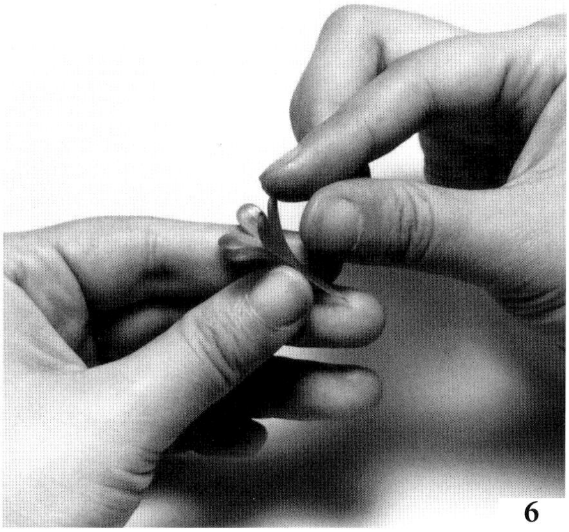

6

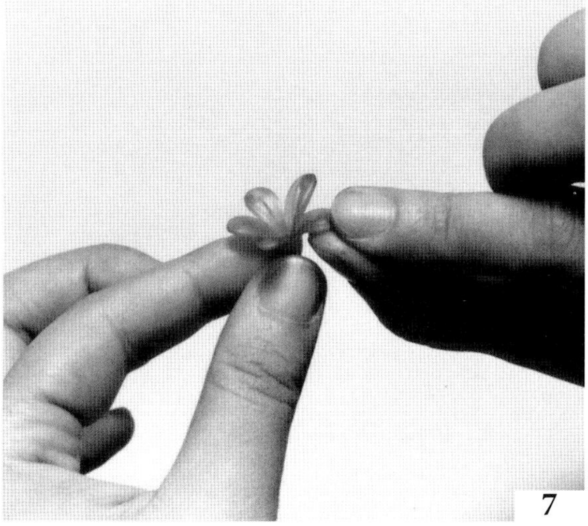

7

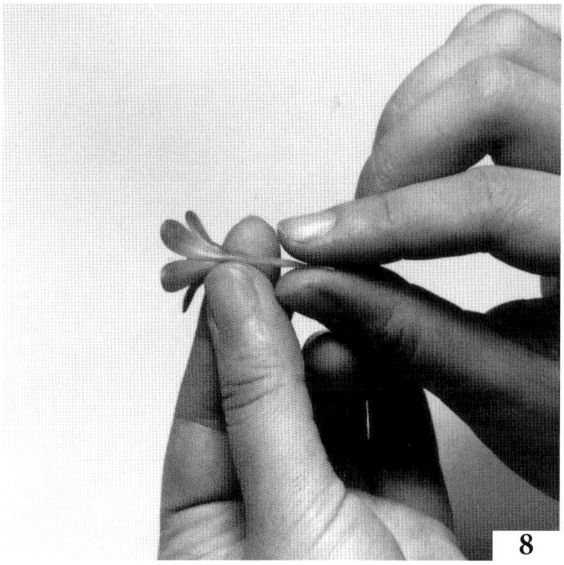

8

Grasp the stem of the flower and arrange all the pieces nicely. Think of the balance as you spread the petals. Bend the outer portions.

After the stem has been stuck well, give it a natural appearance by lengthening and slimming the stem.

Make three small flowers; assemble them together by the stems. Taking care not to spoil the petals, stick the stems together as you warm them with your fingers.

Next, make the leaves. Bring out ample *hikime* and make the long and short parts. Put twists in them as you follow the design for shaping.

9

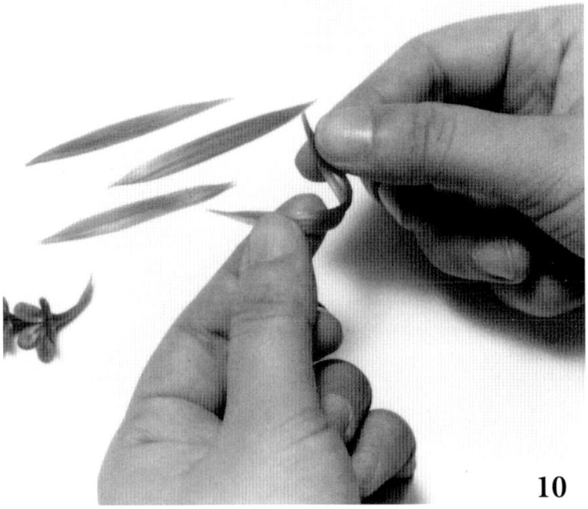

10

11

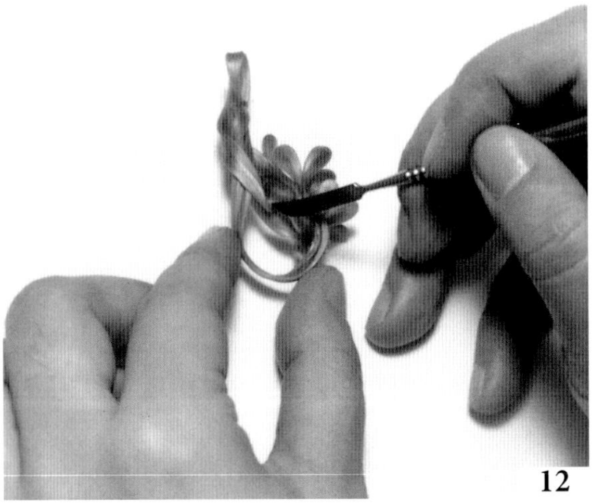

12

As you assemble the parts, check the overall size and balance. Blend the flowers and the leaves together into a natural flow.

After you have welded the points of contact together from the backside, apply additional *mitsuro* to the contact points with a warm spatula. Be certain the added *mitsuro* will not be seen from the front.

MODELING *MITSURO* WITH OTHER MATERIALS

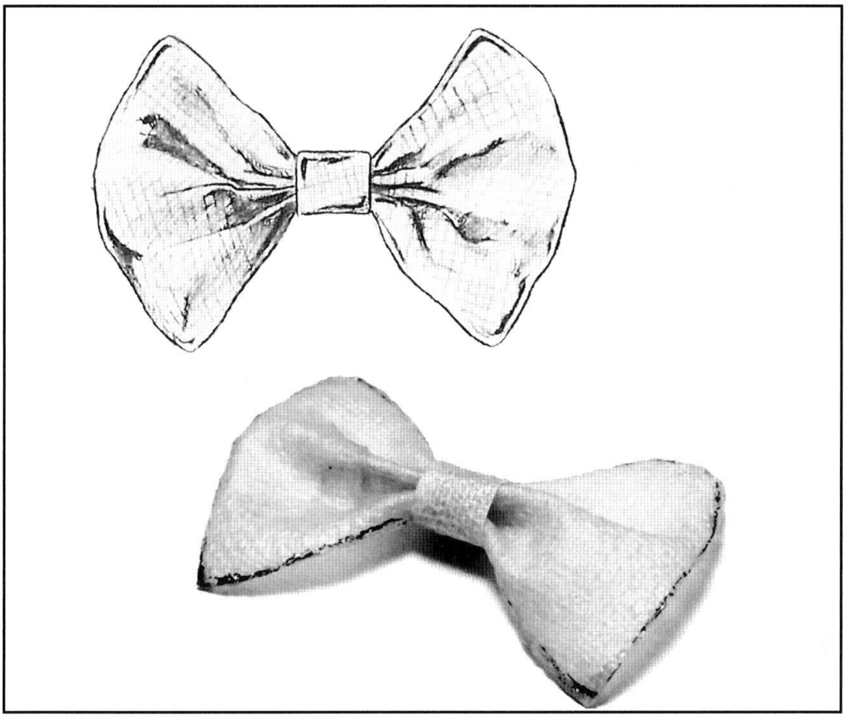

GENERAL DESCRIPTION:

There is a method to modeling, as such, for materials "cooked" with *mitsuro*; materials, such as gauze and lace, which burn out. Here we will use gauze and make a ribbon tie type brooch. The sense of the delicately woven representation of the gauze is produced; a texture which cannot be duplicated on metal directly. Lace may be used in the same method.

WORK HINTS:

1. "Cook" the gauze thoroughly until bubbles no longer appear.
2. Put wax along the borders to add thickness.
3. As the material is flat, bring out the feeling of body.

MATERIALS:

Mitsuro	Gauze
Stove	Perforated metal pad
Chop sticks	Marking pen
Scissors	Spatula

Put the gauze in the pot of melted *mitsuro*. As bubbles will rise, allow the *mitsuro* to completely saturate the gauze until the bubbling stops. Ribbons and lace are treated in the same manner.

1

Pick up the gauze by both corners and suspend it. When it stops dripping, remove it and place it on a spread-out newspaper and remove the excess *mitsuro* completely.

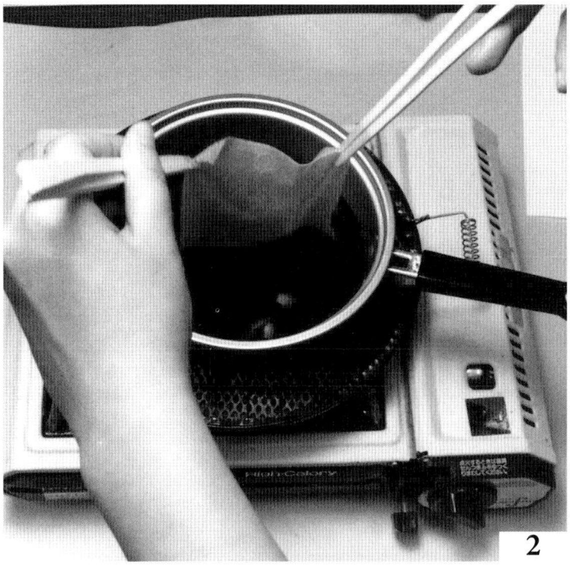
2

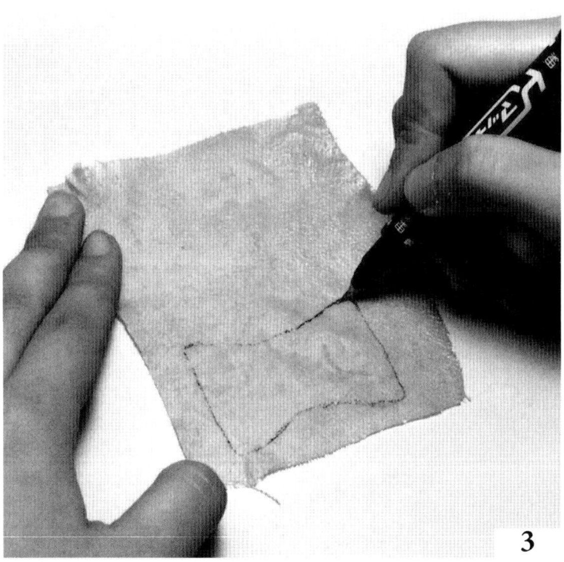
3

After the gauze has hardened to some extent, draw the developed sketch of the brooch with a felt marking pen, do this lightly (pressure). The product will be a ribbon tie.

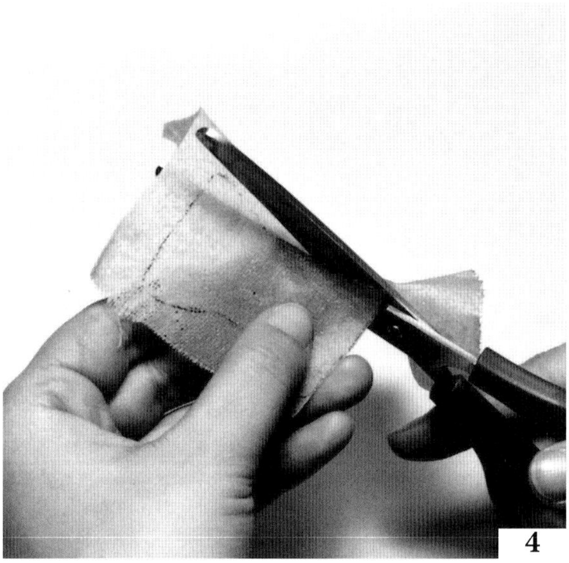
4

Cut the ribbon out with a pair of scissors. Cut the strip for the center tie at the same time.

Using your fingers, form the ribbon. In the event you have difficulties use a *takegushi* or the like to help you form it gradually. Add some plumpness to the folds.

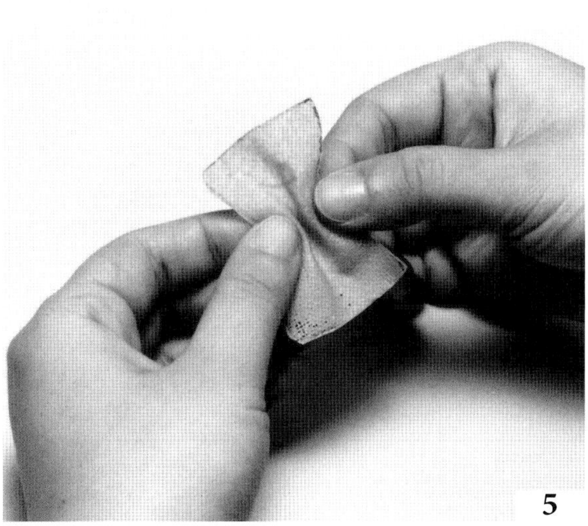

5

Press the edges slightly inward. Give a three dimensional appearance to the ribbon.

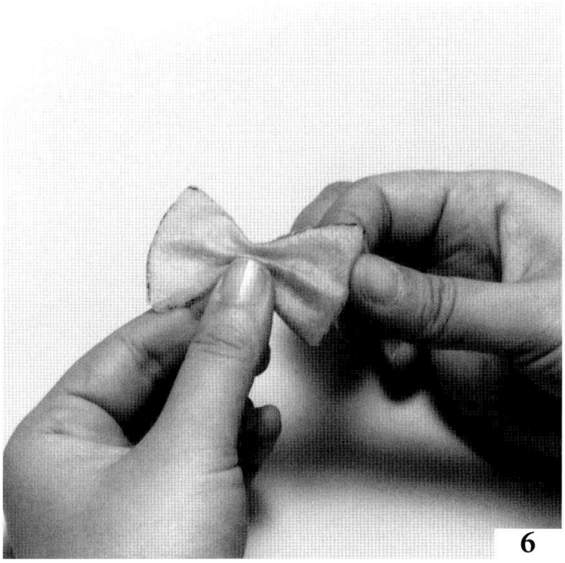

6

7

Add the tie to the ribbon. Cut off the excess on the reverse side of the tie and weld the end down with additional *mitsuro*.

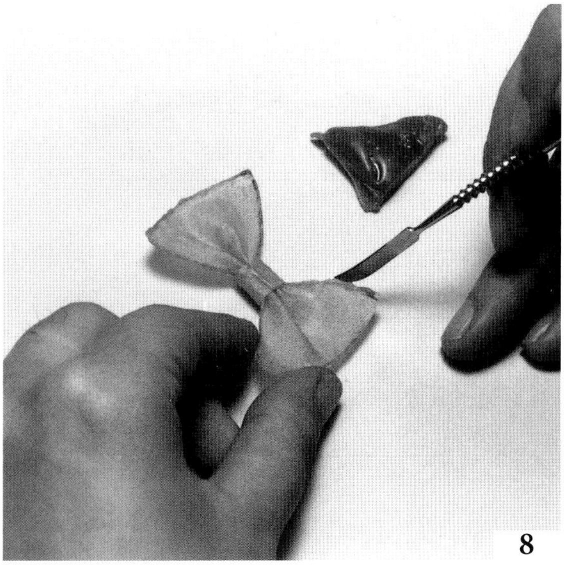

8

Add *mitsuro* along the edges for stiffness to avoid casting problems later.

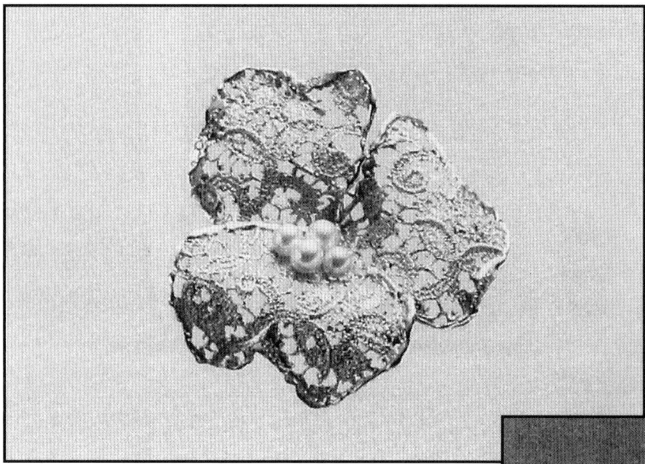

Brooch - Leafy Motif Created with Lace.

Brooch - Basket Created with Lace.

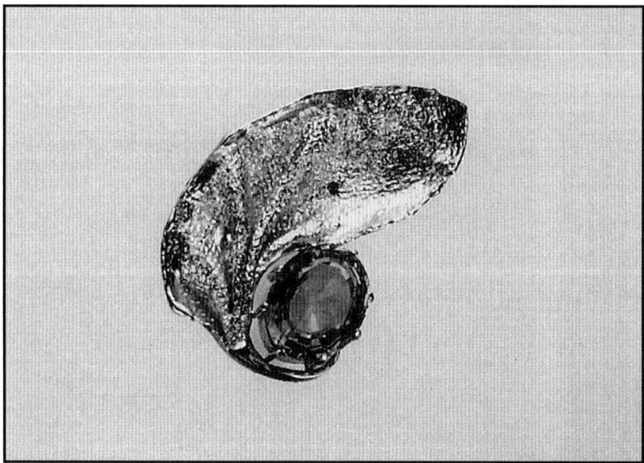

Brooch - Created with Gauze.

Brooch - Three Dimensional Look Created with Lace.

FREE FORMING

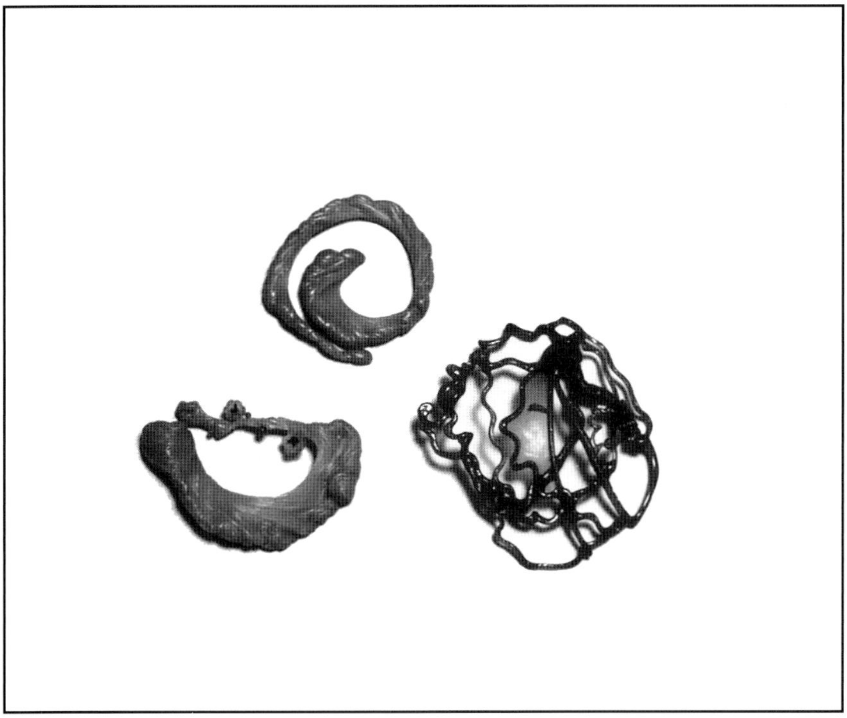

GENERAL DESCRIPTION:

By dripping melted wax into water, a variety of shapes are produced. This method of producing shapes is referred to as "free forming" or "accidentals". Different types of wax will produce different results; the water temperature will create subtle differences on the surfaces of the wax as well. By paying attention when you pour, a variety of shapes may be created. We will make a model using a mixture of hard and soft wax.

WORK HINTS:

1. Know the temperature of the water.
2. Try working with different water temperatures.
3. Develop the knack of dripping the wax.

MATERIALS:

Small amount of soft wax	Small amount of hard wax
Stove	Perforated metal pad
Bowl	Marking pen
Cup	Spatula

Melt soft wax and half as much hard wax (by weight). Use of wax scraps is okay.

1

After the wax mixture has melted, keep it at low heat. Although soft wax may be used alone, the addition of hard wax will improve the forming of irregular shapes and also facilitate hollowing the underside.

2

3

Put water in a large bowl, stir with a spoon and set up a swirling current. The wax will follow the current, and hopefully an interesting form will begin to shape up.

4

Pour the wax onto the water in a small stream without stopping. Be aware that if you pour all of the wax in at one time, it will just form a lump and the swirls will not form.

Pour the wax in the manner you wish it to form. See to it that the water is in constant motion as you pour. Use your hand or a spoon to stir the water gently.

The portion of the wax on the water will harden rapidly, but that portion above the water will not. Before the wax hardens completely, tilt it up from the bottom and spill out the still molten wax.

5

6

7

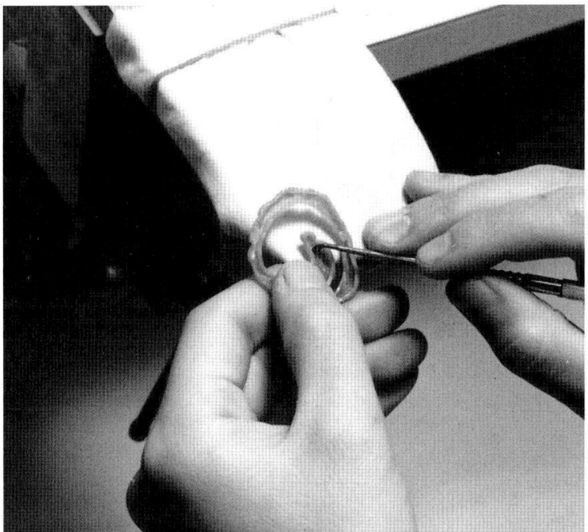

8

After you have selected a piece, immerse it and allow it to cool. Free forming will produce unintentional, interesting shapes. Experiment by varying the flow of wax and the height from which it is poured.

Wipe the piece dry. If it appears that the cast piece will weigh too much, use a carver and remove the excess material from the underside. Since the mixture contains hard wax use the same processing techniques as for hard wax.

You may use plain hard wax for free forming. Put pieces of the wax in a metal container, melt it and pour it into swirling water. However, hard wax has a higher melting temperature so make certain the wax is completely melted.

The results will depend on how you pour. You can produce stringy or lumpy variations. Try pouring in the manner of drawing a picture.

9

10

11

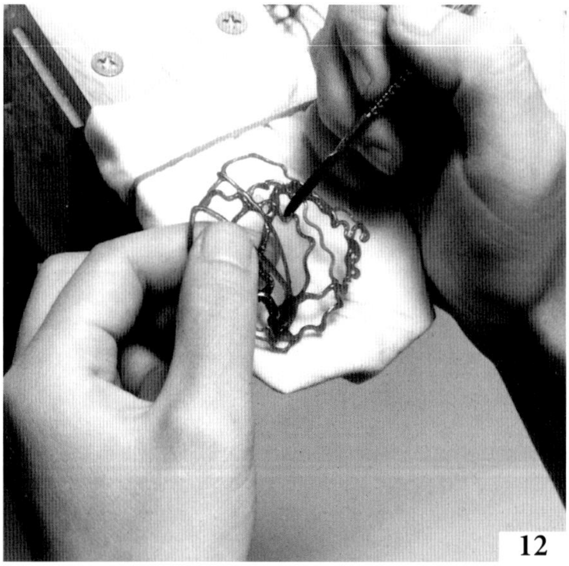

12

If you find some pieces to your liking, immerse them in the water and let them harden. You may cut portions off with a saw or knife and patch them together if you wish.

When you come up with design possibilities, assemble the pieces and hollow out the undersides. Skillful assembly will result in a pleasing brooch or pendant.

Free Form Brooch Made from Two Separate Pieces.

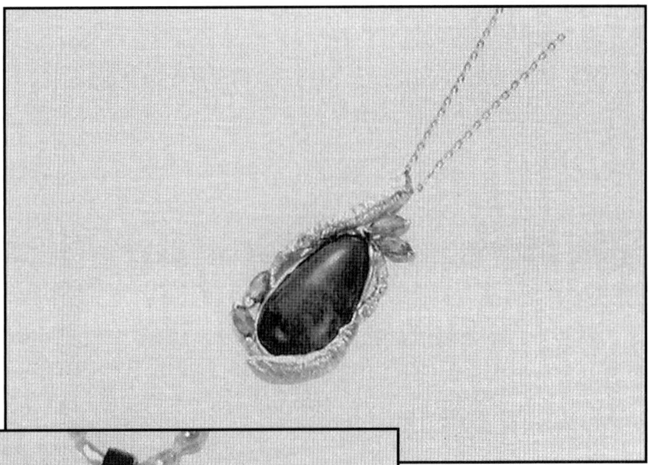

Free Form Brooch with a Wrinkly Texture.

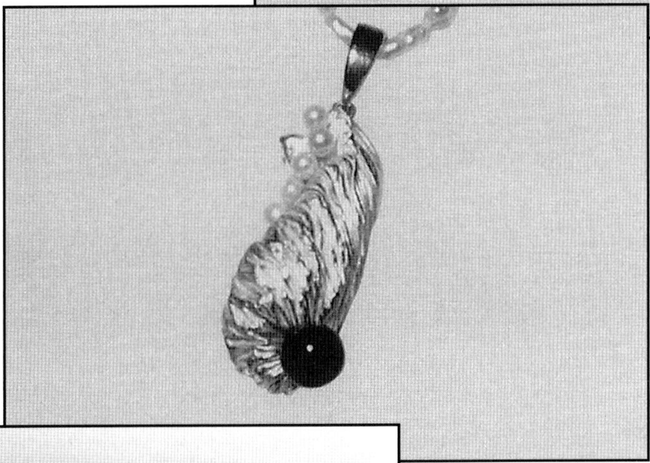

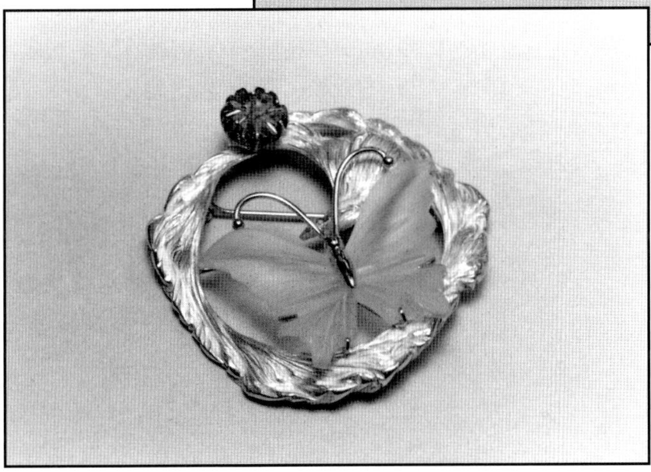

Brooch with a Butterfly in a Free Form Frame.

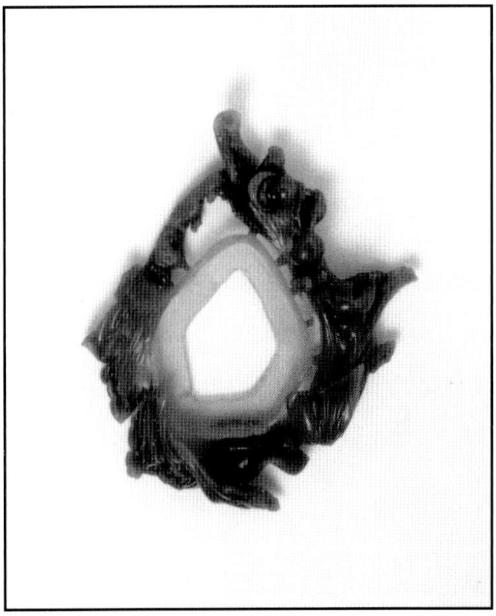

Pendant of Leaf Textured Free Form Pieces.

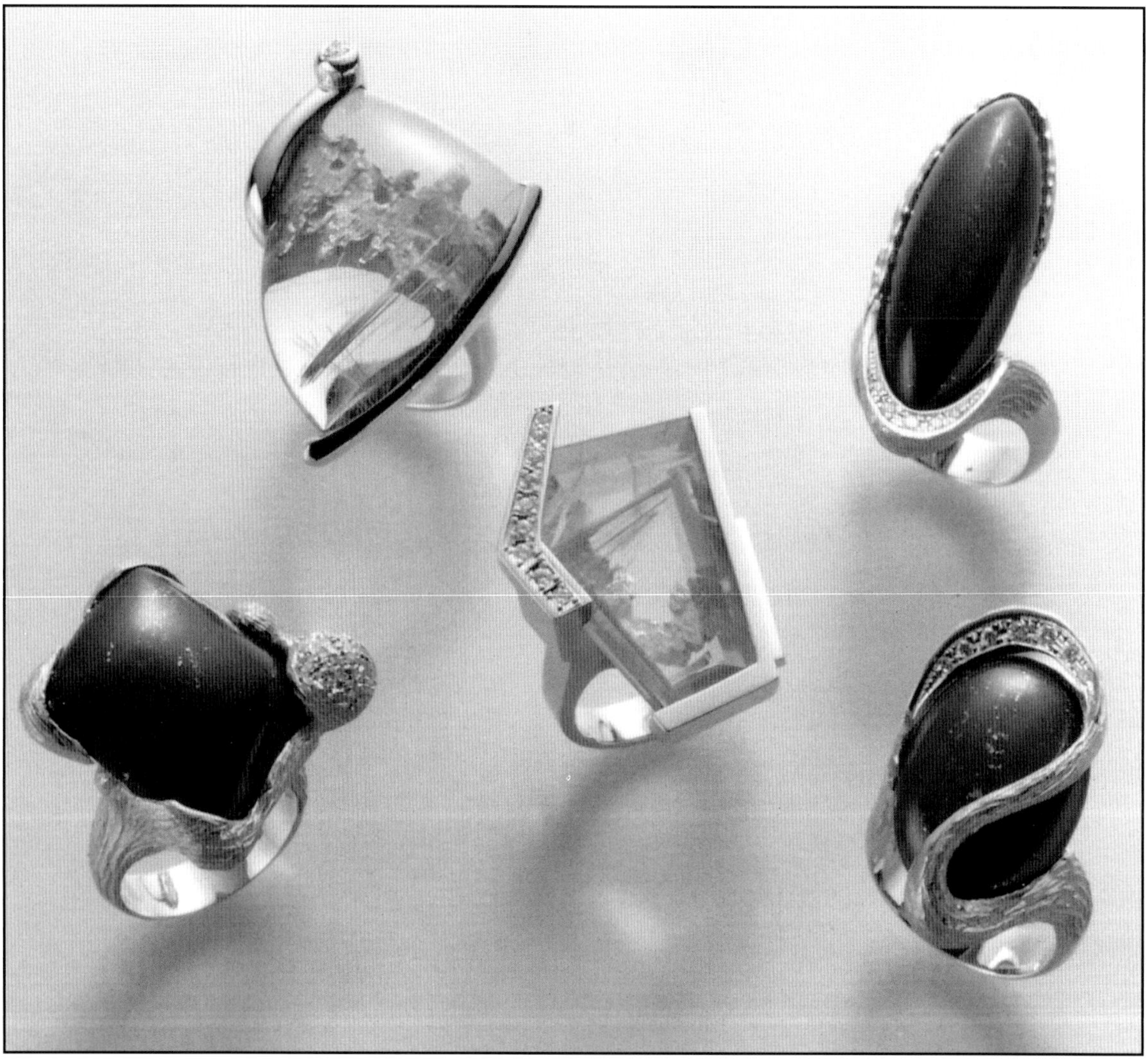

III

MODELING TECHNIQUES WITH GEMSTONES

CABOCHON MOUNTING FOR A PENDANT IN SOFT WAX

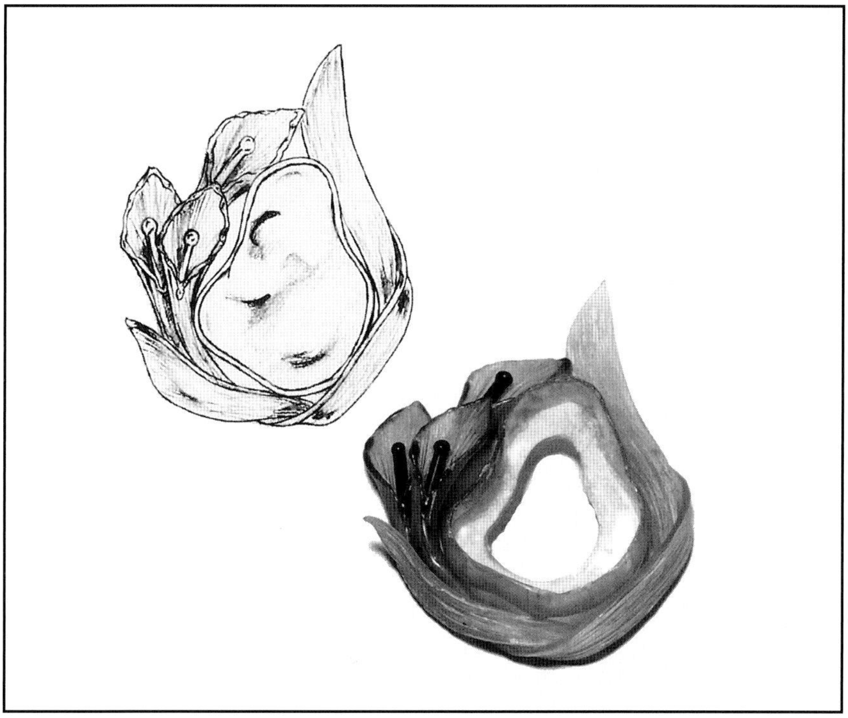

GENERAL DESCRIPTION:

Although it may be difficult to construct a setting for an irregularly shaped stone out of metal, an ornamental setting can be made easily, if you use soft sheet wax. In making a setting from wax a feasible design can be developed, offering a kind of ambiance surrounding the stone. Here, the setting brings a stone together with flowers and leaves.

WORK HINTS:

1. Design a setting which accentuates the shape of the stone.
2. Do not damage the stone while making the model.
3. Maintain good balance to the model as you apply the wax.

MATERIALS:

Soft sheet wax	Wax wire
Stone	Glass sheet
Talcum powder	Scissors
Spatula	*Takegushi*
Knife	Needle
Alcohol lamp	

Place the stone on a sheet of soft wax and cut a piece out about twice the size of the stone, the extra amount about the height of the stone and in its approximate shape.

Put talcum powder on the bottom of the stone and the wax to keep them from sticking together.

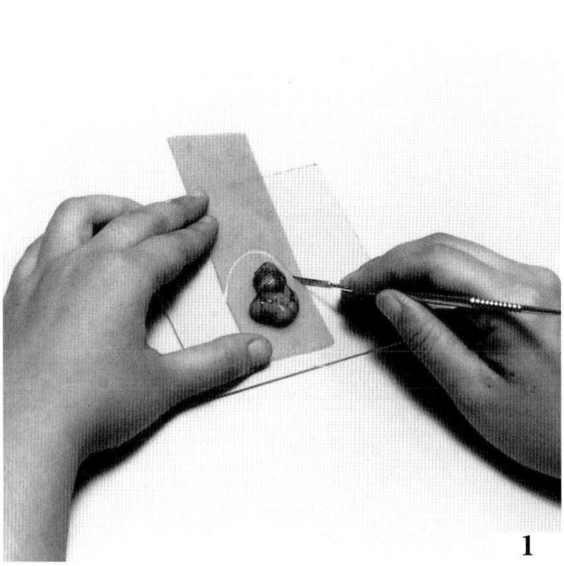

1

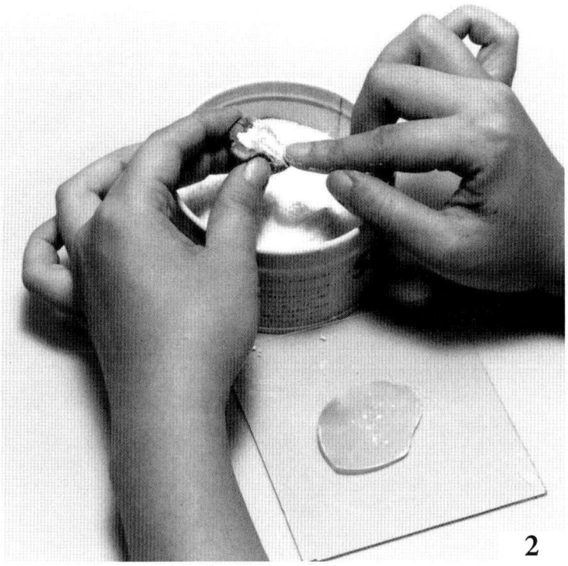

2

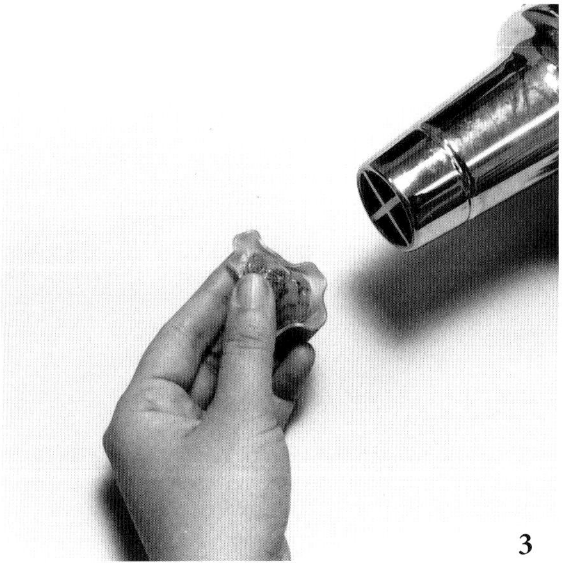

3

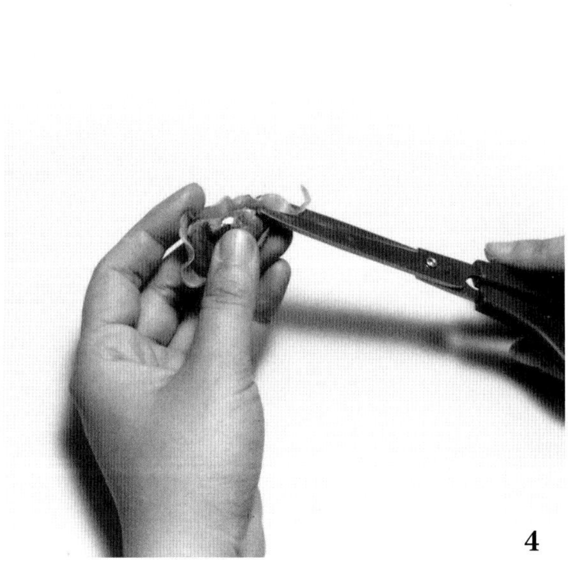

4

Place the stone in the middle of the wax piece and mold the wax around the perimeter of the stone while warming with a dryer. Excessive heat may cause the wax to melt, so be careful.

Cut the excess wax off with a pair of scissors. After cutting, rewarm the assembly with the dryer and trim any excess that may have developed from the heating.

Repeat the process until the stone fits with no gaps. If the wax is bumpy in spots, rub the spots with your finger, while warming, until they smooth out.

Finish trimming the edges with a knife. Take care not to scratch the stone (if it is soft). As the wax is thick trim at an angle with a knife or spatula.

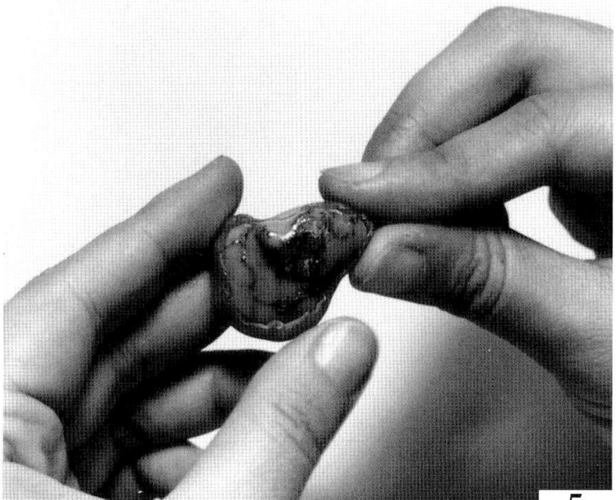

5

6

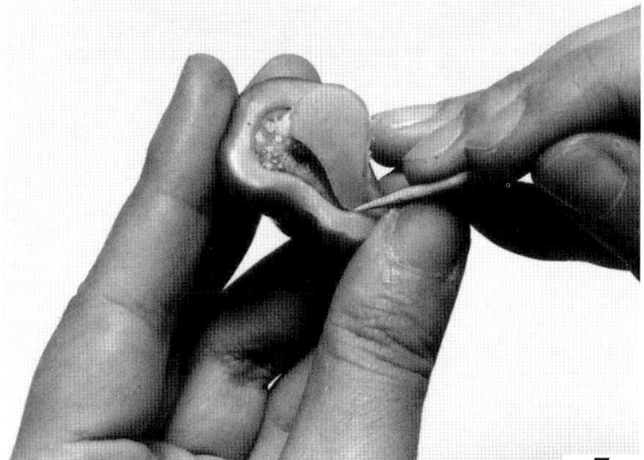

7

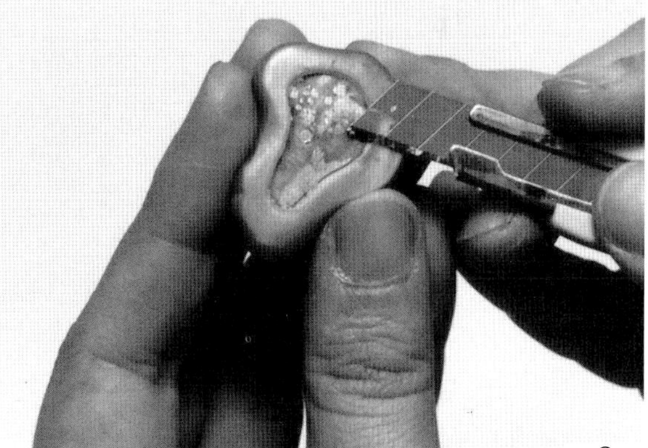

8

Use pointed end of the *takegushi* to cut out the excess wax from the underside (leave enough for the seat). Do not cut it out in one stroke but go around the cut a number of times.

Trim the ragged edges with a knife and burnish with a finger rub.

Remove the stone. If there is difficulty, press the stone out with a *takegushi*. As there is a minute shrinkage in cast metal, make certain the stone has some movement.

Next, make the flowers. Cut them in the "developed" size and add lines for texture on the inner surface. Use a dowel to form the flowers. Add slight in-and-out undulations to the petal, imparting a soft look.

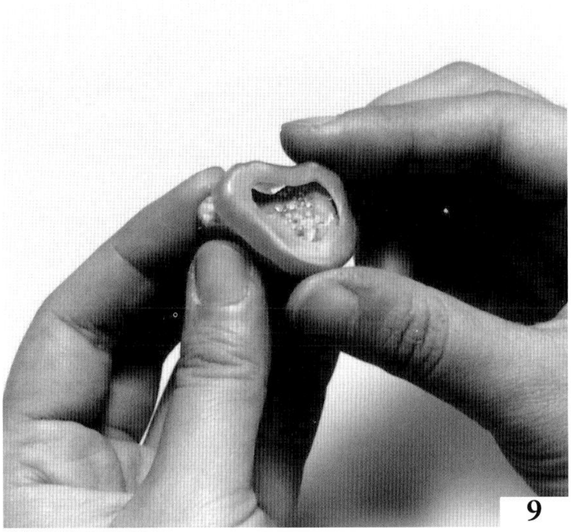

9

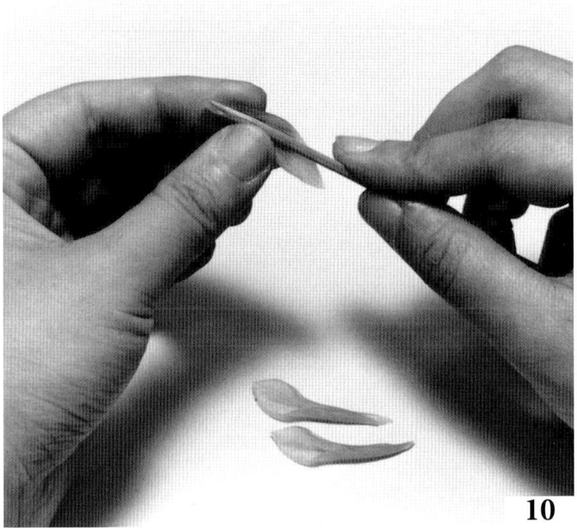

10

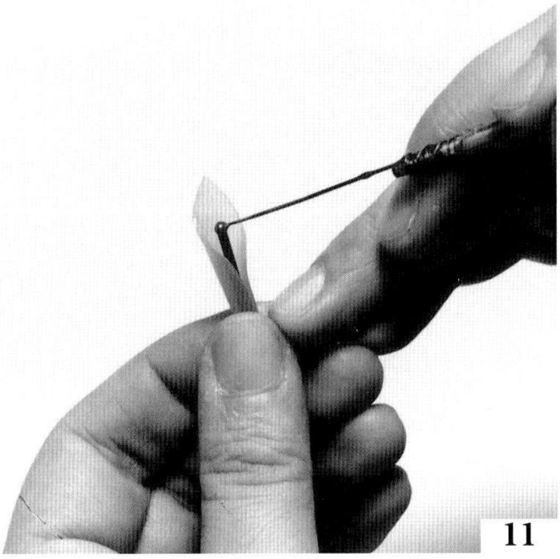

11

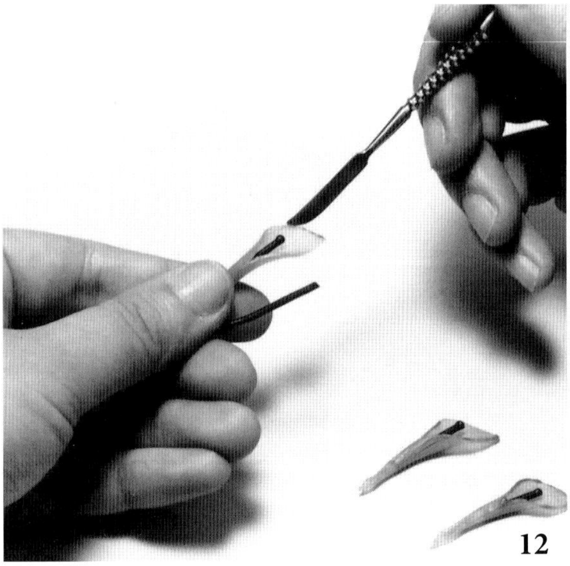

12

After the shaping of the flower is finished, add a wax wire for the stem. Melt the end of the wax wire and form a round head to represent the stamen.

With a heated spatula add wax around the edge of the flower. Make three flowers in this manner.

Make the leaves. Apply texture to the entire surface and give them a natural-looking curve. Use small gauge sheet wax to avoid a heavy look.

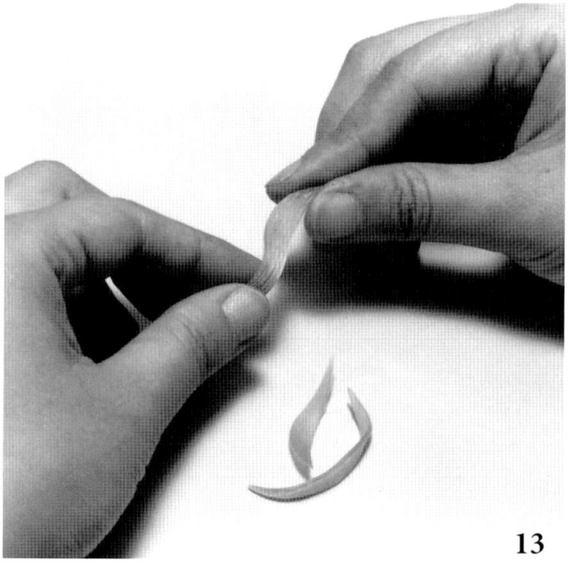

13

As you lay out the parts give thought to the contact points and balance. Should the parts be too large, trim them, mend or remake them.

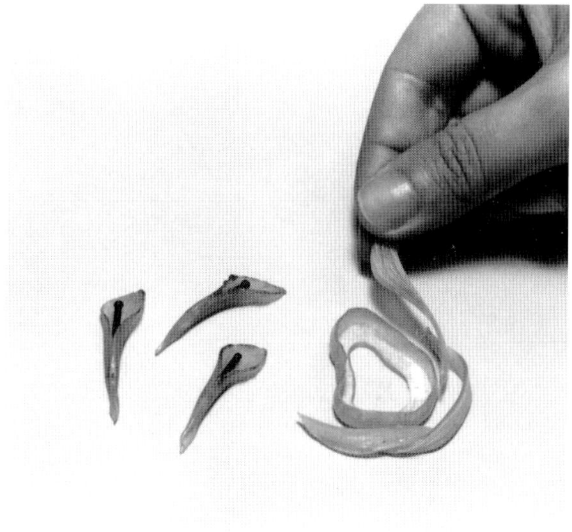

14

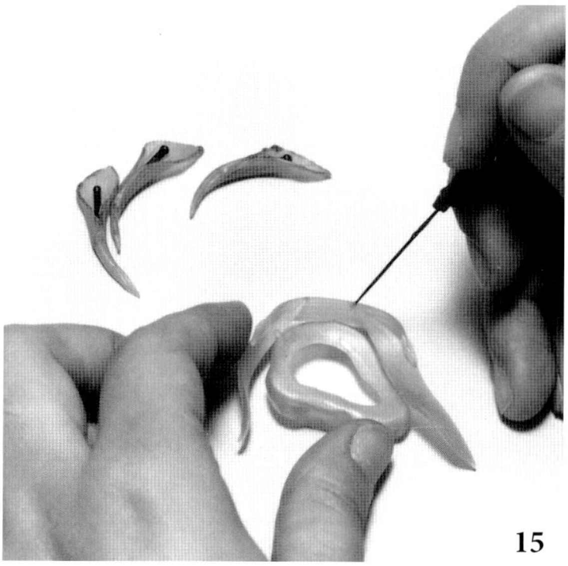

15

Assemble the parts from the reverse side and weld them with a heated needle. If the contact area is too small, add wax and increase the area.

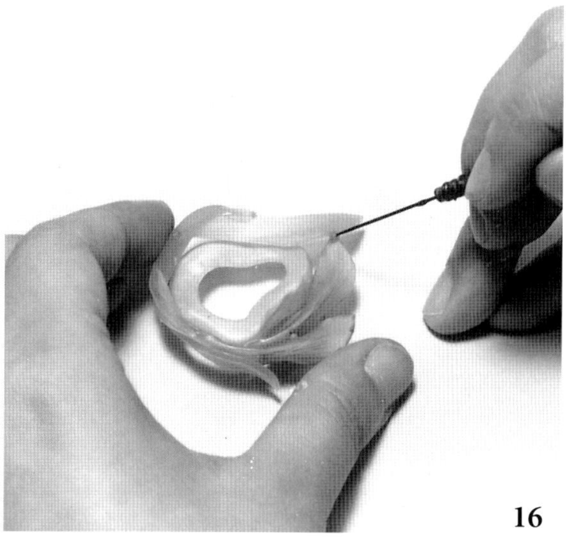

16

After the three flowers have been completed, add them to the assembly. Inspect everything well from the reverse side, adding wax where necessary.

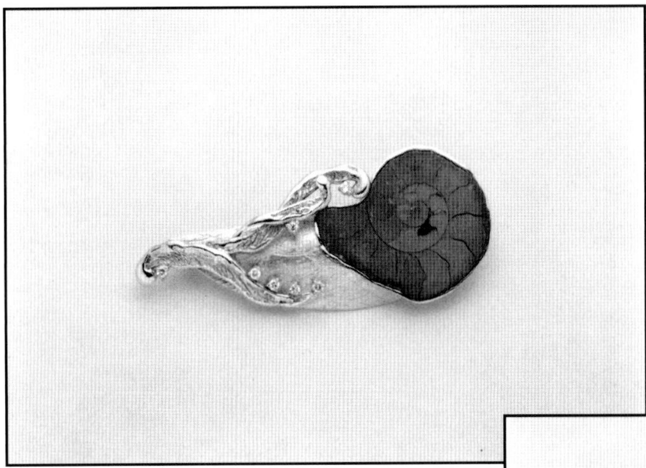

Pendant Featuring an Ammonite Fossil.

Pendant with Stone Settings Added throughout the Design.

Pendant with *Mitsuro*-Made Forms in Irregular Setting.

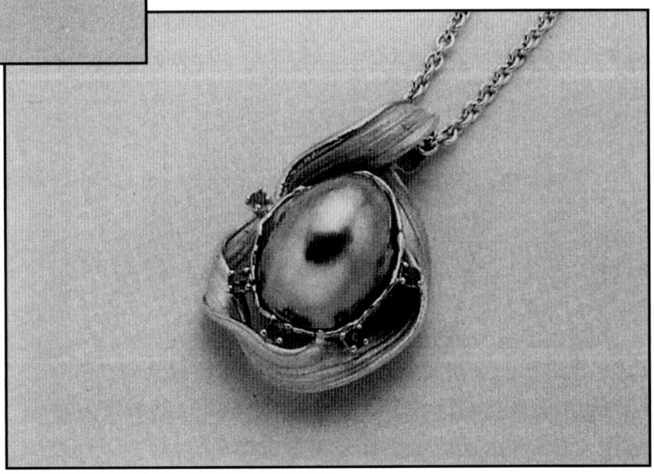

Ring with an Irregular Shaped Bezel.

CABOCHON MOUNTING FOR A RING IN HARD WAX

GENERAL DESCRIPTION:

To make a setting for a precious stone in metal, a hard wax model with a stone seat will be made for the cabochon. Accurate work will be required. As it becomes practicable to add texture to a setting, and in the case of a ring, design the shank and incorporate it into the setting, jewelry fabrication becomes broader in scope. We will add a veinlike texture to the ring.

WORK HINTS:

1. Make the stone seat slightly larger than the stone.
2. When welding parts together, do not cause any deformation.
3. Join the shank and setting accurately.

MATERIALS:

Slice of wax	Off-centered hole wax ring tube
Scriber	File
Jeweler's saw	Spatula
Needle	Abrasive paper
Carvers	

Make the bezel. Use a slice of wax the thickness of the stone, place the stone on top and scribe its outline on the wax.

Cut a hole to the outline. Drill a small hole and widen the hole just to the scribed line with a file, no larger.

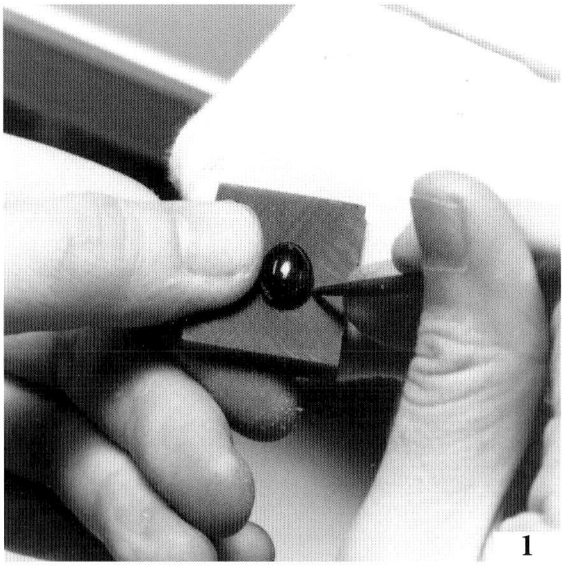

1

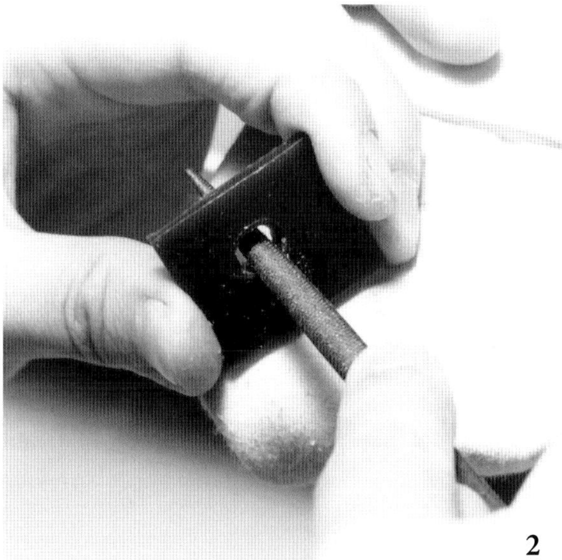

2

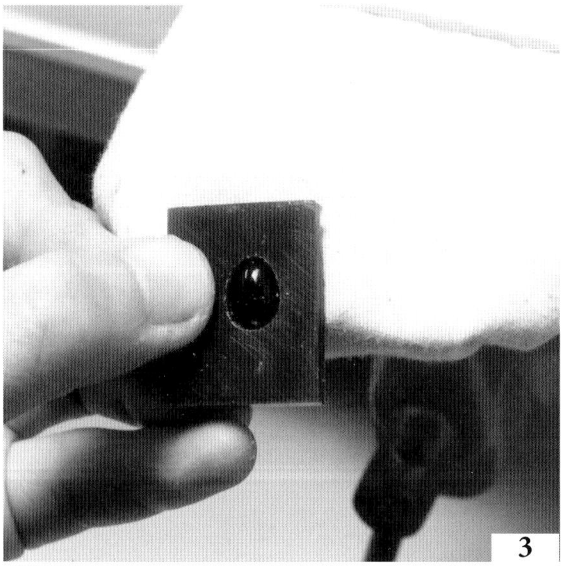

3

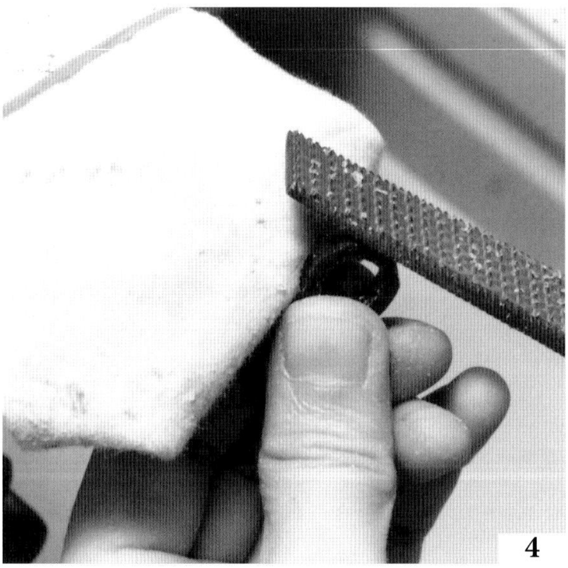

4

Insert the stone and check for fit. After casting there will be some shrinkage, so a slightly loose fit is preferred.

Allowing about a 2 mm wide band around the hole, cut out the bezel with a jeweler's saw and file to shape. Do not file too thin.

Make the seat. Use a portion of a sheet of wax about 1.0 - 1.5 mm and trace the outline of the bezel on it.

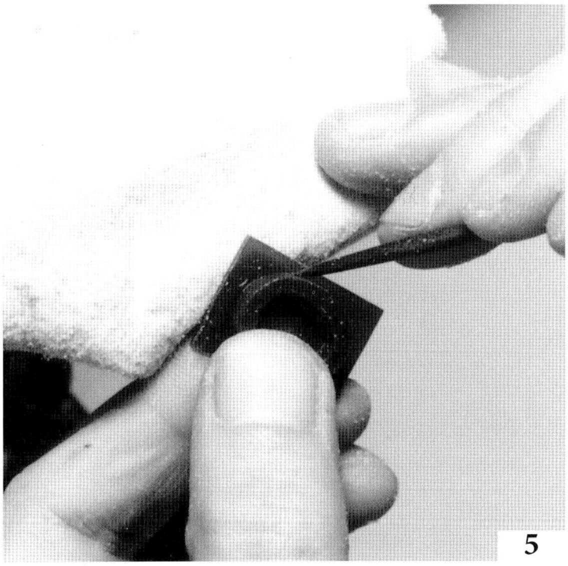

5

Cut the seat to approximate shape with the jeweler's saw and finish up with a file. Remove the material from the center, leaving enough for the stone seat.

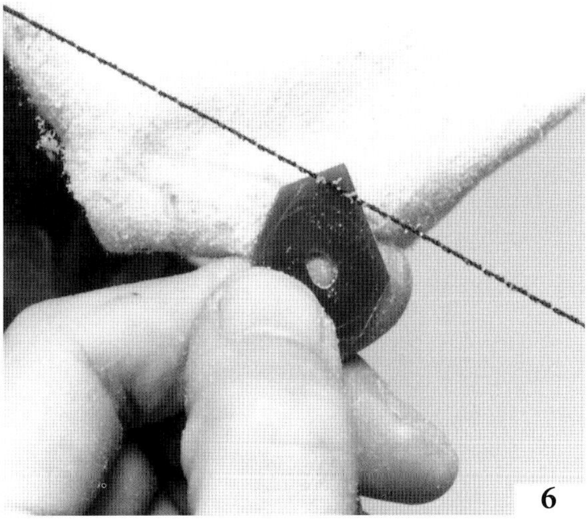

6

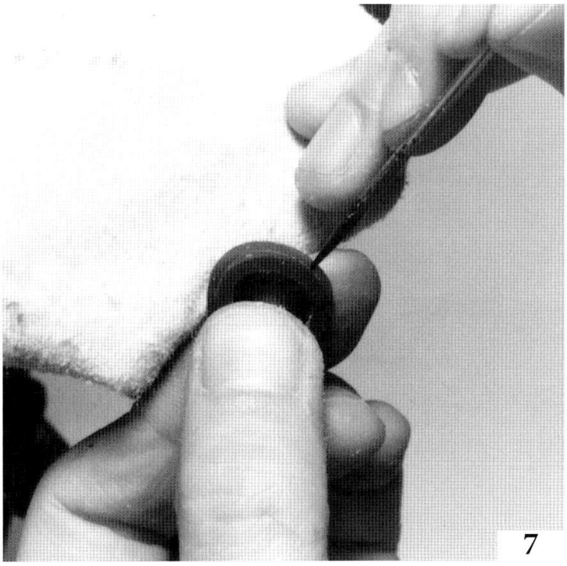

7

With a heated spatula weld the parts together. Run the knife edge on the joint and melt both pieces at the same time for a good weld. Afterwards, fill in the joint with additional wax.

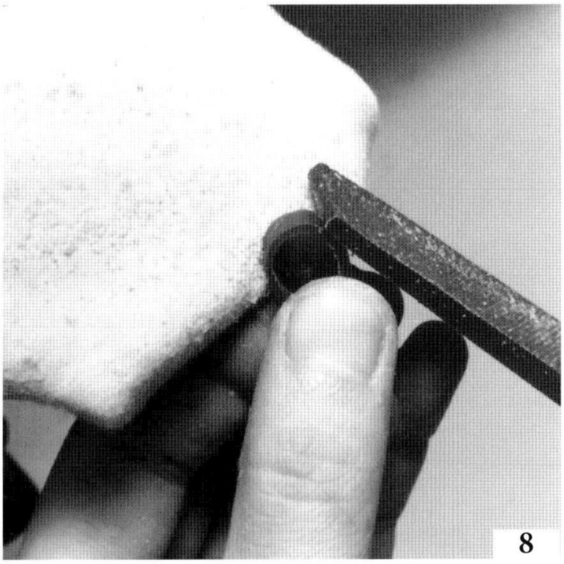

8

After the added wax has hardened, file the outer circumference until the bezel is 1.0 - 1.2 mm thick. Finish the front edge of the bezel.

Construct the ring proper. Transfer the design onto an off-centered ring tube. Scribe the height at the center, the thickness of the shank, and the width, etc., leaving nothing out.

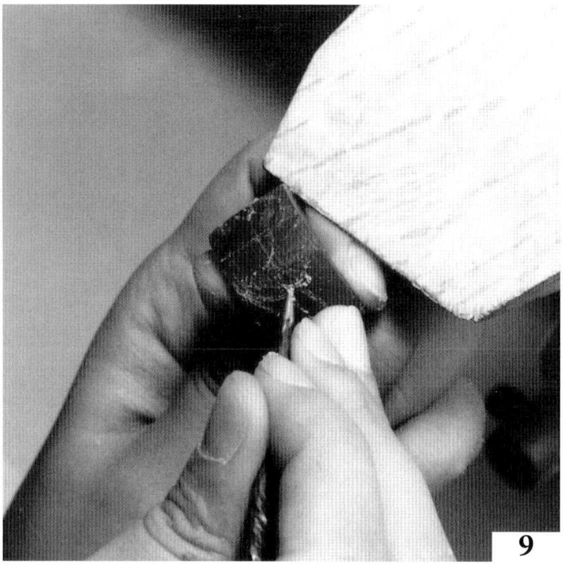

9

Saw out all of the waste. As you get more experienced, you will use the saw to cut out small areas, enabling you to work faster.

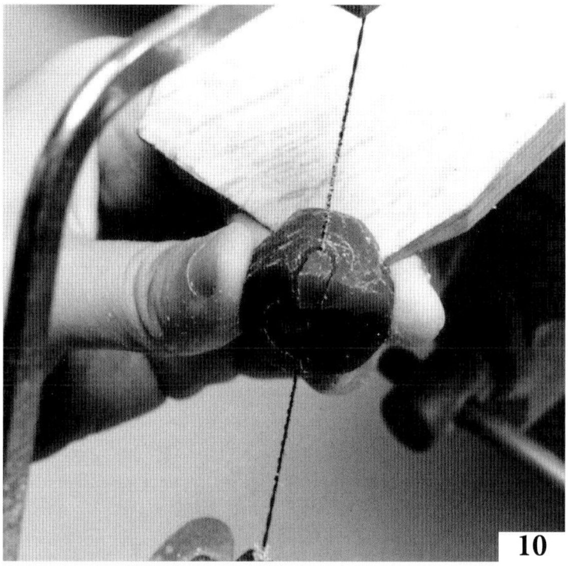

10

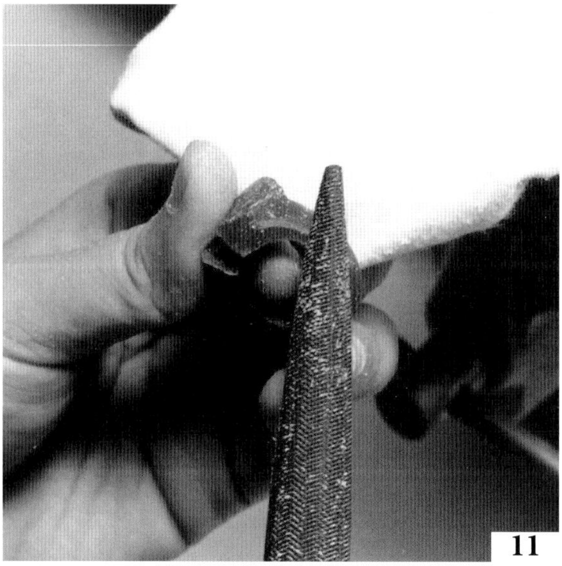

11

After the ring is roughed out, use a file to shape the center area and the shank. If during the filing, pertinent scribed lines are obliterated, replace them each time.

12

Carve a sloping surface in the center area. Make the stone seat opening the same size as the stone. Shape a gradual curve where the wave pattern will appear. Check the shank thickness: pare it down with a file.

Draw the waves with a scriber. Balance the spacing; scribe lines fairly deep and distinct. Incise the curves to swirl towards the finger hole.

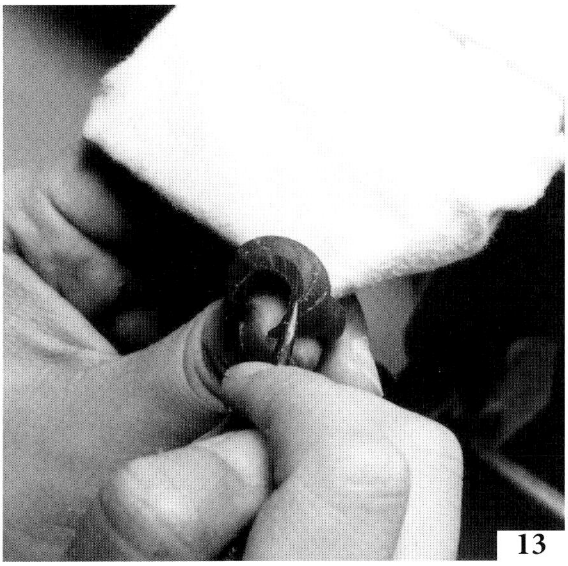

13

Contour the waves with a carver. Carve the inner surfaces deeper to reveal more of the edges. Smooth the surfaces with a fine cut file. Carve to give a flat appearance; finish raised portions and grooves neatly with a *kisage* and *takegushi*.

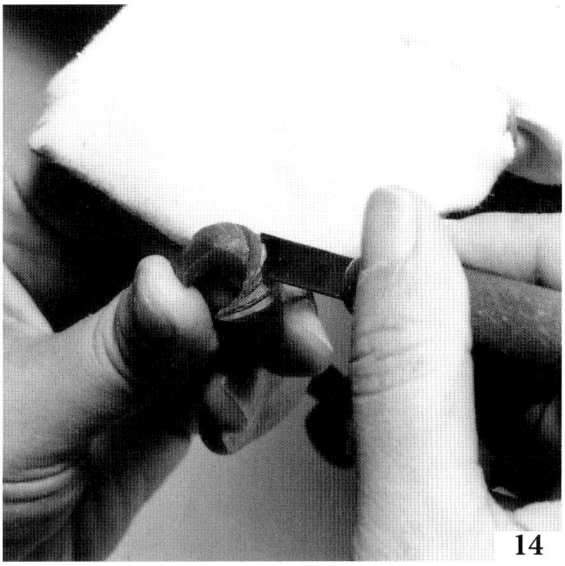

14

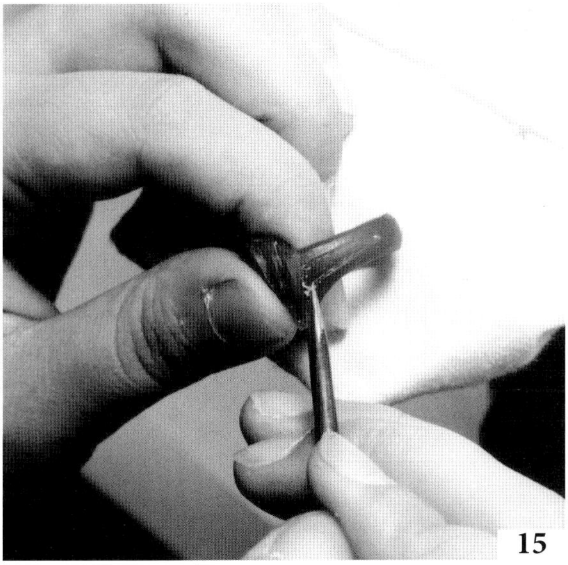

15

After you have finished the center portion, carve three rounded grooves into the shank. Draw in the lines with a scriber, carefully carve along those lines with a knife carver. Because of the curvature take adequate care not to stray from the lines.

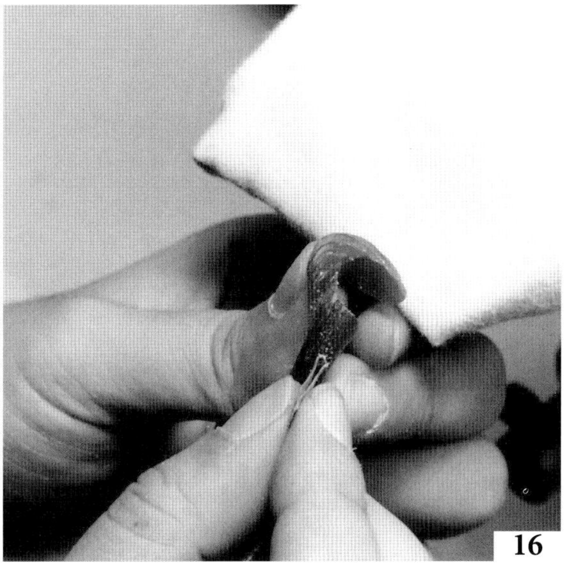

16

Go over the entire ring with abrasive papers. Polish the grooves, tight areas neatly. Extremely close quarters might be accessed with an abrasive impregnated eraser.

Add texture to the waves. With a heated needle, densely cover the waves with minute deep lines.

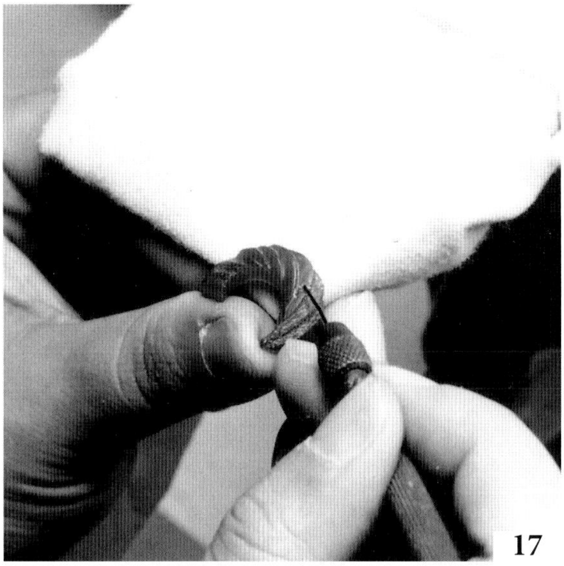

17

After the top is finished, remove material from the underside. Scribe the area to be removed: gouge out the excess with a bur and carvers. Where the stone seat is to go the material needs to be about 2 mm thick.

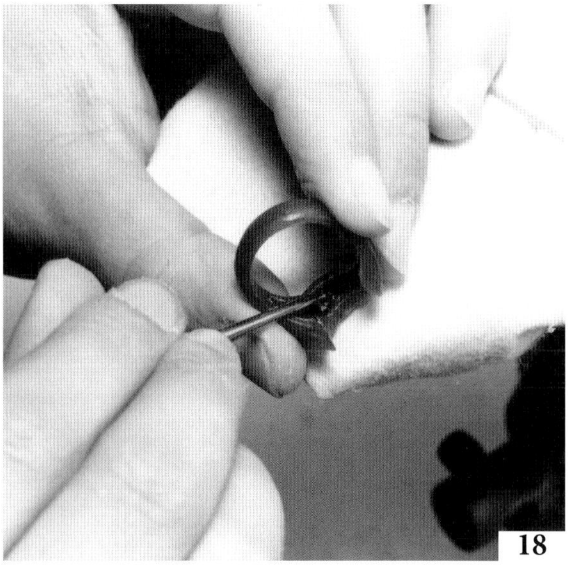

18

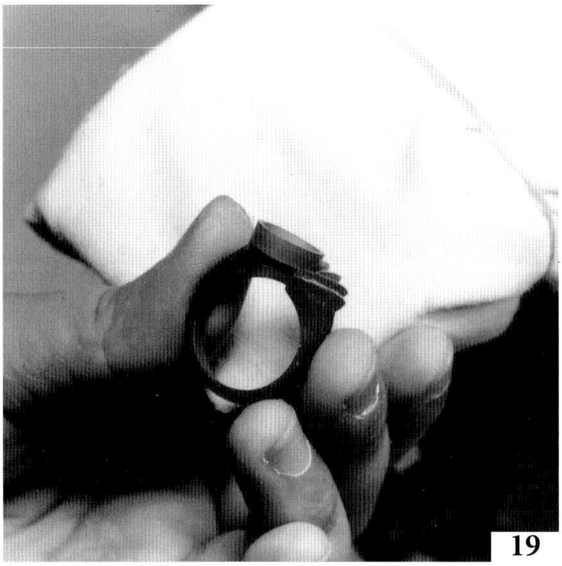

19

Place the stone seat into position. Try to get the seat to fit neatly. Embed about one quarter of the seat depth.

20

When set in place, weld into place from the underside. Pick up wax with a hot needle, apply it in a poking manner.

Wax will be added below the stone seat. Look from the front; the rounded portion of the stone seat must extend to the finger hole. As you build up wax with a heated spatula, be careful not to melt adjacent portions.

Check the ring from the top, make certain there are no gaps. If a gap is present pick up a small amount of wax with a hot needle and fill it in. If you are not able to get the repair wax to run in well, use soft wax.

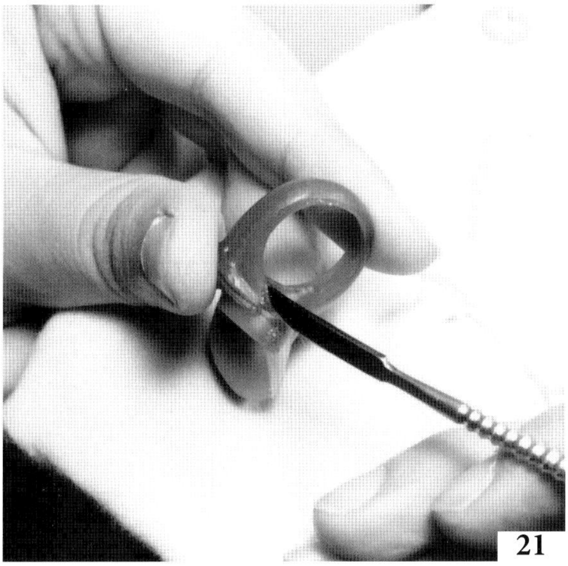

21

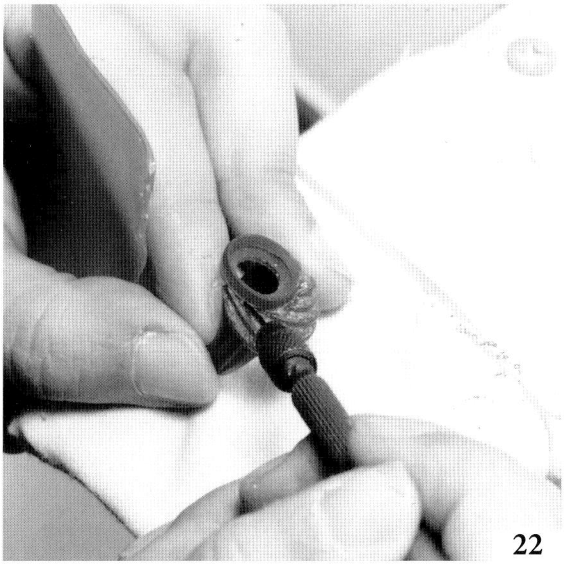

22

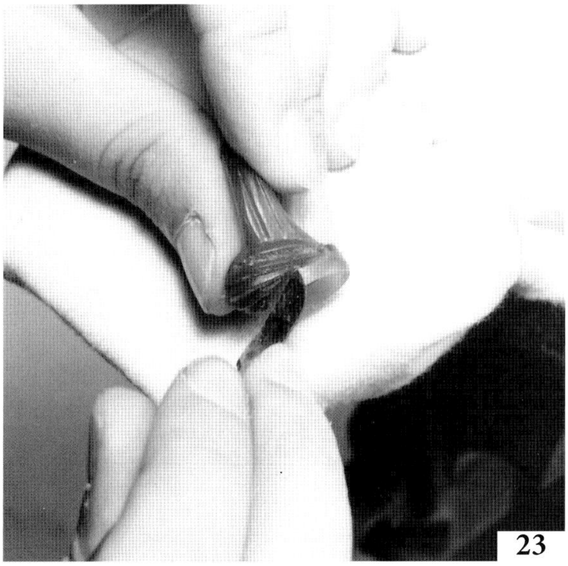

23

24

Clean up any excess wax with files and spatulas. Clean up the corners especially well, inspect the textured portion, if the lines have become obliterated, redo them.

Lastly, finish up the underside. Clean up the welds, get a uniform thickness throughout, grooves under the textured portion. There are thin spots so be careful in the removing process.

Pendant with a Plain Mounted Cabochon.

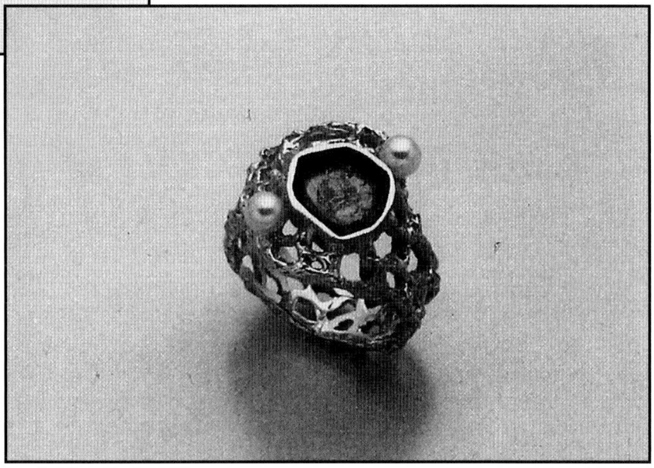

Irregularly Shaped Stone in Ring Fashioned by the Build-Up Wax Process.

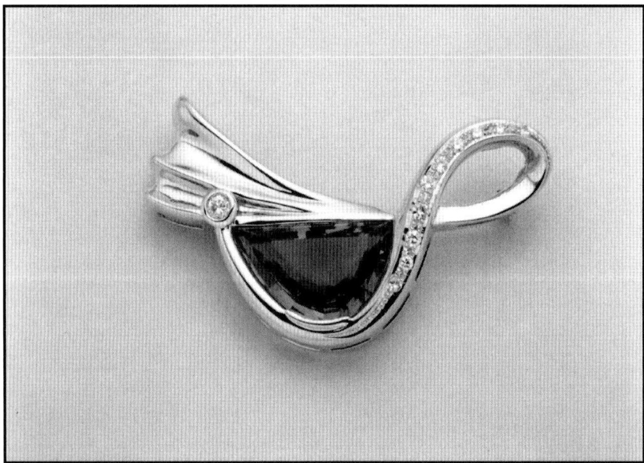

Pendant Design which Brings Out the Special Features of the Stone.

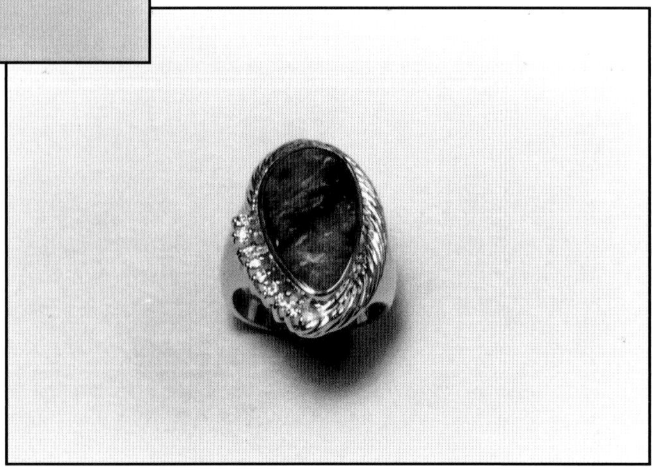

Ring with a Boulder Opal Accented by a Showy Bezel.

IV

OTHER WAX MODELING TECHNIQUES

SIZING

Reduction

1.

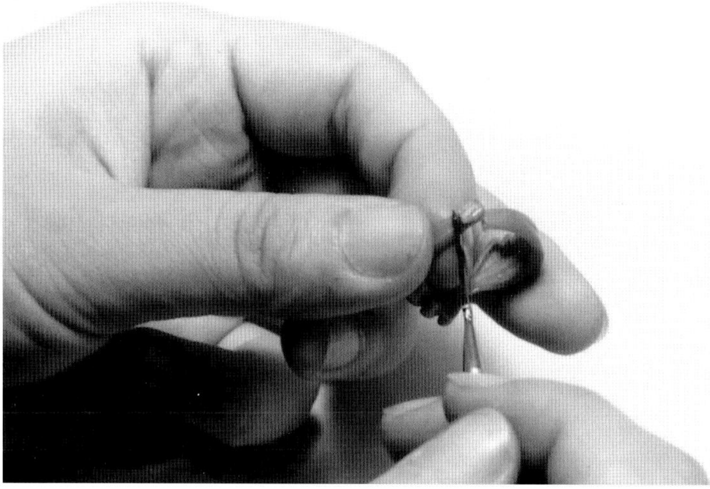

Cut the center of the shank with a warm knife. The standard is one half size = 1 mm. For example, if a 3 size reduction is required, remove 6 mm from the shank.

2.

Press the ring together as shown and with a heated knife weld the joint. Add extra wax if needed. If the required reduction is more than 3 sizes, immerse the ring in warm water before welding. (Treat wax patterns in the same manner).

Expansion

1.

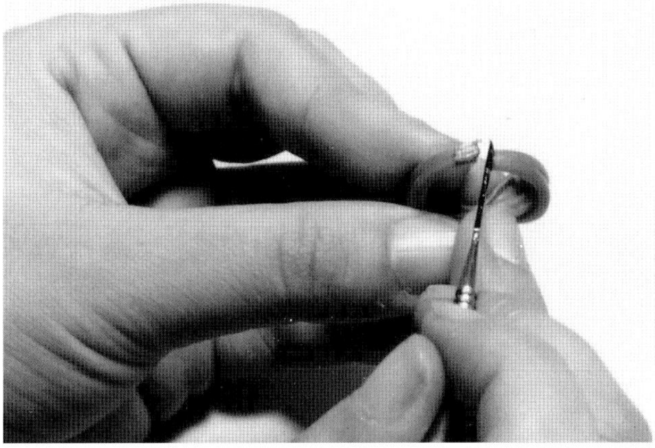

Cut the center of the shank and spread the cut slightly. Insert a piece, slightly thicker and wider but of the proper length, into the gap.

2.

Align the expansion piece in the shank and weld the two joints. Add wax if required. (Treat wax patterns in the same manner).

APPLYING VARIOUS TEXTURES

Lined Texture

1.

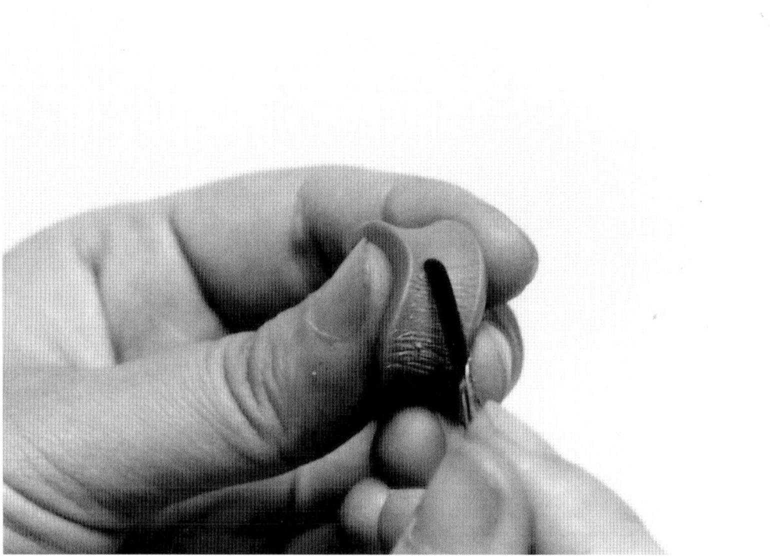

Incise lines uniformly, packed close together with a needle or the pointed end of a carver. Wipe away any dust. This texture is a touch different than that produced with a graver; this texture renders a soft, easy appearance.

Hammered Texture

2.

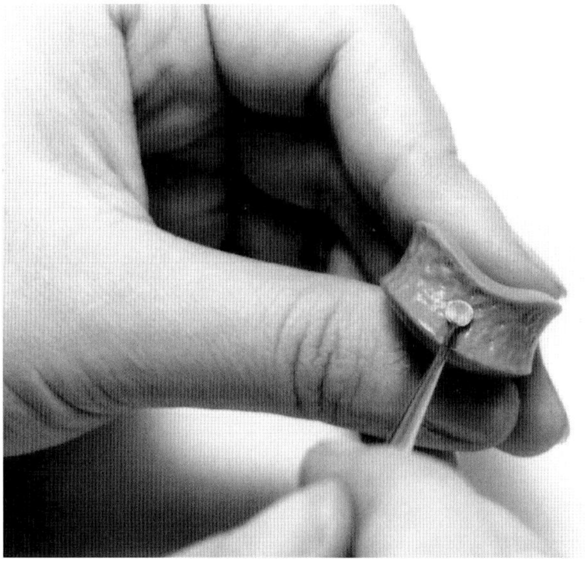

Press the back of a warm, small rounded gouge onto the wax in a random pattern. Where the wax is thin be careful you do not go through.

Sand Texture

3.

Apply with a warm needle or the pointed end of a carver. A small densely packed texture is more effective. When applied, the contrast will effectively improve a bright finish.

Pierced Texture

4.

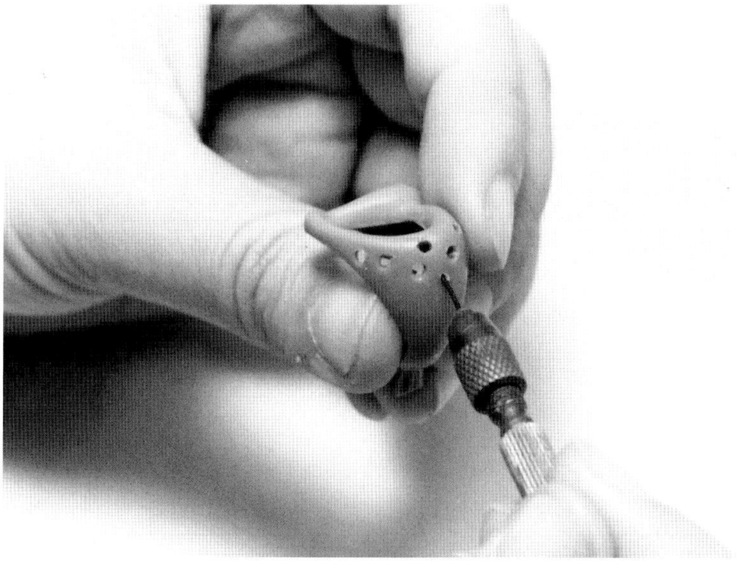

Make holes in sections. Heat a needle or spatula and create holes in the wax. The instant the wax melts, blow the melted wax out of the hole. By shape of holes, sizes and locations, etc. variations are created. (Treat injection wax patterns in the same manner).

REWORKING A WAX PATTERN

Add to a Model

1.

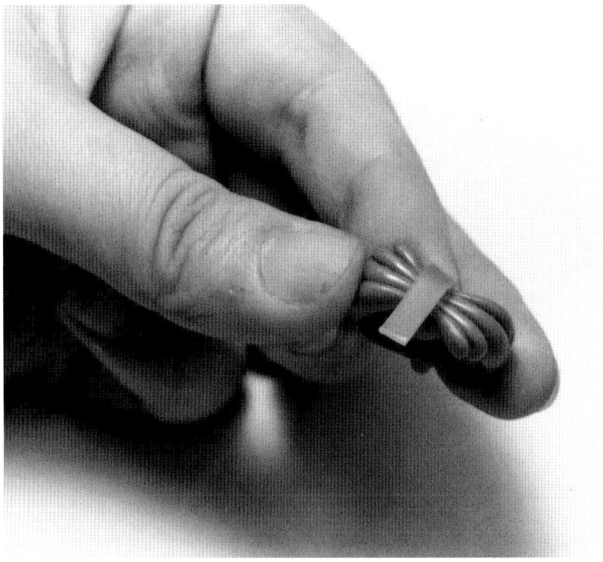

To add a tie to the model shown, cut a strip of sheet wax, bow it slightly. If there is any carving to be made on the tie use a thick enough piece to accommodate it.

2.

Cut the piece off from the underside. Weld the tie in place as you build up the wax. Trim with a knife until it is flat.

Remove Parts and Add Parts

1.

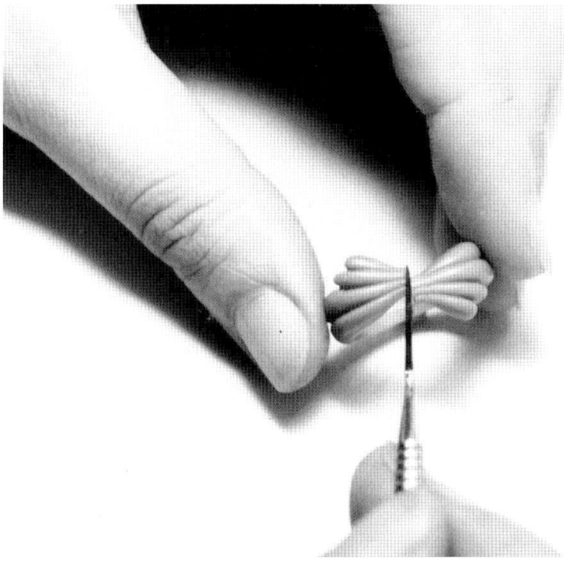

Use a thin bladed knife to separate the center of the design. Twist the shank enough to offset the cut ends to slide by each other a distance of a few millimeters. Weld the contact joint from the underside.

2.

Put the flower part into the niche formed and weld from the underside. Add wax and fix the part firmly in place. In this case, the size will be affected, so check the size.

Use Part of a Model

1.

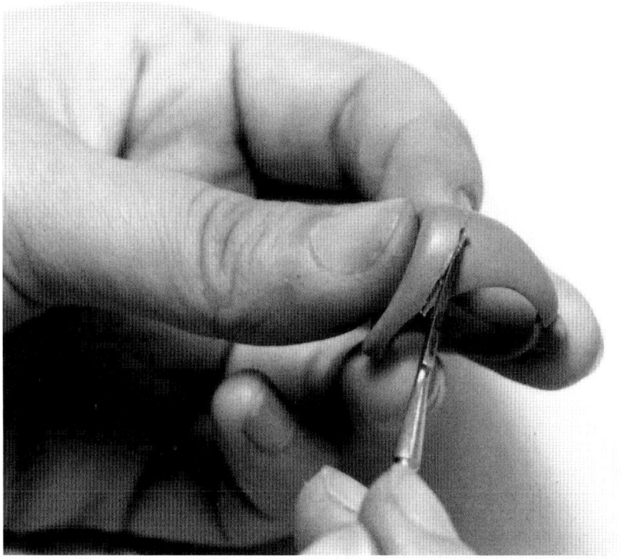

To use a part of a ring for a pendant, cut out the portion with the needed thickness. In the event the portion becomes warped hold it briefly over an alcohol lamp warming it. Bring it back into shape.

2.

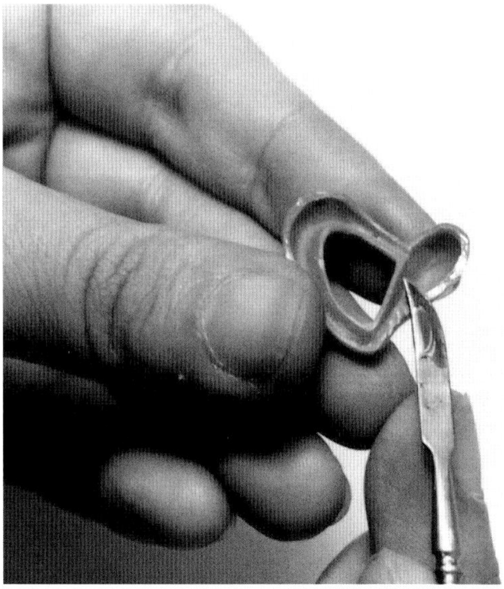

Where you require wax, build it up with a spatula using the pattern wax. Afterward, trim with a knife.

Assemble Parts of a Model

1.

Use the top portions of two wax models. Divide each portion into two parts. Smooth the cuts with a carver. Preserve the original shape.

2.

Assemble the parts. Tack weld from the front and build up wax on the underside, securing the pieces. A number of related pendants or brooches can be made in this manner.

V

CASTING PROCESSES AND RUBBER-MOLD MAKING

CASTING PROCESSES

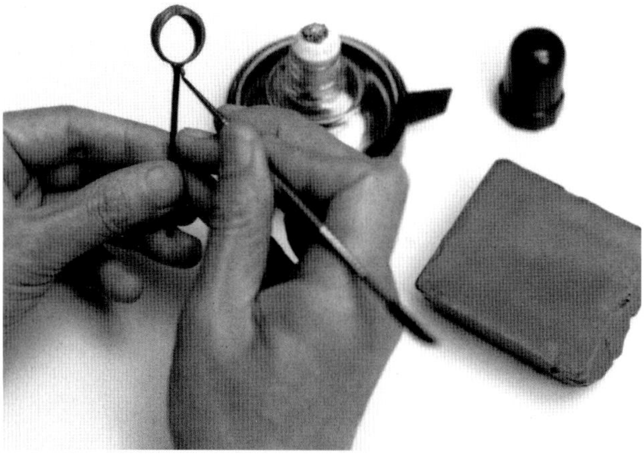

[1] Setting a Sprue:

Set a sprue to the thick part of the body. To connect the model and a sprue, warm up the top of a spatula with an alcohol lamp and make a swell by applying a small amount of wax.
A supplementary sprue might be added to models with sensitive design or larger models.

[2] Assembly:

Install three wax models each with a sprue to a conic base. Set a casting cylinder (iron or stainless) into the conic base and fit the wax models at a distance of over 10 mm from the top and over 5 - 7 mm from the side. Wax models should be lined up at intervals over 5 mm to prevent sticking.

[3] Filling Investment:

Pour investment into the casting cylinder. Investment means materials such as cristobalite, silica or plaster used to make casting models. Generally water (40 cc) is added to the material (100 g). After mixing fully, pour the investment into the casting cylinder using a plaster spatula. Be careful not to touch the wax models directly.
When the wax models are large and the investment might overflow, put adhesive tape around the casting cylinder.

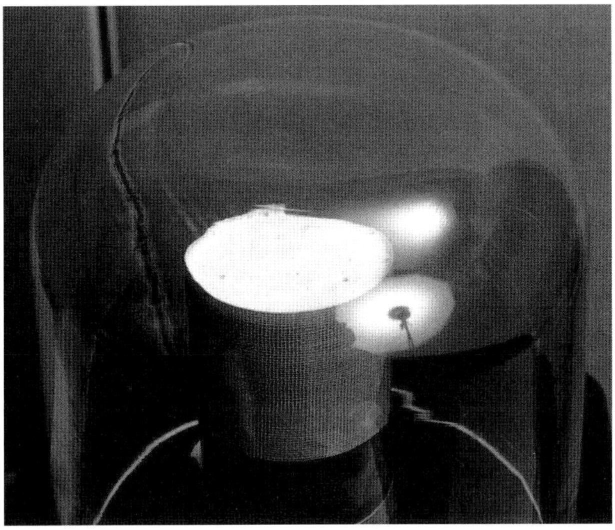

[4] Remove Air Bubbles:

Remove air bubbles in the investment with a vacuum air-removing machine. If air bubbles touch the wax models, they would become metal bubbles and stick to the surface of the base metal. There are two steps for removing air bubbles; primary air-removing which is performed after mixing the investment and water, and secondary air-removing which is performed after pouring investment into the casting cylinder.

[5] Melting-Out Wax and Burning Investment:

After removing air bubbles, dry the investment at normal temperature for 1 - 2 hours. Then remove the conic base and set the casting cylinder in an electric furnace to melt-out wax and burn the investment. As the temperature within the furnace rises and the temperature of the investment becomes around 100° C, water changes to steam and the wax is melted-out.

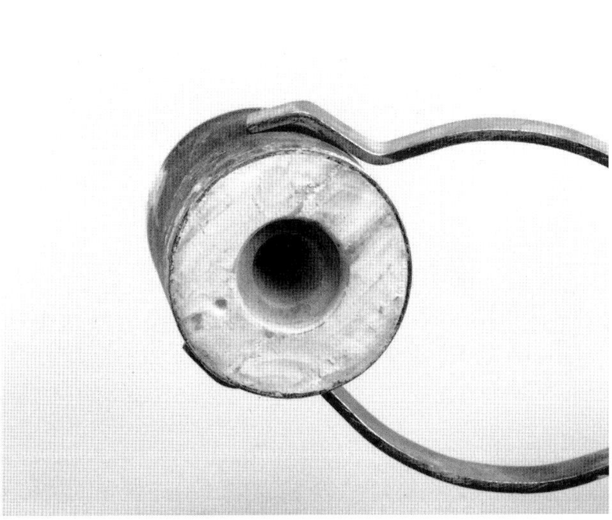

[6] Complete Burning:

Complete burning by gradually raising the temperature in the furnace and then burning the casting models sufficiently. As the term "lost wax" literally means, the wax is burnt to be lost during the melting and burning processes. A cavity with approximately the same shape as the wax model is left there. Then pour the material such as gold, silver or platinum into the hollow.

[7-A] Centrifugal Casting Method

In the Centrifugal Casting Method, melted metal is poured into the casting model by utilizing centirugal force applied to the melted metal.
The casting cavity and a crucible are set to the edge of the arm. The exclusively-prepared frame is wound three times and the stopper is set. After melting the metal, the stopper is released. The frame will spin at a high speed and the metal is poured into the casting cavity through the sprue.

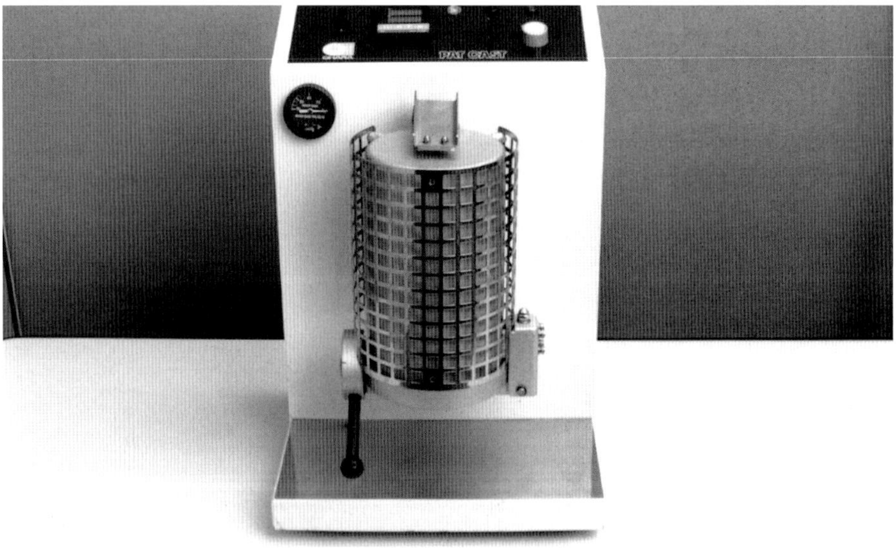

[7-B] Suction & Pressure Casting Method

In the Suction & Pressure Casting Method, melted metal is led to inside of the casting cavity by evacuating the chamber (the cylinder in the center of the photo) using a built-in vacuum pump and applying suction and pressure from outside of the casting model. Air permeability of the investment is utilized in this method.
When the metal is melted by electrically-created heat and the chamber turns around, the air valve on the bottom will be opened and the melted metal will be poured into the casting cavity.

[8] Rapid Cooling

Remove the investment after casting and take out the cast metal. Securely hold the casting cylinder with a casting nipper and soak it quickly in water.
Just as the casting cylinder is soaked in water, the investment is to be shattered and the cast metal will appear.
This is the time you are most tense checking whether the metal is poured into every corner of the cavity.

[9] Cleaning

Clean and remove the investment sticking to the finely designed surface and the reverse side of the metal. Remove the investment on the surface with a metal or bristle brush while exposing it to flowing water. The investment remaining inside or on finely designed parts should be cleaned with an ultrasonic cleaner.
The ultrasonic cleaner washes away the investment through the agency of ultrasonic waves and neutral detergent.

[10] Finishing

When the surface of gold or silver becomes dirty and dark, heat it and wash it with acid. Repeat this process several times to recover the original color of the metal. The weight of metal required for casting can be calculated by weighing the wax and then multiplying it by the specific gravity of the metal to be cast. (For the specific gravity see the Comments section, Proj. 1 of ***Basic Wax Modeling***.)
In addition to the wax used for base metal, extra wax for a sprue is required in actual casting.

RUBBER-MOLD MAKING

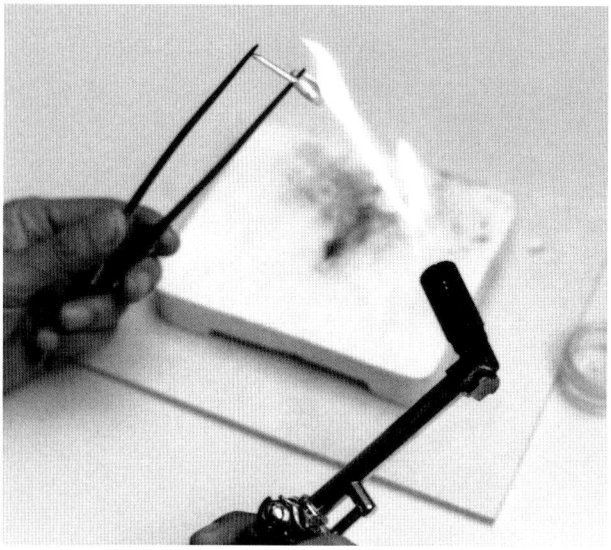

[1] Setting a Sprue:

Wax patterns with the same design can be obtained by making a rubber-mold and then injecting wax exclusively used for casting into it.
First, fit a metal stick 3 mm in diameter and 25 mm in length to be a sprue to the metal model with wax.

[2] Making a Rubber Mold (A):

Hard silicon rubber (silicon containing rubber) is used. Remove oil on the aluminum frame and the metal model. Cut silicon rubber to be laid on the bottom to the suitable size for the aluminum frame and fill it into the frame without leaving a gap. Lay a metal triangular prism and insert the model.

[3] Making a Rubber Mold (B):

Set a silicon rubber plate inside the ring to prevent the metal model from moving. Cut another silicon rubber plate with the same size as the aluminum frame, and put it on the frame. Hold the silicon rubber plate with your fingers so as not to leave a gap.
Be careful not to hold the plate too hard as it might cause transformation of the metal model.

[4] Making a Rubber Mold (with a Presser) (C):

Wrap the metal model in a silicon rubber plate and press it with a hot-press. When a silicon rubber plate is put between two aluminum plates and lightly pressed by a hot-press, it will be hardened. Generally the time for pressing is calculated by multiplying 1 minute by the height of the aluminum frame (mm). As a 20 mm aluminum frame is used here, pressing time is set to approximately 20 minutes.

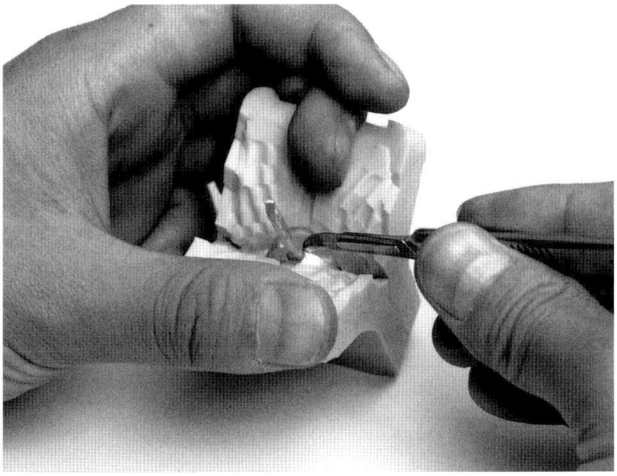

[5] Cutting a Rubber Mold (A):

Remove the metal triangular prism and set a blade to the scalpel holder. Describing an arc, thrust the scalpel towards the model in the silicon rubber plate. Start thrusting little by little from the point around the sprue and make unevenness on the cross section of the rubber mold.
Fully open the rubber with the thumb, forefinger and middle finger of your left hand. Be careful not to damage the model.

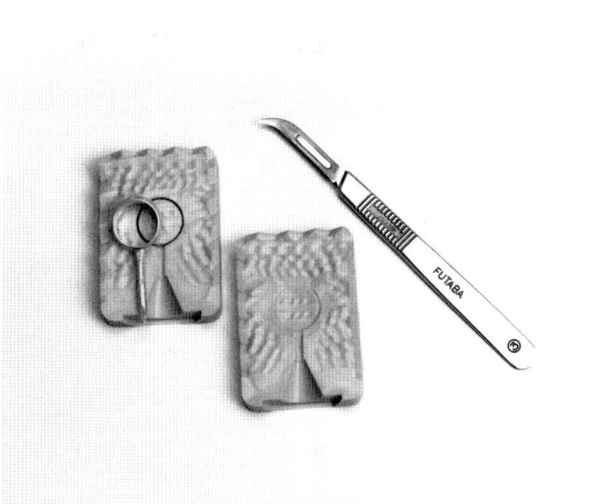

[6] Cutting a Rubber Mold (B):

Make arcs with a depth of 2 - 3 mm on each side of the rubber plate. Then make zigzag waves toward the center. The result of the rubber mold depends on these zigzag waves. As the scalpel for cutting rubber has a sharp blade, be careful not to be hurt. When the metal model is released, the rubber mold is completed.

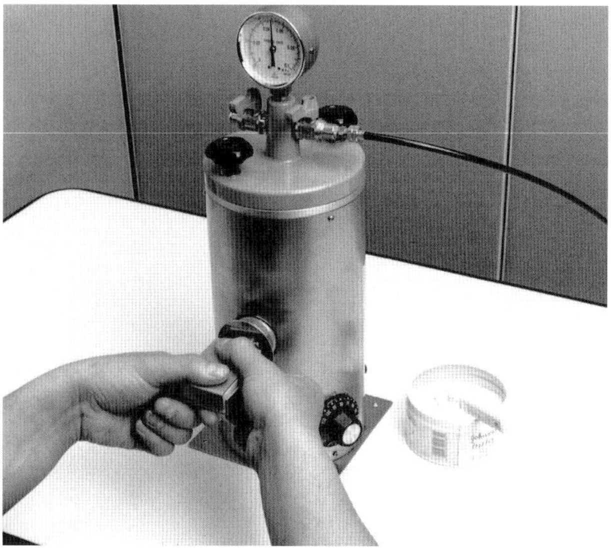

[7] Injecting Wax:

Inject wax into the rubber mold. Set wax in the wax pot. Melt it at 90° C and press it. Fit two rubber molds securely and set them to the nozzle and push. The wax is to be injected into the rubber mold. Spreading some powder as a detachment promoter inside the rubber mold enables easy wax removal.

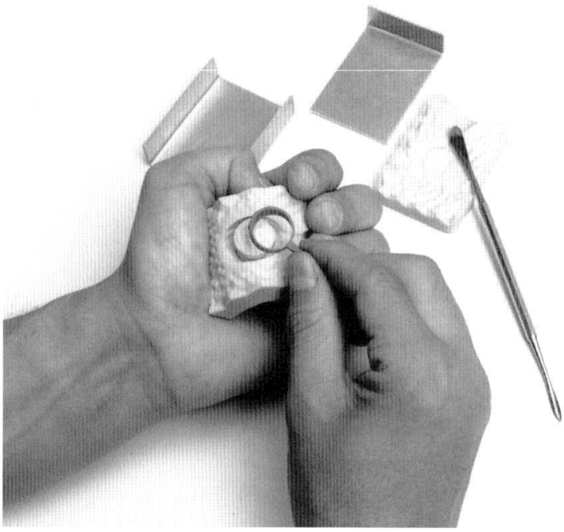

[8] Removing Wax:

Set the part with a sprue upward for three minutes and leave the rubber mold in a cold place for a few minutes. When the wax is hardened, open the rubber mold carefully and remove the formed wax pattern. Bend the rubber mold sufficiently and remove the wax pattern using your fingers or a spatula, starting with the part without a hole. Be careful not to damage the wax.

[9] Correcting Wax:

Correct the wax pattern. If extra wax membrane is produced, shave it with a cutter or remove it by melting the wax membrane using a warmed spatula.
When bubbles are contained in the wax, remove the air with a warmed spatula and then heap up a small amount of wax for correction.

VI

PROCESSING AND FINISHING AFTER CASTING

CLEANING A CASTING

Cutting the Sprue

1.

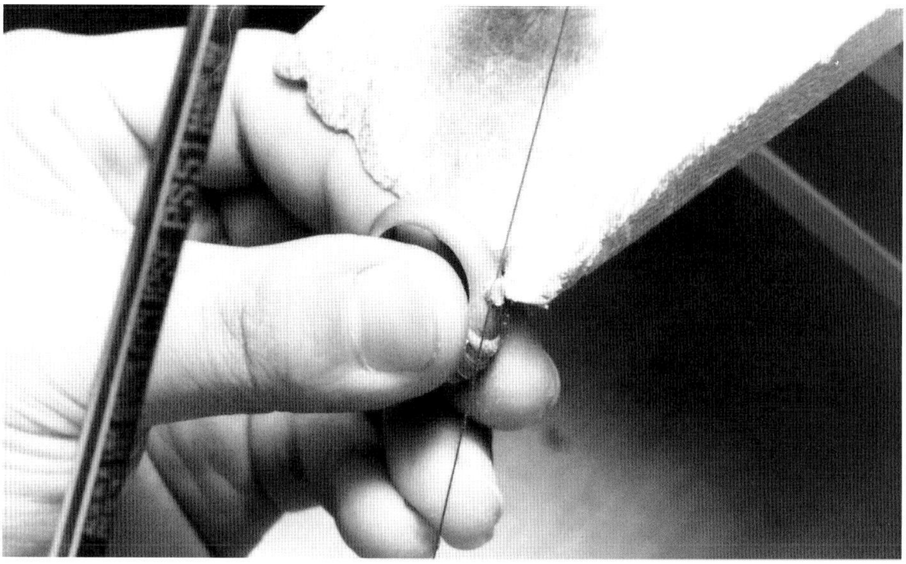

After casting there will be a sprue end remaining on the cast piece. Generally on rings it will be on the shank and on pendants, the rear. Cut the sprue end off with a jeweler's saw.

Filing

2.

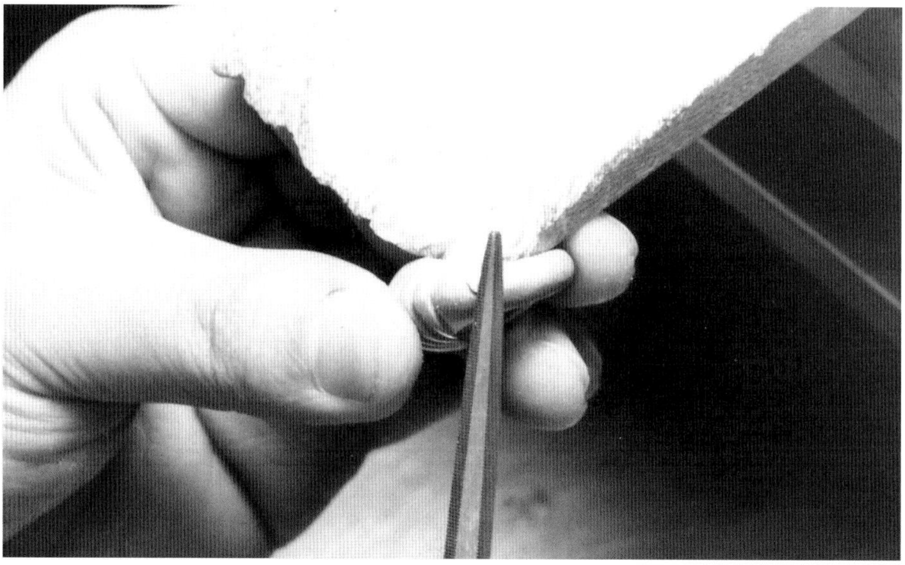

File the stub down with a coarse file. Finish completely with a smooth file.

Finishing with Kisage

3.

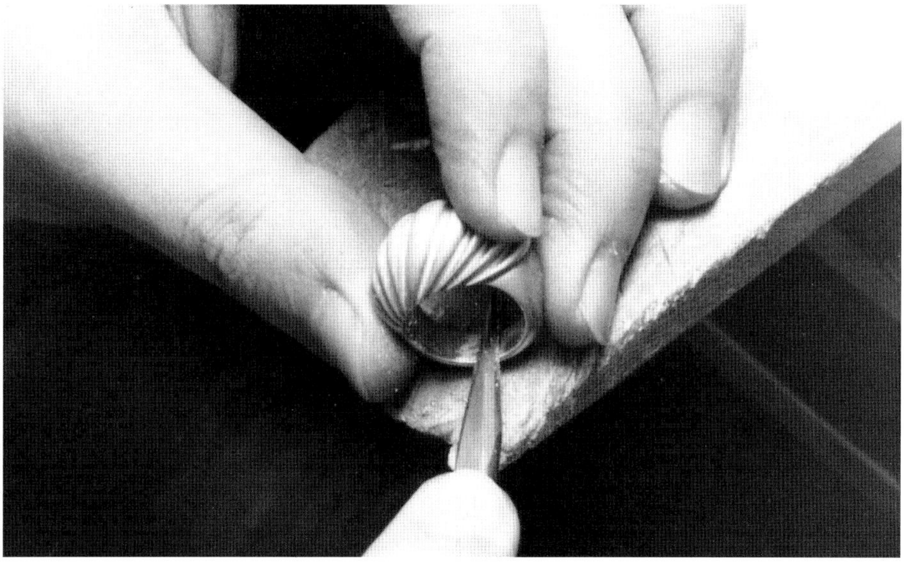

After you have finished with a fine cut file, use the *kisage* in place of the file and finish up neatly. You must keep the cutting edge of the *kisage* mirror sharp at all times. Clean up the inner surface of the shank with the *kisage*.

Finishing with Paper Abrasives

4.

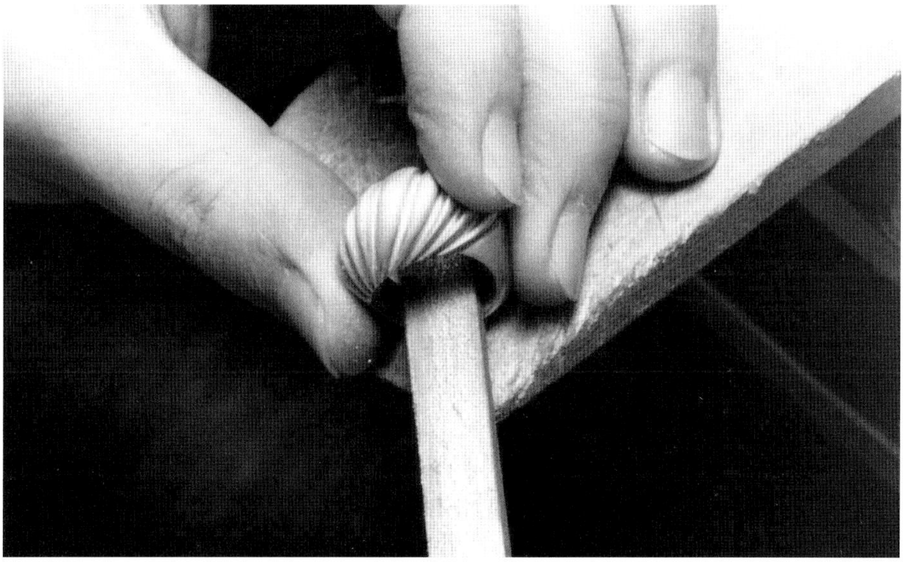

After the *kisage*, finish with paper abrasives (1000 grit or finer). Abrasive paper cemented to a stick is very handy.

Finishing Small Areas

5.

For grooves use the *kisage* and abrasive papers cut into strips. Using abrasive papers in fine to very fine grits will prepare the piece for the next process of buffing to a mirror finish.

Buffing

6.

Use a cloth buff. Apply rouge and polish. As the polishing/buffing machine turns at a high rate of speed, grasp the piece with both hands firmly; take every precaution to keep it from flying out of your grasp. Polish the grooves neatly. Afterwards, place the piece in an ultrasonic cleaner.

REPAIRING A CAVITY

1.

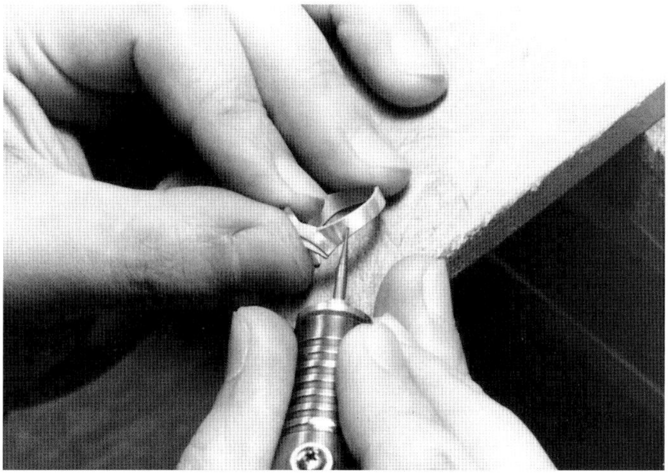

You may find some tiny pits in the cast piece. If it's small, it can be filled. If it is large, bur or use a graver to enlarge the hole.

2.

Place solder in the hole created by the bur. Melt the solder with a torch. Place it in a pickling solution, rinse and finish up with files and abrasive papers. In the case of a larger hole, place a piece of matching metal in the hole and solder.

3.

In the case of coarsely pitted areas, tap the highs down and use solder for the small pits.

MATTE FINISH

1.

Make a saturated solution of borax. Mix an equal quantity of borax and water into a beaker and heat until the solution is thoroughly mixed. Place the article in the solution with non ferrous tweezers.

2.

Remove the piece from the beaker and heat with a torch. As it's heated, white material will accumulate on the surface of the piece. At this time, gradually increase the heat to annealing temperature. A word of caution; if there is any solder it will melt if the heat is excessive.

1.

After the piece has been heated well, allow it to cool slowly, then place it into a newly made pickling solution. After 5 or 10 minutes a matte finish will occur. If it does not come out the first time repeat 2 or 3 times more.

2.

Remove from the pickling solution and rinse. As the entire surface will be matted, stroke a burnisher on the protruding areas to bring out the luster. In this manner contrast can be created.

OTHER FINISHING METHODS

Metal Brush

When you provide a luster finish to an entire uneven surface, use a metal brush. Use a brass or stainless steel brush; luster can be produced in the tiny areas as well. For small areas use a bur with miniature wire brushes.

Electro-Polishing

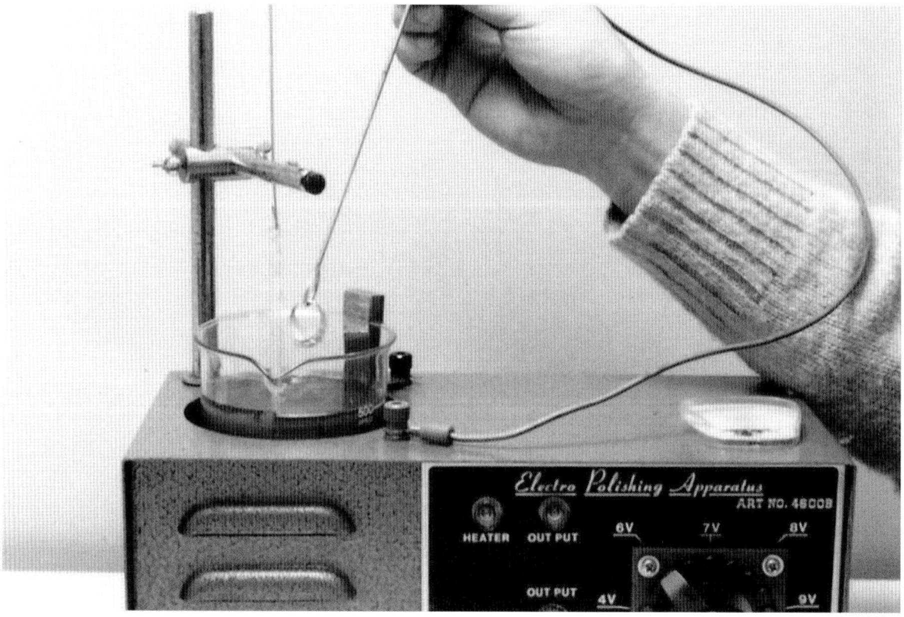

There is an elecrolytic method to remove unwanted metal from surfaces. Be aware that, if an object remains in electrolysis too long, an ecessive amount of material will be removed. Especially objects which have been soldered can be weakened greatly.

AFTERWORD

Practical Wax Modeling was written as an applied compilation for ***Basic Wax Modeling***. Various tools, waxes and their uses, basic wax techniques, etc, were introduced in ***Basic Wax Modeling***. Accordingly, this book has been condensed in those regards.

We recommend the uninitiated learning wax modeling to read ***Basic Wax Modeling*** together with this book Getting you acquainted with the entire wax modeling spectrum through these books has been our objective.

This book, as well as ***Basic Wax Modeling***, was written as part of the curriculum of the Lost Wax Courses of the Japan Jewelry Craft School. The school, based on a long practice in the quality of its curriculum, raised the role and recognition of wax modeling to the production of jewelry, and has been instrumental in the nurturing of a large number of designers and modellers.

Indeed, in the coming years there is much ground to cover, since wax modeling is a relatively new technique. We think many persons using this book as a reference may conceive new ideas in technique and by disseminating these results, will increase our knowledge in wax technology.

Basic Wax Modeling is not only read by jewelry makers and designers but is also widely read by people with an interest in wax modeling and people engaged in marketing and small businesses as well. If these same people use this book and are able to improve wax technology, we will feel fortunate in our contribution.
Lastly, for the cooperation received from the Japan Jewelry Craft School, the school's instructors and students as well as the members of the Pyxis Conference in the preparation of this book, we are deeply grateful.

ABOUT THE AUTHORS

Hiroshi Tsuyuki

President of Japan Jewelry Craft School.
Member of Japan Jewellery Designers Association.
Member of Japanese Society For Science of Design.
Author of: *Kaznri Jewelry Technique*
Practical Jewelry Design
Jewelry Engraving & Gem-Setting
Basic Wax Modeling

Yoko Ohba

Vice President of Japan Jewelry Craft School.
Executive Director of Associate Co., Ltd.
Director of The Pyxis Conference.
Member of Japan Jewellery Designers Association.
Member of Japanese Society For Science of Design.
Member of The Tagane Club.
Author of: *An Introduction To Original Jewelry*
Essence of Jewelry Design and Rendering

APPENDIX

RING SIZE					
Ring Size	Diameter Inches	Length Inches	Ring Size	Diameter Inches	Length Inches
0	0.458	1.4388	6-1/2	.666	2.20923
1/4	.466	1.4640	7	.682	2.1426
1/2	.474	1.4891	7-1/2	.698	2.1928
3/4	.482	1.5142	8	.714	2.2431
1	.490	1.5394	8-1/2	.730	2.2934
1-1/2	.506	1.5896	9	.746	2.3436
2	.522	1.6399	9-1/2	.762	2.3939
2-1/2	.538	1.6902	10	.778	2.4442
3	.554	1.7404	10-1/2	.794	2.4944
3-1/2	.570	1.7907	11	.810	2.5447
4	.586	1.8410	11-1/2	.826	2.5950
4-1/2	.602	1.8912	12	.842	2.6452
5	.618	1.9415	12-1/2	.858	2.6955
5-1/2	.634	1.9918	13	.874	2.7458
6	.650	2.0420	13-1/2	.890	2.7960

PLATE AND WIRE GAUGE COMPARISONS					
B&S Gauge	M/M	Inches	B&S Gauge	M/M	Inches
4	5.189	.2043	16	1.290	.0508
6	4.111	.1620	18	1.024	.0403
8	3.264	.1285	20	0.813	.0320
10	2.588	.1019	22	0.643	.0253
12	2.052	.0808	24	0.511	.0201
14	1.629	.0641	26	0.404	.0159

WEIGHT CHART					
Carat	Gram	Troy Ounce	Troy Pound	Avoird. Ounce	Avoird. Ounce
1	0.2	0.00643	.000536	.007055	.000441
5	1	0.03215	.002679	.03527	.002205
155.517	31.1034	1	.083333	1.09714	.06857
1866.24	373.248	12	1	13.17	.8229
141.747	28.3495	0.9115	.07595	1	.0625
2267.95	453.59	14.583	1.215	16	1

MILLIMETER / INCH CONVERSION							
M/M	Decimal	Inch	Fraction	M/M	Decimal	Inch	Fraction
1	.03937			14	.55118		
		.0625	1/16			.5625	9/16
2	.07874			15	.59055		
						.625	5/8
3	.11811			16	.62992		
		.125	1/8				
4	.15748			17	.66929		
		.1875	3/16			.6875	11/16
5	.19685			18	.70866		
6	.23622			19	.74803		
		.250	1/4			.750	3/4
7	.27559			20 (2 cm)	.78740		
		.3125	5/16			.8125	13/16
8	.31496			21	.82677		
9	.35433			22	.86614		
		.375	3/8			.875	7/8
10 (1 cm)	.39370			23	.90551		
						.9375	15/16
11	.43307			24	.94488		
		.4375	7/16				
12	.47244			25	.98425		
		.500	1/2			1.000	
13	.51181			26	1.02362		

DIAMOND CARAT / DIAMETER TABLE							
Carat Wt.	Diameter M/M	Carat Wt.	Diameter M/M	Carat Wt.	Diameter M/M	Carat Wt.	Diameter M/M
.01	1	.08	2-1/2	.21	3-3/4	.46	5
.02	1-1/4	.09	2-3/4	.23	4	.50	5-1/4
.03	1-1/2	.11	3	.25	4-1/8	.63	5-1/2
.04	1-3/4	.13	3-1/8	.30	4-1/4	.75	5-3/4
.05	2	.15	3-1/4	.38	4-1/2	.88	6
.06	2-1/4	.19	3-1/2	.42	4-3/4	1 ct	6-1/4

BASIC WAX MODELING

The author of ***Basic Wax Modeling***, Mr. Hiroshi Tsuyuki, is the Japanese authority on Jewelry Wax Modeling. In this book he presents 11 basic projects, each one designed to teach the use of certain tools and types of waxes in a progressive manner as one's skills improve.

Each step of every project is accompanied by a photo and text and in some cases supplementary sketches and notes are provided to clarify those particular processes.

Paying careful attention to the photos, noting the demonstrator's hand position and the type of tool being used, eliminates any confusion which may result from reading the text alone.

After each basic model is completed the author offers a number of sketches suggesting design possibilities using the techniques learned in the construction of the basic model.

Mr. Tsuyuki states that by conscientiously completing each project, the student should be well on the way to becoming a designer/modeler.

The author uses an innovative approach. Often a process is easier shown than described in so many words. This book was conceived through Mr. Tsuyuki's teaching experience – more photos and sketches and less text resulting in less over-the-shoulder supervision. By introducing new techniques in each project, his students were able to progress more rapidly towards independence in design concepts.
Projects include models for High Domed Rings, Ripple Patterned Rings, Signet Rings, Box Type Rings, Carved Flat Band Rings, Pendants, Brooches, and others.

Practical Wax Modeling was written as an applied compilation for the book ***Basic Wax Modeling***.

Hardcover, 112 pages, 283 photos and illustrations, ISBN: 978-0-9979798-7-9.

Japan Jewelry Craft School

The Japan Craft Jewelry School is a Japanese jewelry school of international reputation.
Here you will learn jewelry making, jewelry design, gemology and more.
Our school headquarters is located in Okachimachi, the center of the Japanese jewelry industry. There are courses for jewelry designers and creators, courses for non-professionals and hobbyists and courses for qualification in gemology.

■ Full Time Course

These courses are designed to help students aiming to become jewelry professionals. Students acquire comprehensive practical design skill, jewelry making skill and the expertise necessary to enter the workplace of jewelry or affiliated fields. Courses are made up of Creation System Courses concentrating on design and jewelry making skills.

■ Unit Course

These courses are for persons who are now working for another industry and are looking to change to the jewelry industry. They can choose their subjects accordingly. Students choose 3-6 units per week (1 unit = 2 hours and 45 minutes) in the morning, afternoon and evening from Monday to Saturday, and totally acquire the practical technology and the knowledge necessary for working in this field.

■ "Gem-A" Course

FGA (Fellow of the Gemmological Association of Great Britain) is the international qualification for gemmology recognized by the Gemmological Association of Great Britain (Gem-A).
Japan Jewelry Craft School has been offering Gem-A courses to become an FGA since 2012. The courses are run in cooperation with the General Incorporated Japan Gem society (JGS), which is the Gem-A Accredited Teaching Centre in Japan.

■ Unit per Week

This course is a single course that you can attend once a week. It is fun and involves learning jewelry making and design.

ADDRESS: 3-13-10 Taito Taito-ku Tokyo Japan
PHONE: +81 03 (3835) 3388 FAX: +81 03 (3833) 2002
http://www.jj-craft.com   info@jj-craft.com